A Couple State of Mind

A Couple State of Mind is a much anticipated book aimed at an international audience of practitioners, students and teachers of psychoanalytic couple therapy, which describes the Tavistock Relationships model of couple psychoanalytic psychotherapy, drawing on both historical and contemporary ideas, including the author's own theoretical contributions. The book references contemporary influences of other psychoanalytic approaches to couples, particularly from an international perspective. It will be invaluable for all students learning about psychoanalytic work with couples and for other psychoanalytic practitioners interested in this field.

Mary Morgan is a Psychoanalyst and Couple Psychoanalytic Psychotherapist, Reader in Couple Psychoanalysis at Tavistock Relationships.

The Library of Couple and Family Psychoanalysis

A Couple State of Mind
Psychoanalysis of Couples and the Tavistock Relationships Model
Mary Morgan

Clinical Dialogues on Psychoanalysis with Families and Couples
David E. Scharff

Family and Couple Psychoanalysis
A Global Perspective
Elizabeth Palacios

What Makes us Stay Together?
Attachment and the Outcomes of Couple Relationships
Rosetta Castellano

Psychoanalytic Couple Therapy
Foundations of Theory and Practice
David E. Scharff

How Couple Relationships Shape our World
Clinical Practice, Research, and Policy Perspectives
Andrew Balfour

Sex, Attachment and Couple Psychotherapy
Psychoanalytic Perspectives
Christopher Clulow

A Couple State of Mind

Psychoanalysis of Couples and the Tavistock Relationships Model

Mary Morgan

Routledge
Taylor & Francis Group
LONDON AND NEW YORK

First published 2019
by Routledge
2 Park Square, Milton Park, Abingdon, Oxon OX14 4RN

and by Routledge
711 Third Avenue, New York, NY 10017

Routledge is an imprint of the Taylor & Francis Group, an informa business

© 2019 Taylor & Francis

The right of Mary Morgan to be identified as author of this work has been asserted by her in accordance with sections 77 and 78 of the Copyright, Designs and Patents Act 1988.

All rights reserved. No part of this book may be reprinted or reproduced or utilised in any form or by any electronic, mechanical, or other means, now known or hereafter invented, including photocopying and recording, or in any information storage or retrieval system, without permission in writing from the publishers.

Trademark notice: Product or corporate names may be trademarks or registered trademarks, and are used only for identification and explanation without intent to infringe.

British Library Cataloguing-in-Publication Data
A catalogue record for this book is available from the British Library

Library of Congress Cataloging-in-Publication Data
Names: Morgan, Mary (Mary E.), author.
Title: A couple state of mind : the psychoanalysis of couples / Mary Morgan.
Description: Abingdon, Oxon ; New York, NY : Routledge, 2019. | Series: The library of couple and family psychoanalysis
Identifiers: LCCN 2018021795 (print) | LCCN 2018023117 (ebook) | ISBN 9780429451102 (e-book) | ISBN 9781138624948 (hardback) | ISBN 9781138624962 (pbk.)
Subjects: LCSH: Couples therapy. | Couples--Psychology. | Psychoanalysis.
Classification: LCC RC488.5 (ebook) | LCC RC488.5 .M664 2019 (print) | DDC 616.89/1562--dc23
LC record available at https://lccn.loc.gov/2018021795

ISBN: 978-1-138-62494-8 (hbk)
ISBN: 978-1-138-62496-2 (pbk)
ISBN: 978-0-429-45110-2 (ebk)

Typeset in Garamond
by Integra Software Services Pvt. Ltd.

To Philip

Contents

Series editor's foreword by Susanna Abse	ix
Foreword by Ronald Britton	xii
Acknowledgements	xiv
Introduction	xviii
A couple state of mind	xxi

1	A psychoanalytic understanding of the couple relationship: Past, present and future	1
2	Assessment	14
3	Engaging a couple in treatment and establishing a couple analytic setting	34
4	Unconscious phantasy, shared unconscious phantasy and shared defence, unconscious beliefs and fantasy	54
5	Transference and countertransference and the living inner world of the couple	73
6	Projective identification and the couple projective system	88
7	Narcissism and sharing psychic space	110
8	The couple's psychic development, sex, gender and sexualities	126

9 Interpretation	152
10 Endings and the aim of couple therapy	176
References	193
Index	204

Series editor's foreword

It is both a great pleasure and a great honour to write the series editor introduction for this ground-breaking book. This book, first conceived some years ago, may have taken a while to reach publication, but the wait has been entirely worthwhile. The book will become, I am sure, the standard text describing the psychoanalytic approach to couple psychotherapy pioneered and developed by Tavistock Relationships over the past 70 years.

This book which is the ninth in the series of the imprint of *Couple and Family Psychoanalysis* is the first book to describe in detail a method of therapy that has been under development for 70 years, since the founding of the Family Discussion Bureau in 1948. Whilst there have been many fine and important publications in the series, elucidating the techniques, key theories and clinical challenges, none have attempted a systematic description of how psychoanalysis with couples actually works. Indeed, this book is the first text coming out of Tavistock Relationships that has been written by a single author since James Fisher's 1999 classic, *The Uninvited Guest*. Most books in our series have been edited collections of papers offering the reader a rich opportunity to dip and dive into the differing points of view and perspectives of senior and eminent couple psychotherapists in the field. An experience ably offered by the recent publication of *Couple Stories* (2018) edited by Aleksandra Novakovic and Marguerite Reid and by David Scharff and Jill Savege Scharff's excellent *Psychoanalytic Couple Therapy: Foundations of Theory and Practice* (2014). However, single-authored books, such as this gem, are rare and offer quite a different experience for the reader. In this book, we can follow the author's mind and standpoint chapter by chapter, giving a rich encompassing experience akin to the thrilling and intimate experience of a small seminar group, tutored by Mary Morgan.

The psychoanalytic approach developed by Tavistock Relationships has had worldwide impact and influence, but it is also true to say that 'deep' work with couples, which combines intrapsychic understanding with interpersonal dynamics, is not the dominant mode of therapy with couples. Indeed, psychoanalytic treatment continues to face a crisis in many western countries as other approaches have risen in popularity. This loss of favour has come about for several reasons, such as the length of and the absence of clarity of aims of treatment, but most importantly because of the paucity of an evidence base which has made psychoanalytic approaches very vulnerable in the current environment. One essential aspect of developing an evidence base or at least developing evidence that is credible to orthodox organisations such as the National Institute for Health and Care Excellence (NICE) in the UK, is the requirement that the therapy be manualised. Manualisation allows for treatments to be systemised and for researchers conducting randomised control trials (RCTs: the gold standard of research methodologies) to know that the treatment they are studying will follow a rigorous set of procedures and interventions.

Whilst for RCTs there is without doubt an absolute requirement for the principles and strategies involved in any therapeutic approach to be described as systematically as possible, it is clear that this requirement greatly limits the scope and range of problems that can be studied. Further, this limitation means that the difference between how treatment is conducted within the context of an RCT and how a treatment needs to be conducted in real-life practice can be enormous, and this difference can show in the gap between the positive outcomes found in trials which have been difficult to replicate in real-life practice.

At Tavistock Relationships, a different, more pragmatic approach has been taken to studying the impact of treatment which has led to the recently published, largest naturalistic study of couple therapy (outcomes gathered from normal clinical practice) (Hewison et al., 2016). This study looked at the outcomes for 877 people who came with both depressive symptoms and difficulties with their relationship and who had had a minimum of two sessions of psychodynamic couple therapy. The results showed that there were significant improvements in both their mood and in their satisfaction with their relationship, and these results were comparable with the results of other kinds of couple therapies evaluated via RCTs. As a result of this finding, Hewison et al. argue in the paper that naturalistic effectiveness studies should hold greater weight when evaluating which therapies actually help our patients.

Whilst this new book is not a manual, it does present a comprehensive framework of the key theoretical and technical aspects of post-Kleinian psychoanalytic work with couples, and this achievement will, alongside Tavistock Relationships' growing evidence base, make a large contribution to ensuring that this comprehensive, in-depth methodology grows in influence and stature.

However, I am sure Mary Morgan would agree that this book, which manages to be both erudite and full of creative ideas, is not the ultimate exposition of our craft. Practice changes and develops; new influences come along and new voices emerge. This is why manualised therapies, in the end, cannot be the way forward – the human spirit demands more than a manual, it demands a dialogue and a developing approach – both of which are fundamental to Mary Morgan's approach in this book.

Susanna Abse
Senior Fellow, Tavistock Relationships
Series Co-Editor, The Library of Couple and Family Psychoanalysis

Foreword

This book, which describes and illustrates the approach to couples that has developed in Tavistock Relationships, is vivid in its immediate account of the work whilst thorough in its discussion of the theory underpinning it. The names have changed more than the methods or the clinical understanding, and those changes from Marital Therapy to Couple Relationships reflect more on cultural and social change than psychological entities. This in itself speaks to the basic understanding of a special, shared object relationship that is basic to the approach whatever its title. The formal bond is love, but as experience shows, it will include also hate and knowledge. These three, as St Paul almost said, love, hate and knowledge, but the greatest of these is love.

Three is, paradoxically, the crucial number of positions needed in a couple relationship as Mary Morgan describes: the third being the position the couple needs to occupy to view and reflect on their shared relationship whilst maintaining their own subjective positions in the relationship as individuals. The therapist or therapeutic couple may be the original 'third' performing this function in the hope that it can be introjected by the two parties of the relationship.

The notion of couple therapy began at the Tavistock when there was, just after the Second World War, a great outburst of creative applications of psychoanalytic understanding and wartime experience of social relationships. It was as if there was, in current parlance, a sudden proliferation of 'Apps': marriage, childbirth, death and mourning, life in the workplace were selected for exploration and experiment.

Amongst the survivors of these Tavistock Relationships is notable and it has accumulated considerable clinical experience as well as adding new items to its storehouse of psychoanalytic theories. The notion of there being a relationship with its own psychological elements contributed by the couple that then forms a living net that holds and binds them is a very fruitful one. We could describe it as a container in which the two contained individuals live. As has been described by Bion (1966/2014), the relationship of the contained to the container can be symbiotic, commensal or parasitic. Put another way, it might be enhancing or it might be claustrophobic. The devil will certainly be in the detail and as is well illustrated in this book, it is detailed work and hard thinking that are needed and provided. I am sure all those who have embarked on providing couple therapy or are thinking of training to do so will find it enormously helpful as a stimulus and as a comfort in difficult land.

Dr. Ronald Britton
Fellow of the Royal Society of Psychiatrists and
Distinguished Fellow of the British Psychoanalytical Society

Acknowledgements

Many people have, in different ways, contributed to the writing of this book. First, I would like to thank my family for their encouragement, support and love. Philip, Oliver and Willow, Stanley and Peggy, Jack and Thelma. Philip, my husband, has been a tower of strength in so many ways, including reading more drafts of chapters than anyone else and in helping me think and rethink.

There are many colleagues I wish to thank. When I joined Tavistock Relationships (then the Institute of Marital Studies) as a student in 1988 and staff member from 1990, we were a small group working closely together. My first co-therapists were Chris Vincent and Warren Colman and the opportunity of learning alongside them was a memorably rich experience that has stayed with me. They, along with Di Daniell, helped me begin to find my way as a psychoanalytic couple therapist. Chris Clulow led Tavistock Relationships for many years and encouraged me early on to write this book, and although it was perhaps too soon for me, his belief in my capacity to do this has stayed. Stan Ruszczynski was the Deputy Director for many years and he and James Fisher were close colleagues and friends with whom I had many conversations and learnt a great deal. Their book *Intrusiveness and Intimacy* (Ruszczynski & Fisher, 1995), Stan's *Psychotherapy with Couples* (Ruszczynski, 1993a), and James's *The Uninvited Guest* (Fisher, 1999), along with Francis Grier's *Oedipus and the Couple* (Grier, 2005a) I think of as some of the classic texts elaborating Tavistock Relationships' couple analytic approach. Other colleagues in those early years were Joanna Rosenthall, Lynne Cudmore, Nina Cohen, Felicia Olney, Lynette Hughes, Paul Pengelly, Malcolm Millington, and a little later, Dorothy Judd, Monica Lanman, Francis Grier, David Hewison and Avi Shmueli. We were a close working group, who shared and developed many ideas and I feel lucky to have had the opportunity to work with you all. Of course, this was a snapshot in time; Janet Mattinson, Douglas Woodhouse and Barbara Dearnley had recently left, but their influence was still felt by us and there have been significant colleagues before and since, many of whom are referenced in this book and who can be discovered in Tavistock Relationships' numerous publications.

James Fisher helped me send off for publication one of the first papers I wrote, 'The Projective Gridlock', by 'explaining' to me that my delay in getting it published (and endless writing of drafts) was a 'narcissistic problem', since writing did not have to be perfect but was simply a contribution to the field and a way of communicating with, and thinking together with, colleagues. I have tried ever since to pass on this message to others. Francis Grier and I trained alongside each other as psychoanalysts at the Institute of Psychoanalysis, while both working at Tavistock Relationships, having many evening conversations as we made our way to seminars, about the fruitful interplay between psychoanalysis and couple psychoanalytic work. He, along with a small number of psychoanalysts in the British Psychoanalytical Society (BPAS), holds a place for psychoanalytic work with couples. In some other psychoanalytic societies around the world there is more interest in psychoanalytic work with couples and families, and I hope this will develop further in our own.

In recent years Tavistock Relationships has expanded enormously – its trainings, clinical service, research and collaborative projects spanning parenting work, mentalisation-based therapies, dementia, old age, alongside its core psychoanalytic clinical service and training. So here I can only mention a few names, they are among those who have heard and discussed earlier versions of some of the chapters and in their different ways supported the writing of this book. I would like to thank Susanna Abse, Chris Clulow and Andrew Balfour, who entrusted me to write this book which, although it is my personal view and understanding of the work, attempts to capture and represent some of the key theory and practice of Tavistock Relationships over the last 70 years. Thanks also to Catriona Wrottesley, Julie Humphries, David Hewison, Krisztina Glausius, Viveka Nyberg, Leezah Hertzmann, Limor Abramov, Maureen Boerma, Pierre Cachia, Damian McCann, Marian O'Connor and Kate Thompson for their warm and collegiate support. I hope you like the way I have put together our approach to analytic work with couples. I have not really attempted to pull together differences in emphasis or approaches in our thinking – I feel it is better that these are allowed to exist, interact and keep our thinking alive.

As I suppose is often the case, the decision to write this book came about through a series of synchronous events. One was a 'meet and greet' occasion with Tavistock Relationships' new Chair of Trustees, Nick Pearce, who asked me to describe our theoretical framework and the way we understood couple relationships. In that moment something came together in my mind which I felt might have coherence. This formed the basis of the theoretical overview in Chapter One. Shortly after, two colleagues I was working with both became rather insistent that this book needed writing, and I was the person who had to do it! Thank you, Viveka and Leezah, and to Viveka who then took on running the Psychoanalytic Couple Training for a year, so that I could have some more mental space to do the thinking and writing. Leezah and Susanna also read and gave me helpful comments on earlier chapters. Catriona was amazing in this respect. She read every chapter and returned them to me quickly and with incisive comments; I felt she was alongside me in the writing process. Hilde Syversen a friend and journalist, generously gave an early proof read of chapters and Stan Ruszczynski read a final version of the whole book, which meant a lot to me and for which I am very grateful.

My thanks also to colleagues at Routledge for their care in bringing this book into fruition, in particular Russell George, Lauren Frankfurt, Helen Lund, Klara King, Seth Townley and Elliot Morsia. I would also like to thank Sophie Bowness and the Hepworth Wakefield for kindly allowing me to use an image of Barabara Hepworth's Curved Forms (Pavan) for the cover. This sculpture captured for me something of the creative interplay between the partners in a couple, showing both space and connection.

I realised that despite many important publications over the last 70 years, we at Tavistock Relationships had never produced a book describing our model. In fact, it was from teaching in other countries and from colleagues referring to the Tavistock Relationships model, that it dawned on me that we had a model. We didn't talk about it in this way at Tavistock Relationships, this was just what we did. Of course, somewhere it had been in my mind for a long time to write this book, originally to be jointly written by Stan Ruszczynski and me, but for various reasons not possible at that time.

For many years I have led the MA and Couple Psychoanalytic Psychotherapy training at Tavistock Relationships and taught and supervised students, many of you whom are now colleagues. You are too numerous to mention here which is a shame, as it is of course from you that I have learnt so much. Thank you.

There are several groups of colleagues whom I have worked with over many years that I would like to thank. First, John Zinner and Joyce Lowenstein at the Washington School of Psychiatry, and David Scharff and Jill Savege Scharff, formerly at the Washington School and now at the International Psychotherapy Institute, which they founded.

Between 1992 and 1995, Warren Colman, Paul Pengelly and I travelled regularly to Sweden to teach on a training course in psychoanalytic couple therapy that Tavistock Relationships had set up with colleagues there. I learnt a great deal during those years. I particularly want to thank Gullvi Sandin who imaginatively and generously was instrumental in this collaboration, which has continued in other ways ever since, and to Ann-Sophie Schultz-Viberg, Anna Kandell and Christina Noren-Svensson. A similar training was set up in San Francisco and later developed by the San Francisco Bay Area Psychoanalytic Couple Psychotherapy Group (PCPG) into their own training, based on the Tavistock Relationships approach. Shelley Nathans, Julie Friend, Leora Benioff, Milton Schaefer, Rachel Cook and Sandy Seidlitz: thank you, all of you, it has been such a pleasure to be part of your journey and I have valued the thoughtful and thought-provoking discussions with you and your students.

During the writing of this book, I have had the chance to try out 'chapters' and develop ideas with other colleagues, particularly in New York, Helsinki and Warsaw. Thank you to all of you and a special thank you to the Specialized Marriage and Family Counselling Clinic Warszawa-Bemowo, led by Jaroslaw Serdakowski, to Iwa Magryta-Wojda and Barbara Suchańska for their tireless translation of my papers so that we could have a dialogue, and to Rafal Milewski for his encouragement and interest in this book.

I would also like to thank all the members of the International Psychoanalytical Association (IPA) committee on Couple and Family Psychoanalysis (COFAP), past and present, especially Isidoro Berenstein who welcomed me onto that committee so warmly, and to the current Chair, David Scharff. David Scharff and Jill Savege Scharff and I have collaborated for many years through Tavistock Relationships and the International Psychotherapy Institute (IPI), and I want to thank them for their generosity and passion for this field, particularly their inclusivity and the way they have reached out and taken couple and family psychoanalytic work to many parts of the world. The committee brings together many different perspectives and for me it has been important to have this 'out of London' *and* 'out of the British Object Relations perspective', and readers will see some of the influence of this, particularly from South America, in this book. In this regard, I especially wish to warmly thank Monica Vorchheimer and Elizabeth Palacios. I would also like to thank my colleagues on the board of the International Association of Couple and Family Psychoanalysis, currently led by Rosa Jaitin, for their collaboration in bringing together different perspectives, in particular Link Theory and Object Relations.

There are many psychoanalytic colleagues too who have influenced me and helped me. I am especially grateful to Irma Brenman Pick, Ron Britton and Michael Feldman. Finally, thank you to all my patients, individuals and couples.

Introduction

This book is written for students and colleagues in the field of couple and individual psychoanalysis. Although not exactly a text book, I hope it will help students in engaging in psychoanalytic work with couples and provide a psychoanalytic framework for any clinician in thinking about the couple relationship and the couple analytic process.

It is not possible to disentangle how much of this book is me and how much is Tavistock Relationships, since I have worked there for so many years, been influenced by the thinking of our founders and colleagues over the years and also myself contributed to the theory and technique. My training as a psychoanalyst within the Kleinian tradition has had an influence here, so in that respect there are areas not covered or developed in this book that another author might include; for example, the interest in attachment theory and attachment-based couple therapy (on which there have been many excellent publications, particularly by Chris Clulow) or mentalisation-based couple treatment, Improving Access to Psychological Therapies (IAPT) couple therapy for depression or psychodynamic sex therapy. There are also areas that I have not been able to cover in any depth; for example, working with couples' different sexualities, which I hope will be rectified in a future publication.

For analytic colleagues elsewhere, either from a different couple analytic perspective or from psychoanalysis, I hope by describing this approach as clearly as I can, that you can engage with it, and our dialogues can continue creatively.

The book starts with a description of the concept of a couple state of mind and how this might be of value in couple analytic work.

Chapter One is an overview of Tavistock Relationships' theoretical approach. Part of the nature of being a human being is that we are continually trying to work through and resolve or defend against and deny earlier experience and intrapsychic tension. This affects all our relating and all our relationships and is particularly acute in the adult intimate couple relationship. Determinants from the past that shape the couples relating are thus an important component. The couple's psychic development in becoming a couple is another theoretical strand. The way we relate to an intimate other in the present, as well as what a couple creates together potentially in the future, are also described as part of this theoretical overview.

In Chapter Two I explore what I consider to be key elements of a psychoanalytic couple assessment – providing containment, formulating an initial understanding of the relationship problem, assessing the couple's suitability for treatment, including an assessment of risk. These different aspects can be difficult to hold together. Couples often feel ambivalent about seeking psychoanalytic treatment – differences between the partners in wanting help, fears about the relationship and family life falling apart, and anxieties about what therapy might mean for them all play a part. In Chapter Three, I describe this process and how to create a couple analytic setting in which the therapy can take place. The Tavistock Relationships frame, including the possibility of co-therapy, is described. In this way Chapters Two and Three provide a guide to starting treatment with a couple.

The next few chapters, Chapters Four to Seven, explore some key areas of theory and technique in couple analytic work. Chapter Four focuses on the concepts of unconscious phantasy, shared unconscious phantasy, unconscious beliefs and fantasy, which I distinguish from each other and consider how they are all useful concepts in thinking about and working with a couple. In Chapter Five, I explore the field of transference and countertransference in working with couples. It introduces the idea of the living inner world of the couple and how this might be accessed by the therapist's lived experience of the couple in the room. How to gather the transference in a couple relationship is described and illustrated with clinical material. Working with both the 'couple transference relationship' and the 'therapeutic couple transference and countertransference' is described. In Chapter Six, central concepts in work with couples, the concept of projective identification and the couple's projective system are explored. Not all projective systems function in the same way, and I emphasise the importance of considering the *nature* of the projective system which can span from being quite flexible and developmental for the individuals within it, to one that is very defensive, controlling and claustrophobic. The key concepts of unconscious choice of partner and couple fit are also described in this chapter. Chapter Seven looks at what is both an ordinary problem and a more disturbed dynamic in considering narcissism and the couple's capacity to share psychic space. Several clinical examples of working with these issues are given.

Chapter Eight provides a different lens on intimate relating, that of psychic development and state of mind. I trace how through earlier stages of development we become an adult intimate couple and why for many this is not an easy process. All couples move between the different states of mind depicted by those stages. This perspective also helps us in relation to what it means to be part of a couple and how this might be defined, albeit with a never-ending level of variation with which each couple defines their own relationship. I also explore sex and the couple's sexual relationship and a frequently reported problem, loss of desire.

Chapter Nine is possibly the most technically focused chapter in this book as I look at the field of couple interpretation and other interventions that the couple therapist makes. I describe how with a couple state of mind it is possible to direct interpretations to the different relationships and dynamics in the room, working towards 'couple interpretations'. What is meant by a couple interpretation and why this is important in helping the couple themselves to develop a 'couple state of mind' are outlined.

The final chapter, Chapter Ten, is about endings, but in the process of thinking about ending, we also have to think about the aim of couple analytic work. I suggest a way to formulate this which is consistent with the theme of this book, about the couple themselves introjecting a couple state of mind.

Before ending this introduction, there are two things I wish to draw the reader's attention to. The first is that throughout the book, when I refer to Tavistock Relationships, it is to the organisation and thinking that has evolved over the last 70 years, though called by different names through its history. It started as the Family Discussion Bureau, then became the Institute of Marital Studies, the Tavistock Institute of Marital Studies, the Tavistock Marital Studies Institute, the Tavistock Centre for Couple Relations and is currently called Tavistock Relationships.

The other issue is another but different one about names. At Tavistock Relationships we call our analytic training the MA in Couple Psychoanalytic Psychotherapy and consequently those trained with us call themselves Couple Psychoanalytic Psychotherapists. But in other parts of the world, even without this level of training, practitioners refer to themselves as Couple Psychoanalysts. This is reflected not only in organisations of psychoanalysts such as the IPA committee on Couple and Family Psychoanalysis (COFAP), but in others such as the International Association of Couple and Family Psychoanalysis which Tavistock Relationships is affiliated to, never mind our own international journal *Couple and Family Psychoanalysis*. The Tavistock Relationships model I am presenting is undoubtedly psychoanalytic, but at the moment we describe what we do in different ways as you will see through this book – for example, couple psychotherapy, analytic work with couples. I think for Tavistock Relationships and those working in private practice within our particular culture, there is a concern that using the name 'couple psychoanalyst' could alienate couples seeking help. I think this is perhaps different in other societies and countries. I think it also reflects the fact that we are at a point in time when thinking about and attending to one's couple relationship is not something that is commonplace in society. As a friend pointed out to me a while ago, we don't go to dinner with friends and ask each other, "How is your relationship going"? In the same way, most couples don't think about seeking *psychoanalysis* as a couple, though some do. So, this is something that is somewhat unclear in the profession, but hopefully not in this book which is about psychoanalysis of couples.

A couple state of mind

The development of the concept

The idea of a couple state of mind is rooted in the discoveries of the clinicians and theoreticians at what is now known as Tavistock Relationships (TR), previously known by other names (see Introduction) and also by Dicks and others at the Tavistock Clinic, who recognised that, to understand a couple, the focus had to be on the couple's *relationship*. In other words, a couple's relationship is more than the sum of the two individuals; it is what the partners create between them consciously and unconsciously. The relationship becomes a psychic object in its own right which the couple relates to symbolically and can feel contained by (Colman, 1993a; Ruszczynski 1998; Morgan, 2005). This has been expressed in different ways and is embedded in concepts such a 'shared unconscious phantasy' (Bannister & Pincus, 1965), and more recently the idea of a 'creative couple' (Morgan & Ruszczynski, 1998; Morgan, 2005). But what specifically do I mean by a couple state of mind – the theme running throughout this book?

Before describing this, it is important to acknowledge that the application of post-Kleinian theory, while not being the only theoretical influence, has had quite an impact on the clinical work and theory at Tavistock Relationships, particularly since the 1990s (see, for example, Ruszczynski, 1993a; Ruszczynski & Fisher, 1995; Fisher, 1999; Grier, 2005a). Of particular significance has been the work of Britton. In my own writing, his work on the Oedipus Complex (1989), triangular space (1998a), narcissism (2000) and unconscious beliefs (1998b), has been particularly important.

I first thought about and began to conceptualise the idea of a couple state of mind when undertaking consultations at Tavistock Relationships in the 1990s. At that time, I was seeing a lot of couples for initial consultations and I became aware that what I later came to think of as a 'couple state of mind' (Morgan, 2001), was an important part of the therapeutic and containing nature of this first contact with a couple (see Chapter 2). Writing about couples seen for consultations and drawing on Britton's work, I described the following:

> What might be of most help to the couple in this situation is the therapist's capacity to hold a 'couple state of mind', an important component of which is the capacity to take a "third position" (Britton 1989) in relation to the couple – that is, being able to be subjectively involved with both individuals, but also, at the same time, being able to stand outside the relationship and observe the couple.
>
> (Morgan, 2001, p. 17)

I realised how important and containing it could be for a couple to have the experience of being with a therapist who thinks about their *relationship*, that is, what they create together. Of course, this is such an obvious point – the couple is approaching a couple therapist for help with their relationship. Only I realised that might not be how the couple experiences it. Often, they were coming for help with their partner who was seen as causing them unhappiness and therefore they wanted help from the therapist to change their partner. Sometimes, one partner who felt to blame was reluctant to come. It struck me that some couples may not previously have conceived of themselves having a relationship in the sense that they were creating something together.

Part of the Tavistock Relationships' approach was to think about couple therapy as a treatment of choice rather than an adjunct to individual work. Assuming the couple was suitable for psychoanalytic treatment, the view was that this was the arena in which it made sense for them to do this analytic work, which could help them as a couple and as individuals. Sometimes either or both partners might have been in individual psychotherapy or go on to this after the couple work, but we saw it as part of their psychoanalytic journey. But what was interesting to me was why couples *did* come for psychotherapy together, something that at the time Fisher was also thinking about, asking the question: "In order to think about whether or not any given couple can benefit from analytic therapy, we need to think about why anyone would want to engage in the analytic process *as a couple*" (1999, p. 123; emphasis in original).

Because of our understanding of the interlocking nature of the couple's unconscious relating, we knew that the couple relationship was sometimes the arena in which disturbance arose. All couples form a unique unconscious link based on the way each partner's subjectivity comes together with the other's, creating tensions, some irreconcilable, some potentially creative. But, as well as that, I came to see that couples came for help because the 'couple state of mind' was missing as a function of their relationship. In other words, they were not able to take a third position in which they could observe themselves and think about themselves *as a couple* and what they were creating together, positively and negatively.

I came to think that this was something missing in many couples coming for help and what they unconsciously sought in the figure of the therapist.

The couple therapist stood for the relationship, observed and interpreted what they were creating together as a couple. Being with a therapist who had a couple state of mind changed the atmosphere in the consultations (and the ongoing therapy). It became less blaming and the couple felt they could move from a fairly powerless position of feeling the other was responsible to a change of position in which they could think about what was happening between them. In the best consultations, they even started to feel a bit curious about this entity they realised they were part of, 'their relationship'. This realisation, which might only be fleeting in a consultation, sometimes seemed to make even the most unmotivated couple want to come back for another consultation or to commence therapy. The therapist's 'couple state of mind' stance introduced a new way of understanding what was happening to them.

A couple state of mind as an aim of couple psychotherapy

The most important thing about a couple state of mind is that over the course of the therapy, if the therapy progresses well, this becomes internalised by the couple as part of their own relationship. The capacity of the couple to hold a couple state of mind can be seen in the unfolding of the therapy as the couple starts to think together about what is happening between them. They still have arguments, but they start to report that they were able to talk about it the next day and reflect on what might have gone wrong, and they develop more insight into themselves and their relationship. In this way, monitoring the internalisation of a couple state of mind is diagnostic and helps the therapist think about when the couple could end therapy.

A couple state of mind as part of the therapist's analytic stance

From the beginning of treatment, a couple state of mind guides and grounds the therapist. It manifests in the setting – the way the therapist approaches the initial contact, the way she sets up the consulting room, the way she communicates with the couple between sessions by keeping them both in mind. It also helps the therapist manage aspects of the countertransference as although the therapist has as her focus the couple relationship and what the couple creates between them, this is not always easy or possible. Each partner may see the other as the problem or agree between them that one of them is the problem, and sometimes the therapist initially also sees one of them as the problem. But a couple state of mind provides an internal position in the therapist in which this perception can be challenged and a couple state of mind rediscovered.

If a couple state of mind is securely in place it provides the therapist with flexibility in the work. For example, it would not be possible to see one partner without the other, as I describe in Chapter Two, without a couple state of mind as the therapy would shift from couple to individual work. Contrary to popular belief, couple therapists are not only interpreting to the couple as a couple. But with a couple state of mind, all interpretations are to the couple, because even if addressed to one of the partners, the other, their response, is taken into account, and may be the basis of the next interpretation. The flexibility a secure couple state of mind provides makes it possible to interpret in relation to the different relationships in the room, leading towards a 'couple interpretation' which addresses what is happening unconsciously between the couple.

A couple state of mind and the creative couple

Sometimes, perhaps in my own writing too, the idea of a couple state of mind and the creative couple are not clearly distinguished. In an attempt to be clearer, I would like to say that I locate the achievement of the creative couple, as an internal object, as part of an individual's psychic development (Morgan, 2005; and see Chapter 8). It is a stage of psychic development which follows earlier developmental struggles and is the foundation for a healthy adult couple relationship, as well as other kinds of adult relationships. A feature of this development is a couple state of mind. But in addition to a couple state of mind as a function of the couple's relationship, the couple can use their couple state of mind to think creatively together. They can tolerate differences, not necessarily knowing if and how these differences can be brought together, but nonetheless hold the belief, sometimes realised, that their differences can lead to a creative outcome, something 'new' between them that neither could have discovered alone. And one of the triggers for the creative couple developmental process is being with a therapist who expresses a couple state of mind because of her own internal creative couple development.

Chapter 1

A psychoanalytic understanding of the couple relationship

Past, present and future[1]

The understanding of the couple relationship has been at the heart of Tavistock Relationships since its inception in 1948 (then called the Family Discussion Bureau). Set up in post-war Britain amid political and social concern about family and marital distress, there was growing recognition that psychological as well as material help was needed. The pioneering family caseworkers turned to psychoanalysis to help understand the conflicted and distressed couple relationships they were encountering.[2] Over the last 70 years, this work has developed into a specific psychoanalytic theoretical and clinical approach. As this thinking developed, it has been influenced by a broad base of analytic thinking, but particularly from the 1990s, by post-Kleinian ideas. The model that has evolved concerns the complex unconscious interplay between the two people in a relationship, their internal object relations, unconscious phantasies, conflicts, anxieties and defences, and how these interact with another psyche and create something new.

There are several strands to this thinking that have developed and had prominence at different periods in the history of Tavistock Relationships, but all form part of the current body of thought. These I have conceptualised as the influence of the past on the relationship, the nature of the relationship developmentally and dynamically in the present, and the potential for the relationship in the future. Central to the Tavistock Relationships technique is the therapist's 'couple state of mind'. These areas, brought together here in this overview of Tavistock Relationships theory, will be elaborated further in subsequent chapters.

The influence of the past

This concerns the unconscious determinants that bring the couple together based on their past experience, and how their new relationship is shaped by these, and is perhaps set up to repeat, manage or work through unresolved early conflicts and anxieties. Pincus, for example, wrote:

> Although there is often a wish to start afresh in marriage and to escape the frustrations or disappointments of unsatisfactory early relationships, the strong unconscious ties to the first love-objects may help determine the choice of partner with whom the earlier situation can be compulsively re-enacted.
>
> (Pincus, 1962, p. 14)

The meaning of the unconscious choice of partner and the unconscious contract that the couple sets up, and the projective system in which each partner splits off, projects into and carries aspects of the other are analysed. In more defensive relationships, there is the wish to keep these aspects located in the other, but in developmental relationships, there is more flexibility and these aspects of the self have the potential to be reintegrated, leading to growth in the individual and the relationship. Early clinical publications traced in detail the meaning of the object choice, the couple fit and the complex unconscious arrangements the couple made to find equilibrium in their relationship.

The defensive version of a couple's transference relationship – a repetition of an early, unresolved relationship or internal versions of this – was noted by Freud in *Beyond the Pleasure Principle*. He gives examples of individuals whose relationships all seem to have the same outcome, whereby a similar object is repeatedly chosen, but nothing is worked through; no new relationship develops. For example, he speaks of, "the lover each of whose love affairs with a woman passes through the same phases and reaches the same conclusion" (1920, p. 22). He says:

> If we take into account observations such as these, based upon behaviour in the transference and upon the life-histories of men and women, we shall find courage to assume that there really does exist in the mind a compulsion to repeat which over-rides the pleasure principle.
>
> (Freud, 1920, p. 22)

In this sense, the new relationship becomes a version of an old relationship. What these early clinicians understood was that there was often both the wish to repeat *and* the wish to create something new; for example, Balint observed that:

> One of the most striking, and perhaps encouraging, things that psychoanalysts have discovered, is that people never give up trying to put things right for themselves and for the people they love. Even when they may appear to be doing just the reverse, we often discover that what appears to be the most desperate and useless behaviour can be understood as an attempt to get back to something that was good in the past, or to put right something that was unsatisfactory ... We

could say then, that in marriage we unconsciously hope to find a solution to our intimate and primitive problems.

(Balint, 1993, p. 41)

The relationship is thus seen as potentially containing for the couple in that it can provide an opportunity for working through and development. If the projective system is flexible enough, parts of the self are not lost, but are held by the other and within the safety of the relationship and, over time, can be reintrojected. Ideally, each partner continues to work through, individuate and develop within the context of the relationship which functions as a psychological container (Colman, 1993a). In this sense, the adult intimate couple relationship provides a special opportunity for the individuals within it to both regress and develop or individuate as some earlier clinicians described,

> The marriage relationship provides a containment in which each feels the other to be part of themselves—a kind of joint personality. What at first attracts and is later complained of in the other is often a projection of the disowned and frightening aspects of the self. It might be imagined that the best thing to do with unwanted aspects of the self is to project them onto someone or something and get as far removed as possible. That would, however, be placing a part of oneself in danger of being lost forever, and of losing one's potential for becoming a more complete person.
>
> (Cleavely, 1993, p. 65)

All these writers speak about the tension between the developmental and the defensive needs inherent in most relationships. But essentially this is quite an optimistic view of the couple relationship as potentially therapeutic, with the capacity to repair the past and enable the individuals in the relationship to work through earlier conflict.

A further important thread in this thinking was the idea of shared unconscious phantasy (Bannister & Pincus, 1965). It was observed that, as well as repeating or reworking the past, couples brought to the relationship shared or similar ways of experiencing the world through unconscious phantasy; as, for example, the unconscious phantasy that love or hate are dangerous. It could be seen how couples set up shared defences to manage shared unconscious phantasies, leading to a relationship in which, for example, strong feelings are avoided and the presenting problem is a lack of intimacy and sex. More recently, very fixed and more deeply unconscious phantasies that grip a relationship have been thought about as unconscious beliefs about being a couple (Britton, 1998c; Morgan, 2010; Humphries, 2015).

Much of this thinking was prevalent from the 1960s to the 1980s and can be seen in the publication, edited by Stanley Ruszczynski, *Psychotherapy with Couples* (1993a).

The present

There are two areas of thought that relate to the nature of the relationship in the present, which I describe as the relationship *developmentally* and *dynamically* in the present.

The couple's psychic development in becoming a couple

Becoming a couple is part of a process of psychic development from birth onwards, but development can become stuck before becoming a couple is achieved, or if development towards being a couple is not secure. In a paper on being able to be a couple (Morgan, 2005), I describe this process of the couple's psychic development, in which the relationship to the primary object, working through the Oedipal situation and adolescence are all crucial. Therefore, sometimes as couple therapists we ask what kind of couple exists in the present; do the partners feel part of a couple and, if so, what kind of couple is it?

It could be that the relationship is set up unconsciously to create an idealised version of a mother–baby dyad. Or there may be problems in being able to take a step into being an adult couple because of difficulties relinquishing an earlier stage of psychic development, such as the adolescent sense of autonomy. It is not infrequent to see couples try to create a perfect unity, holding the belief that this is what a couple relationship is, or should be. Equally, we see individuals who are terrified of making the commitment to be a couple, as if they would get lost in, or consumed by, this idea of coupledom.

The relationship dynamically in the present

Unconscious phantasy

Unconscious phantasy, although inevitably having roots in past experience, also shapes the way the couple relates in the present. The way we experience the world, including those we are in a relationship with, is filtered through the lens of unconscious phantasy. In a healthy relationship, this is a two-way process, these unconscious phantasies are brought into contact with external reality and are modified. But couple therapists also observe the partners perceiving the other in repetitively familiar ways and misperceiving each other. It is like another unconscious conversation going on between the couple of which they are not aware.

Some unconscious phantasies dovetail in the couple relationship around significant areas – for example, dependency, separateness or intimacy – and the couple's unconscious struggle with these areas can be thought of as shared unconscious phantasies. The couple relates to the shared issue in particular ways and can induce the partner to play a part in their phantasy. As this happens both ways around, the couple creates a shared 'story'. In the process of the couple repeatedly bringing different versions of this story, which the therapist is unconsciously invited to participate in, the therapist can build a picture of the shared unconscious phantasies underlying it.

Unconscious beliefs (Britton, 1998c) are conceptualised as a type of unconscious phantasy that has not developed and remains deep in the unconscious in an unchanging state. Sometimes the couple or one partner holds unconscious beliefs about the meaning of being a couple (Morgan, 2010). The belief is like an ever-present backdrop to the relationship. In the unconscious, it is experienced as a 'fact' and therefore does not need to be questioned. The partner not fitting in with the belief is seen as a betrayal which justifies criticism and attack. It is harder to make contact with these beliefs, but when they break through into consciousness, sometimes through an enactment or through making sense of a disturbing, elusive countertransference, the present but unseen backdrop of the belief can for a moment come into sharp focus.

Narcissistic relating

Related to this, but opening up a broader question, is how does a couple manage the reality or fact of being in a relationship with an 'other' who is separate and different, but also intimate? This, I think, is both an ordinary difficulty as well as a more narcissistic problem. Being in a relationship (unless the relationship is very fused) faces the individual on a daily basis with the reality of there being another view, a different experience, and perhaps one that cannot easily be engaged with or understood. Even if we consider the couple relationship to be constructed on the basis of object seeking, inevitably there are aspects of the 'other' discovered in the relationship that cannot be anticipated and will be challenging – not all of the other can be assimilated, known or even tolerated. This reality can hit some couples hard and it is not uncommon to see couples expending an enormous amount of psychic energy in trying to deny this fact. The therapist's exploration here is not so much about why two people come together based on unresolved aspects of their past and what the relationship might help them work through or defend against, but rather about the impact on each partner of being with an 'other'.

For some, the fact of there being a separate other is intolerable and couples resort to primitive defences to try to deal with this situation. One common solution is the attempt to force the other to fit in with one's own view, resulting in endless conflict, or a sado-masochistic dominance and submission. In another solution, which I have termed a 'projective gridlock' (Morgan, 1995), the couple collapses into each other. Here projective identification is used to create a sense of living inside the object, or the object living inside the self, as a way of managing and denying the other's actual separateness and difference which are experienced as too threatening to the self. We see with couples the way in which this psychic arrangement can create a comfortable sort of fusion, but it usually becomes something that feels very controlling and rigid, trapping the couple in the gridlock they have created.

These ideas about narcissistic relating in the couple were developed in Tavistock Relationships from the 1990s onwards and were described in *Intrusiveness and Intimacy in the Couple* (Ruszczynski & Fisher, 1995) and in *The Uninvited Guest: Emerging from Narcissism towards Marriage* (Fisher, 1999). Here, Fisher suggests an ongoing tension between narcissism and the psychological state of marriage:

> The capacity to pursue the truth of one's own experience and also to tolerate the truth of another's experience, acknowledging and taking the meaning of the other's experience without losing the meaning of one's own, especially when these experiences not only differ but conflict, is a major developmental achievement ... The achievement of this capacity is not a fixed state and in intimate relationships they are always under pressure of our own infantile wishes, fears, and anxieties to redraw the boundaries between self and other.
>
> (Fisher, 1999, p. 56)

Sharing psychic space was the subject of the Enid Balint Memorial Lecture in 1999 given by Ron Britton. Giving the response to that paper, I was very struck, as I imagine Britton was from his use of metaphors in that lecture, by the parallels between the analytic (patient/analyst) relationship and the intimate couple relationship. In particular, Britton described two kinds of narcissistic relating – 'adherent' and 'detached' – which can result in disturbing kinds of 'couple fits'; for example, in which one partner takes all the psychic space in the relationship while the other is hidden or absent (see Chapter 7), or in which each member of the couple acts as opposite poles preventing any kind of intimacy (Britton, 2003a; Nyberg, 2007).

Both Ogden (1994a) and Pickering (2006) describe the individual's confrontation with what they call "alterity" – the otherness of an 'other'. This affects our sense of who we are and "does not allow us to remain who we were" (Ogden, 1994a, p. 14). Thus, intimacy is not just about being close while remaining separate – each member of the couple is changed through the encounter with the other. The fact that the way the self is changed cannot be known and is not conscious helps us see why, for some, contemplating a relationship may be experienced as a frightening step into the unknown.

Again, drawing fruitfully on the work of Britton and the development of triangular space, as an outcome of working through the Oedipal situation, couple therapists in different ways have applied this to the couple and to analytic couple therapy. Ruszczynski has written about "the marital triangle" (Ruszczynski, 1998), and more recently, Balfour (2016) has highlighted the special potential of the triangular situation in couple therapy for creating more psychic space. I have proposed the notion of "a couple state of mind" (Morgan, 2001) as something that is often missing in couples seeking help and that can be provided by the therapist and gradually internalised by the couple as an outcome of treatment. The couple state of mind is a third position symbolised by the couple's relationship itself, and helps the couple to be themselves, while also seeing themselves, in the relationship with the other. This is important in potentially containing the turmoil that is inevitable in an intimate relationship in which both the otherness of the other and the impact on the self have to be managed, particularly when we consider that the self in this relationship is no longer the self from before.

Berenstein (2012) from the perspective of the "link" (*el vínculo*) describes the notion of "presence", meaning the presence of the other, and how this impacts on the self as an "interference". He says:

> Interference is what is produced in the space in between as a result of there being two or more subjects whose presence generates something new and unknown. The unknown forces these subjects to do something with it, to inscribe it, and to attempt to produce a *becoming* based on difference while dealing with the uncertainty about what they may be able to achieve.
>
> (Berenstein, 2012, pp. 575–576)

The similarities and differences between object relations theory and the link perspective is a creative area of study now both within the current International Psychoanalytical Association Couple and Family Psychoanalysis committee and within the International Association of Couple and Family Psychoanalysis. This work is captured in a number of recent publications (Scharff & Savege Scharff, 2011; Scharff & Palacios, 2017; Scharff & Vorchheimer, 2017).

Projective identification and the projective system

The understanding of the way in which projective identification works in couple relationships has been central in Tavistock Relationships' thought from early on. It is part of the couple analytic concept of a 'couple projective system'. This concept underpins the idea of a 'joint marital personality' (Dicks, 1967), unconscious choice of partner and marital or couple fit. It is also a way of understanding why some individuals have to seek therapy as a couple, as part of each partner is located in, and only known about, in the other. Pincus describes this in the following way:

> [T]he person who complains of his partner's depression, dependence or dominance may well, by denying his own, leave the partner to express a double dose and, at the same time, by developing defensive opposite attitudes to the denied ones, increase the stress and the estrangement in the marriage.
>
> (Pincus, 1962, p. 18)

The couple's projective system contributes to an understanding of why couples who want to separate cannot. All couples have some kind of projective system and what is important is the nature of this system. How communicative and flexible it is or defensive, rigid and intrusive rests on the way that projective identification is being used by the projector and experienced by the recipient. As described earlier, the couple's projective system can be containing for the couple. If flexible, it can lead to growth in the individual partners and the relationship, as it adapts to changing needs and external reality. Over time, projected aspects, lived with in the partner, can be reintrojected. Alternatively, if the projective system is very defensive and controlled, it can manifest as something very narcissistic and anti-developmental.

The future

My third area, the future, returns to the idea of the adult couple relationship as having the potential for development. In contrast to the earlier ideas that emphasise working through the past, this is about the relationship creating something new. That which gets created in the coming together of the two people is unique to that configuration. Here, I want to bring together the idea of 'the creative couple' with the notion of *el vínculo*, each stemming from different psychoanalytic traditions. Berenstein describes the link between the couple as follows:

> Its product is an expanded, modified, renewed subjectivity that makes it possible to negate the ego's (narcissistic) confinement in its identity and to establish this subjectivity as novelty. The couple has its own life as an aggregate, which is different from the sum of its parts. Its members carry in them the psychic developments of their own history and childhood as well as those produced within this aggregate, which is ceaselessly being constituted in each of the numerous "nows" they experience together. The present time gives rise to a past, a history, and a future in the form of a project that may not necessarily be realized but is a determining factor nonetheless.
>
> (Berenstein, 2012, p. 573)

The whole point of being in a relationship is that there is an 'other' and a continuous exchange between the partners who are together, but also, separate and different. They come together, are changed by each other, and have the capacity to produce a third between them, symbolised by the 'baby'. Rather than 'third', perhaps I should say 'thirds', as the couple who function creatively produce many 'thirds' as an outcome of their relationship.

In psychoanalytic couple therapy, we are interested not only in whether the couple can discover their relationship as a resource, something they can turn to in their minds to contain them, but also whether they can use their difference and otherness to create something new – new thoughts, resolutions and ways forward. The internalisation of a couple state of mind helps the couple find the capacity to observe themselves in a relationship with the other. This helps them manage difference and conflict through achieving a perspective on the dynamics of their relationship, and on what each partner brings to it based on who they are, including their past experience. But in order for the couple to be creative, something else has to happen with these differences: "the foreign aspect of the other", as Berenstein describes it, has to be engaged with (Berenstein, 2012, p. 576)

Psychoanalytic couple theory takes as its focus not only what each partner brings from the past to the present relationship, but the new and unpredicted ways in which their separate inner worlds impact on the other in the present. If the otherness of the other can be engaged with, the individual's own psychic development continues, not only in terms of working through the past, but through a new potentially creative couple relationship in the present.

Before ending this theoretical overview, I want to note, perhaps rather obviously, but nonetheless I think interestingly, the way in which the view of relating in the 'analytic couple', patient and analyst, referred to earlier, is different from that in the 'adult intimate couple'. Working analytically with individuals, we try and observe our developing and changing relationship to our patient over time and from moment to moment, drawing especially on our countertransference and the ways we are unconsciously nudged into enacting our patient's inner world. This helps us understand their inner world. Of course, we are not completely neutral objects and some schools of psychoanalysis would emphasise this more strongly. In analytic couple therapy, the therapist is also observing a couple (and sometimes she is a participant in the couple as I will describe later – see Chapter 5), and here we can see the way that the relationship is not only determined by each partner's past, including their own 'couple relationship past', their two internal worlds, but also that what each brings to the relationship affects the other and creates something new, that is always changing, in the present. In this way, I believe analytic work with couples provides a vantage point from which to observe and understand the complexity of relating, which might be of interest in psychoanalysis beyond the couple field wherein it is observed.

In summary, the way I have conceptualised a psychoanalytic approach to understanding the couple relationship is: first, what the couple brings of their past and how this is responded to defensively and developmentally; second, how the couple is progressing developmentally in the process of being 'a couple' and how the partners manage the dynamic of there being an 'other'; and third, how they might carry on developing in the context of a relationship that could be creative for them both together and individually.

The following clinical example illustrates some of these ideas – the influence of the past and the attempt to work through unresolved early experience, and also the couple's projective system, transference relationship, and the way in which feeling less in the grip of these, other difficulties emerged, but also something more creative and 'new'.

David and Kay: a couple who struggled with love and hate
I have chosen this couple and one central aspect of the work with them, their difficulty in managing love and hate. Kay, aged 45, and David, aged 55, had been married for 5 years. It was David's second marriage, his first wife having died 10 years previously in a car accident. He had two children in their mid-twenties.

When I first met them, I was struck by Kay's vitriol – she was so angry, felt the relationship was ruined, and said she would be better off on her own. She then started screaming, and explained she had seen her doctor as she felt close to breakdown. David was very alarmed; he could not understand how things had gone so badly wrong and perhaps irrevocably broken down between them. He said he loved Kay and could not bear to see her like this. The couple seemed in a traumatised state. As she cried, he reached out to comfort her and she angrily pushed him away. It was a shocking moment and made me wary of reaching out to her myself.

When Kay recovered herself, she told me about the "abominable behaviour" of David's children, a daughter and a son, who within the first few years of their marriage had moved back home and exhibited very demanding and dependent behaviour. Kay was appalled that they were like regressed adolescents – invasive, rude, untidy, selfish and demanding of their father financially, physically and emotionally. She believed that, "like birds", at a certain point, babies are pushed out of the nest and have to fly. It seemed that while secretly Kay had hoped that they would have all got on together as a family, she in fact found herself furious that David's children should use him in this way, and that he allowed them to do so. David had felt it was natural as a parent to try and help his children, particularly as they were having real problems. Neither had any secure employment; his daughter was receiving help from mental health services, and his son had a medical condition for which he was not following the prescribed treatment.

As often happens when treating couples, I initially had a very uneven counter-transference response to the couple. I felt sorry for David, who had lost his first wife, possibly now his second, and who was extremely worried about his children.

Kay was so harsh, hostile and ungiving that I wondered if I would ever be able to make emotional contact with her.

Something must have happened. It may have been simply the consistency of the setting, and the fact that, although I could not make much contact with Kay, equally I did not let her push me away, as, a few months into the therapy, she felt safe enough to tell me that in her relationship with David, she had allowed herself to become "excited for the first time ever in her life". I wondered what it was that she felt excited about. She said that she had found "love". This was said in such a way that for a moment we were all silenced. After a few minutes, I said I thought she was telling David and me about an experience of finding the capacity to both love and be loved.

Kay then told me about the following events. She grew up in an orphanage overseas, without contact from her parents. When she was 7 years old, her mother came to see her. At first, she could not believe the visitor was for her, as up until then she had had no family visitors and did not know her mother. She felt excited by the visit and obtained the promise from her mother that she would return in a fortnight. She remembered vividly the next 2 weeks of anticipation, thinking and talking of nothing else. When the day came, she waited in anticipation, time went on, other visitors came and went, and she eventually reached the painful conclusion that no one was coming for her.

I now knew it was not that Kay did not have any love, but that she was extremely frightened of it. I now understood what a risk it had been for her to allow herself to feel excited and hopeful about a chance later in life to have the love she had been so deprived of earlier. Melanie Klein points out that it is not just bad aspects of the self that are split off and projected, but good aspects too, because one feels one does not deserve to have them (Klein, 1946). I think Kay had found someone in David into whom she could project what remained of her loving feelings for safekeeping as she felt that inside her they would not flourish or would be destroyed.

David started off his life in more affluent circumstances than Kay and with his family intact. However, his father's business failed during David's childhood, plunging the family from wealth to poverty. The family, which included two younger brothers, had moved around the country living hand to mouth from relatives. David thought that his mother never recovered from the shock of their changed circumstances and her health failed. David was bright and did well at school, but the family could not afford any further education.

David presented as a warm and caring man, but I realised he lacked any aggression and the firmness he needed. While Kay was frightened of love, David was frightened of hate. It was many months into the therapy before he could start to express how angry and let down he felt by his parents, who in his eyes both collapsed in his childhood and never recovered. Any contact with his anger and hate had to be warded off as in unconscious phantasy he feared that it might kill off his parents altogether. Instead, he had taken on the role of carer of his mother and later of his first wife. This caring aspect of David was what had excited Kay so much – as she put it – he seemed to have "an excess of love". Through him she felt she might risk being loved and also felt she might be able to recover (reintroject) some of her own loving feelings. David, on the other hand, felt drawn to Kay's robustness and the way in which she could express negative, even hostile feelings, and nothing terrible seemed to happen. He may have thought, less consciously, that Kay coming into the family might be just what his children needed too.

One could see that for this couple, their unconscious beliefs that love and hate were dangerous were being challenged in their relationship through experiencing, in the other, a different connection with these powerful feelings that had been kept at bay for most of their lives. When David's children came to live them, however, their respective traumas began to recur. David feared that the children were getting worse, and Kay was breaking down, just as his parents had. Kay felt abandoned by David, "pushed out of the nest", just as she had been by her parents (and others) who left her.

These earlier feelings in relation to fragile and abandoning objects were re-evoked in the transference between them, intensifying anxiety for them both. And their projective system, in which Kay could see her split-off loving feelings lived with in David and David could see his hate – which in a benign form stood for firmness, robustness and boundaries – lived with in Kay, also intensified, gripping the couple in a stranglehold they could not see their way out of. Instead of a reintrojective process occurring, as the projective processes continued, the couple became polarised, each partner even taking possession of the projected aspects.

An understanding of the roots of their anxieties, brought alive again in the present, helped to lessen the grip of their projective system. In parallel to this, there was a shift in the transference to me, and in my countertransference. As Kay started to feel more secure in her relationship with me, I started to feel annoyed and irritated with David. Why was he not more robust with his children? Why was he always such a benign figure in the room, as if he had taken possession of all the good aspects and left Kay to complain and criticise – a feeling that was taking hold of me too in my countertransference. He was, of course, frightened that any anger expressed towards any of us would be destructive. I had a sense of this destructive anger located in Kay, when she had shown her hostility in the first session. Although her rejecting response to David was not an unusual event for a couple in therapy, her expression of it had conveyed something so killing off, of human, emotional contact.

A turning point came a few months into the work when I noticed Kay unexpectedly expressing some warm feelings towards David's children. When I pointed this out to her, she realised she had surprised herself – she had not meant to. It did not feel a very safe place for her, but I felt she also took a tentative bit of pleasure in freeing herself, even temporarily, from her fixed role in relation to them, of being a hating, abandoning object. This was the beginning of a loosening of the projective system and of developing a more realistic connection to, and integration of, the love and hate in each of them.

As things slowly improved in this family, other difficulties emerged. Further into the therapy they struggled with their differences and, as the idealised phantasies of what the relationship could provide for them were brought into more contact with reality, they were faced with its limitations. It could not repair everything in the past, but they did manage to limit the degree to which they recreated the past in the present. When David's children did leave home, Kay felt sad about the fact that they would not have children together. This loss, important in its own right, also gave a platform to them both to grieve earlier losses that had never been worked through.

This mourning process and the loosening of their projective system produced new challenges in the relationship. They had to struggle more with who the other was and not only those aspects of the other that through projective identification they had honed in on. As David became able to demand more of his children, he also expressed more of his needs to Kay and this was difficult for them. Kay did not see herself as someone who could nurture and David was worried about demanding things for himself. Each had to struggle not only with real aspects of the other that they had not previously encountered, but with emerging aspects of themselves that could take them by surprise.

At the point of ending the therapy, it seemed the couple had more of a capacity to relate to the other as an 'other' rather than as a figure saturated and heavy with transference and projections. It was not that they didn't relate to the other in these distorted ways, but some light was getting in now. Freeing themselves from a very fixed projective system meant being more in contact with the loving and hating aspects of themselves, which caused anxiety in each of them and challenged their relationship. However, the relationship was less constrained now, enabling them to work through with me some of the disappointments about each other and the relationship. Although not easy for them, this made room for some 'new' possibilities between them and I felt some optimism about them.

Notes

1 A version of this chapter was presented at the European Regional Couple and Family Psychoanalytic Conference, "Understanding Couples and Families—Similarities and Differences between Object Relations and Link Theory Perspectives" on 14 November 2015, held at Tavistock Relationships, London. It was later published in *Couple and Family Psychoanalysis*, 6(2), Autumn 2016, and also in D. Scharff & E. Palacios (2017), *Family and Couple Psychoanalysis. A Global Perspective* (pp. 21–26). London: Karnac.
2 Enid Balint (Balint, 1993), Lily Pincus (Pincus, 1960) and Kathleen Bannister (Bannister & Pincus, 1965), have been referred to as the founding mothers of Tavistock Relationships (Dearnley, 1990). Other influential colleagues in the Tavistock Clinic were Dicks (Dicks, 1967), Gill and Temperley (1974) and Teruel (1966); other early writers and clinicians in Tavistock Relationships were Mattinson (1975) and Lyons (1993a, 1993b; Lyons & Mattinson, 1993).

Chapter 2

Assessment

The first real encounter a couple has with psychoanalytic couple therapy is when they meet with a therapist for an assessment or consultation. Both the couple and the therapist are in particular states of mind at this point and there is often an intensity to the encounter. The couple is often ambivalent about seeking help, sometimes one partner 'brings' the other. They may be in a crisis. They are not sure what couple therapy is or if it can help them. They can have a strong reaction to the assessing therapist, from whom they need help, but at the same time, can feel hostile to her, because of inviting this 'third' into their relationship and feeling anxious about what might develop. They may also feel both very relieved, having taken this step, and contained in this initial encounter. The reality of what it means to engage in a therapeutic process will take time to digest and they may not be able to make much sense of this at the beginning.

The therapist is also in a particular state of mind as she prepares to meet a new couple and to make space in her mind for them. Often the constraint of assessing within a limited time frame raises a certain amount of anxiety about the task, but even without this pressure, the nature of a psychoanalytic assessment itself is complex.

In this chapter, I explore what I consider to be key elements of a psychoanalytic couple assessment and how these are not easy to hold in tension together. First of all, the therapist is attending to the presenting concerns of the couple coming for help, experiencing and observing the live dynamic encounter in the room as a way of gaining insight into their way of relating and their internal worlds. But, as well as this, she needs to gather current and historical information, formulate an initial understanding of the problem, assess suitability for therapy, which might include an exploration of risk, and give information if needed. These elements are there in any psychoanalytic assessment, but in an assessment for couple psychotherapy, there are differences in focus and also in the way a couple presents, that need taking into account.

Assessing a couple for psychoanalytic therapy

First of all, unlike assessing an individual, the focus is on the couple's relationship and what they create together. As Lanman describes, "couple psychotherapists ... extend the thinking about relating, which is employed by contemporary psychoanalysis, beyond the therapist-patient relationship, to include the relationship between the partners, to explore the unconscious 'fit' between their internal worlds" (Lanman, 2003, p. 310). But this exploration can prove difficult. Quite often only one partner really wants to be in the room, the other feels they have to come because the relationship, which may include children, is under threat. They might not see the problem as being about their relationship, but as about the other. Thus, an important task for the therapist making the assessment is to maintain a couple state of mind in which she can engage both members of the couple in the process. For example, it is not a matter of 'cajoling' the reluctant partner to consider therapy, but of making room for each partner's different position to be expressed.

Second, while some couples have thought for some time that there are difficulties in their relationship that could be helped by engaging in analytic therapy together, this is probably not the case for most couples. Often there is a crisis in the relationship, something has happened that throws the relationship into turmoil, or long-standing problems suddenly become acute and the couple, feeling distressed, and sometimes desperate, looks for help from outside. Providing containment is, therefore, an important part of a couple therapy assessment.

Third, in this state of mind, the couple often has an agenda, wanting advice or a 'quick fix' to solve the problem. The couple may have little idea of what psychoanalytic couple therapy is and need help in engaging in an analytic process. In their minds, they are coming to an 'expert' but not really wanting therapy, or at least the kind of therapy being offered. The therapist, by holding a couple state of mind and providing a different kind of space, a couple analytic space, offers the couple, as a couple, containment which, while not what they imagined, they do indeed quite often respond to.

These factors, often present in the initial consultation, are also part of engaging a couple in therapy which I discuss more fully in Chapter Three, but I want to highlight them here because, if it is not attended to in the assessment, the couple may not feel held or may embark on a therapy only to drop out after a few sessions.

The assessment within the setting

What couple psychotherapy assessment actually means and how the assessment is structured are usually influenced by the setting. In the setting of the Tavistock Relationships clinic, the assessment process is designed to respond quite quickly to the couple, to be a gateway into the clinical service and provide holding until their ongoing therapy (often with another therapist) can commence. The disadvantage of this approach is that the couple often has to manage a transition from the assessing therapist to the ongoing therapist which is not always easy. In public service settings, the couple may have had to wait for some time to be seen and there will be constraints on resources and on what can be offered to the couple, both of which will have to be taken account of in the assessment.

In more complex cases, or where it is not clear if a psychoanalytic approach would be helpful, a fuller assessment may be undertaken, perhaps over several sessions. This kind of extended assessment provides the opportunity to see how the couple has experienced the previous consultation, and to take into account what happens between the meetings, as an indication both for the couple and the therapist regarding the suitability of ongoing analytic therapy. If appropriate, it can also give time to liaise with other involved professionals in the couple's network.

There is always a balance to be struck between offering an extended assessment and establishing the couple in regular treatment. In extended assessments, the couple may feel they have already begun to engage in the process of therapy with the therapist and feel dropped and resistant to starting again. On occasion, this can lead to splitting between the 'good' initial therapist and the 'bad' or disappointing, ongoing therapist. For this reason, a key element in assessment, especially extended assessments, is working with the process of transition to another therapist, if this is to occur.

In private practice, the initial meetings with a couple might be thought of more as an 'initial consultation'. The couple comes and meets with the therapist, someone they have found through professional networks or who has been recommended. Sometimes one of the partners is in therapy or analysis and has been referred by their analyst. Many of the same areas may be covered as in a couple therapy assessment, but if there may be more likelihood of continuing with the therapist, time can be taken to gather information and explore the couple's difficulties.

Sometimes a limited number of consultations are offered as a contained piece of work in itself. For some couples, even this brief intervention of several consultations might be enough. The couple might feel contained by the consultations and, having had the opportunity to think through their current crisis, can decide to try and move forward by themselves. I suggest that for these couples, a couple state of mind has already been in existence as part of their relationship, but has temporarily broken down. The experience of the consultations helps begin to re-establish it.

Although I have made a distinction between the term 'assessment' and 'initial consultation', for the remainder of this chapter I will use the terms interchangeably to refer to the dynamics in both.

Responding to the initial contact with the couple in mind

The initial contact with the therapist is often made by one partner. The therapist usually does not want to hear too much about the presenting problem on the phone or in an email exchange, both because, as with all patients, it is difficult to contain in this situation, especially with a patient you have not yet met and particularly with a couple, because the therapist is only hearing one partner's view. When the couple attends for the initial consultation, reference to the initial contact can be made, so that what took place outside the couple setting can now be gathered up into it. At this stage, little or much may be made of this initial contact. It may be that the couple had agreed who would make contact and the resulting discussion with the therapist was shared or the emails copied to each partner. On the other hand, either member of the couple might experience their partner contacting the therapist as the creation of an alliance between that partner and the therapist. Referring to the initial contact may reveal that the other partner did not want to come. If the consulting room is arranged with one chair nearer the door, this is often the one that partner chooses. (In fact, having done several consultations recently, I have noticed that, without exception, the partner who made the initial contact has taken the chair further into the consulting room and the other closest to the door.) The way the couple is responded to at the point of the initial contact is the beginning of establishing the couple's relationship as a focus, in which both partners are brought into the frame.

How are assessments structured?

Clearly there is no exact formula to a couple therapy assessment – it depends on the way the therapist works and the way the couple presents. However, we might think about some guiding principles.

- The first thing that usually happens in an initial meeting is that each partner is given the opportunity to give his or her view or experience of the problem and why they have come. It is important that both partners have a fairly uninterrupted space to do this. If this is not possible, then the therapist is already party to a dynamic that is diagnostic – perhaps about the threat the 'otherness' of the other imposes on the partner or the lack of psychic space in the relationship. But otherwise at this stage the therapist is listening and observing both partners and getting an early sense of what has brought them to seek help. From the beginning, she is trying to create a couple analytic space in which both partners feel properly heard, if not by each other, then at least by the therapist. For example, the therapist might note the differences in how they see things, but through her couple analytic stance can convey that there is room for their differences and, although causing conflict, these differences potentially might come together in less destructive, even creative ways. In this way, the therapist tries to create a little more psychic space in the couple's experience of the relationship.

- The therapist also listens carefully to the presenting problem, what it is that has brought the couple for help and perhaps why this particular issue is a problem for their relationship now. Sometimes this is more obvious – for example, with an affair – but at other times less so; there may have been many affairs, but the recent one threw the couple into crisis. The couple may feel it is obvious that if 'X' has happened, the relationship is in crisis, but for the therapist it is not so obvious because the meaning for the couple is not yet understood.
- As each partner talks and interacts together with the other, the way they relate to the therapist, the therapist's own response and the emotional atmosphere in the room give the therapist a preliminary sense of the nature of their relationship, not so much from what they are saying but from how they are being.
- As the consultation proceeds, the therapist comments on her preliminary understanding of the couple's relationship. Giving an interpretation is not only important in offering something that could be helpful to the couple, but also useful in a consultation in gaining a sense of how the couple is able to respond to and make use of it. It helps the therapist as part of assessing if the couple is receptive to help and to a psychoanalytic approach, or possibly quite hostile to it.
- Although the therapist will want to gather information, particularly about history, such information gathering can get in the way of a dynamic encounter with the couple and can also lead them to feel unheard. They might not want to talk about facts in their life or their past but to convey what is distressing them in the present. By hearing about this first, the subsequent gathering of information can be seen to have a meaningful link with their current plight.
- The therapist may be alerted to areas of risk that need exploring and this might take time and need another or several consultations.
- Towards the end of the assessment, if it seems that the couple is likely to come into therapy, there needs to be a discussion about the frame; for example, the establishment of regular session times, policy about missed sessions, holiday breaks and a negotiation of the fee. Sometimes at this point the couple wants to ask questions about the therapist or other issues about treatment that might concern them. These questions are perfectly reasonable and the therapist makes a judgement about how much of this 'conversation' is necessary for the agreement of a therapeutic contract and how much might also need interpreting. Later in treatment,

if such questions arise again, they are more likely to be analysed as part of the couple's unconscious communication, because they have already been addressed in a practical way at the beginning.

Key elements of a couple psychotherapy assessment

I think that there are three key elements to a couple therapy assessment – containment; a focus on the relationship and formulating the couple problem; and assessing the couple's suitability for psychoanalytic couple therapy, which includes assessing for risk, which we might think of as a fourth element.

Containment: maintaining a 'couple analytic space' and the pressure for enactment

Considering some of the difficulties couples present with, it can feel, within the limited time frame of an assessment, difficult to contain them. Often one partner is considering leaving the relationship, or something has happened in the relationship that throws the relationship into crisis, perhaps a sudden eruption of violence, an argument that goes beyond what the couple could imagine and feels unable to recover from, or the realisation that the relationship is causing damage to the children. Of course, the therapist can't 'solve' any of these problems, but she can provide a different state of mind and try and provide a 'couple analytic space'. However, faced with a couple in crisis this is not easy to do.

The therapist can struggle to resist certain transference and countertransference pressures that, if enacted (as they easily can be), undermine the couple analytic space. While the therapist tries to provide this, the couple can put pressure on the therapist that undermines this capacity:

- The couple tries to put the therapist into a position in which she is to judge who is right and who is wrong, or whose reality *is* reality, and it can be hard to establish the idea that there is room for both realities, even when they appear to be in conflict. However, conveying this is often a relief for the couple, though not always easy for them. The couple's

    arguing and fighting over conflicting factual accounts is a way of expressing their difficulty in tolerating the reality of the other's emotional experience, especially when either it differs from what they expect or want it to be, or it has an unwanted impact on them.
    (Fisher, 1999, p. 152)

- The couple hopes that the therapist could magically put things right, or relieve them of psychic pain, so while the therapist may disappoint the couple in this respect, she also attempts to convey that it's possible to stay with and work through painful experiences. Both of these dynamics of judge and magician are described by Vincent in consultations with couples wanting to divorce or separate. Where the pressure is to act as judge or magician, the therapist is turned to, to act as a "rescuer who might provide either a decision or a solution which would release one or more of the participants from intolerable stress". Where one partner wants to leave the relationship, there is often an "unconscious hope that separation could happen without turmoil and pain and that the consultant would provide the magic formula for this to be achieved" (Vincent, 1995a, p. 679).
- The therapist may feel, as 'couple expert', under pressure from the couple to advise them what to do. They may feel some action has to be taken – for example, one partner moving out of the marital home – and the therapist may indeed get caught up in feeling that some action has to be taken or that she has to decide something for the couple. The therapist can feel swept up in the anxiety and while sometimes, if there is risk, action needs taking, usually the couple needs help to think, not act. As Grier points out, in relation to couples asking the therapist to

> Just tell us what to do. It is very hard at such moments for couples to perceive that, were their request granted, it might well signify the therapist's despair of the couple actually finding and making active links with their own, innate resources to produce a creative solution to a problem.
>
> (Grier, 2001, p. 4)

- In relation to the process of therapy, anxiety can lead to the couple demanding to know what the outcome of therapy will be, sometimes one partner only agreeing to come if it can be guaranteed that it will not lead to them separating, otherwise they may as well separate now. In fact, no one in the room knows the answer to that question, but the therapist can convey the idea that therapy might help them work this out more thoughtfully, more carefully and that what they may be feeling now, positively and negatively, might change in ways that can't be predicted.

Formulating the couple problem

Gathering information and attending to the dynamics in the room

Lanman has argued that understanding the couple problem in an assessment requires two potentially conflictual lines of enquiry.

If one gets too involved with asking questions, about family or psychiatric history, or even just about the problem the couple is bringing, one can easily lose sight of the dynamic being enacted in the room, which is, of course, the most alive version of the problem. On the other hand, if one doesn't ask those questions one may end up overlooking information crucial to the assessment.

(Lanman, 2003, p. 309)

However, as Lanman suggests later in her paper, these two areas are not necessarily in conflict, as "the dynamic implications of asking such questions, and the answers produced, would of course be thought about in the same way as any other 'event' in the interview" (Lanman, 2003, p. 316). Equally, the therapist's own experience of gathering information can shed light on the couple dynamic; for example, the therapist may notice she is asking too many questions, or avoiding the emotional atmosphere between the couple and herself, or between the couple. Some of this is illustrated in the example below:

Clinical example: Leroy and Roxanne

Leroy and Roxanne came for an initial consultation; they were in their 60s, both previously married and now a widower and widow, and had been together for just 18 months. Leroy wanted them to move in together, but Roxanne was not sure. Leroy was frustrated as he was convinced they could have a great life together if they made this step. The couple gave quite a lot of information about themselves, their backgrounds, similarities and differences and how they got together. They talked about what was difficult in the relationship including Leroy's feeling that he always had to take the initiative. It was when this fragment of information was shared that I became aware of my emerging feeling of needing to pull everything together and come up with a 'bright idea' for the couple. I then became more aware of the very heavy feeling in the room, a sense of inertia and it seemed to be something about the way the couple were talking and my own difficulty in staying interested in what they were saying, despite the fact that they were volunteering potentially interesting material. I also realised that I was rather too focused on gathering information. I arranged to see them for a second consultation. Following the initial consultation, I found myself reflecting on this heavy inertia and wondered if it was to do with some unresolved loss or depression. Perhaps my impulse to come up with a 'bright idea' was a manic defence in relation to something unbearable or unresolved, and maybe Leroy's wish to move in together was something similar. In the second consultation, Roxanne told me she had been diagnosed with breast cancer, for which she had been receiving treatment and this was what Leroy's late wife had died of. The meaning of this and the fact that it had not been brought to the initial consultation shed light on what the couple was struggling with in their relationship. Between them there was a shared anxiety about moving forward with their relationship as it evoked for them many losses of significant others in the recent and more distant past. They were anxious about deepening their attachment which unconsciously they linked with further loss.

The therapist attends to the dynamic encounter with the couple, particularly processing her countertransference, in trying to formulate the problem. It provides a way of giving meaning to other aspects of the consultation, information about their histories together and separately or their description of the problem now. The way the couple is in the room and the emotional atmosphere they create give the therapist a lived experience of what it is like to be inside this relationship. Although it may not make sense immediately, allowing the emotional experience to come together with the more factual content of the consultation provides a closer understanding of the couple.

A note on theory

We do also need theory to help us conceptualise the couple problem, but it is important that theory doesn't intrude in our minds to the detriment of staying close to the clinical material. After all, theory, good theory, is rooted in clinical practice and is the clinician's attempt to conceptualise that experience. If theory is useful it should come naturally into mind as a way of helping us think about what we are feeling. In other words, theories, if turned to in the light of the clinical experience at hand, can contain feelings aroused in the therapist and help develop thinking.

At times in the consultation, the therapist will be listening to one of the partners, perhaps empathising with their experience, she may be trying to help the couple listen to each other and deescalate a fight, she may feel pulled between one partner and the other. But from time to time, she can get herself into a third position and ask herself, "What does this tell me about the relationship?" And theory can be helpful here. It can of course be used as a defence and retreat from difficult dynamics in the room, and an attempt to make sense of something which doesn't yet make sense, that which Britton and Steiner have called an 'overvalued idea' in contrast to a 'selected fact'.

> It should be the analyst's mind primed with its theories which awaits as a receptacle for its expectations to be fulfilled by the experience of the patient. This requires a capacity to wait, and if the analyst is unable to tolerate the uncertainty of not understanding he may turn to his theory as a source of reassurance and look for a patient to act as a container for the theory. Bion emphasises that the analyst's pre-conception has to act as a container for the realisation, and 'NOT' the other way round (Bion, 1962).
>
> (Britton & Steiner, 1994, p. 1076)

In the case of Leroy and Roxanne, I had to wait until the second consultation in which the heavy and manic countertransference in the first one connected with new material that the couple brought in the second, and threw light on the couple's deeper anxieties about coming together.

Some theories about couple dynamics and levels of functioning

Different writers in the field of couple psychoanalysis have formulated types of couple dynamics as ways of helping to conceptualise the clinical experience. For example, Mattinson and Sinclair identified three types of defensive couple dynamics, based on splitting – 'babes in the wood', 'net and sword' and 'cat and dog'.

> When two people use this type of splitting mechanism as their predominant defence, their marriage becomes a useful vehicle by which the conflict can be externalised either between themselves (one spouse expressing one side of the split, the partner the other), or between them as a strongly identified pair on the one hand and the outside world on the other.
>
> (Mattinson & Sinclair, 1979, p. 54)

In the babes in the wood marriage, both partners defend against anger which is projected outside the relationship, while the couple only express need and yearning between them. In the cat and dog marriages, the couple is caught up in an excited way fighting together, with a denial of more dependent feelings; and in the net and sword marriage, the split is between the couple, one expressing need, the other anger and rejection, but this can easily switch between them. Although one of these combinations may be predominant, Mattinson and Sinclair didn't think of them as types of marriages, but 'systems of splitting behaviour' (1979, p. 55) which could be used by the same couple. To these three types, Hewison has added a 'Dolls House' couple (Ibsen, 1996) and a 'projective gridlock' couple (Morgan, 1995) (Hewison, 2014a, p. 163). Hewison suggests that the Dolls House couple is like the babes in the wood couple, except if a child enters the relationship, he or she may have to carry the feared aspects projected outside the couple's relationship. These aspects, now in closer proximity, threaten to destroy the couple relationship. The projective gridlock couple, fused through the belief of not being separate and different either maintain a cosy but ultimately deadening relationship, or the relationship has a more sado-masochistic dynamic; these dynamics I discuss more fully in Chapter Seven.

Keogh and Enfield (2013) have also described couples as functioning at different developmental levels, each of which require a different approach from the therapist, from more primitive anxieties in the autistic-contiguous stage, to those in the paranoid schizoid stage and to more depressive position anxieties (see Chapter 8). These ideas have some parallels with Fisher's ideas of the move between narcissistic relating and the psychological state of marriage and the post-Kleinian thinking about the oscillation between the paranoid schizoid position and the depressive position, also discussed by others (Steiner, 1987, 1992; Britton, 1998d; Fisher, 1999). Buss-Twachtmann and Brookes, drawing on Colman's work on 'Marriage as a psychological container' (Colman, 1993a), suggested that "couples coming for therapy can be classified according to the current state of their marital container" (Buss-Twachtmann & Brookes, 1998, p. 4). None of these writers are attempting to pigeonhole couples into a particular category, but each have developed ways of conceptualising the type of dynamic or level of functioning a couple might present with and how the therapist might best respond. Conceptualising in this way might help the assessor not only in the couple diagnosis, but might also be an indication of the treatment path.

The presenting problem and the nature of the relationship

Each therapist will draw on their own analytic framework to try and understand the clinical picture before them. The different conceptual frameworks referred to above are examples of this. For myself, in thinking about the couple in an initial consultation, I find it useful to try and conceptualise both the specific difficulties they are presenting, and also what is the *nature* of the relationship, the way it is functioning. All couples have difficulties, but the way they are functioning as a couple may be part of the reason they are not able to work through those difficulties.

To take the consultation with Leroy and Roxanne, the presenting problem was a difference between them about entering into a more committed relationship, one of them wanting to take this initiative, the other not so sure. The issue was becoming somewhat polarised as Roxanne was digging her heels in and Leroy was becoming manic with enthusiasm. There was information in their backgrounds which threw light on why it became polarised in the particular way it did. However, while this was all being talked about and I was making links which seemed to help, I was also able to take up a more 'third position' perspective and wonder if these links were more helpful to me than to the couple because there was something heavy in the atmosphere. At that point, it was difficult to make sense of this thought. Later I realised this was a couple who shared unresolved loss from early in their lives, something they unconsciously recognised in each other, felt they had overcome between them, but now once again felt overwhelmed by. They were functioning through the use of a defensive projective system – with one manic, the other depressed, and this was leaving them unable to move forward.

It may be that an understanding of the couple's specific difficulties comes from listening carefully to the presenting problem, elaborating this and gathering further information about them, including making links between current difficulties and earlier experience. An understanding about the *nature* of the relationship comes more from the dynamic encounter with the couple. The therapist has an alive and immediate experience of the couple, the way they interact and the emotional atmosphere of the sessions, which conveys something of what it is like to be in their relationship.

Drawing mainly on the current Tavistock Relationships body of thought, I have outlined five key areas in this book: (1) shared unconscious phantasy and beliefs; (2) transference in the couple's relationship; (3) the couple's projective system, including unconscious partner choice and couple fit; (4) narcissism and the sharing of psychic space; and finally (5) the psychic development of the couple, including, importantly, their sexual relationship. These areas, manifested in the couple's unconscious relating to each other and the therapist, together form another conceptual framework that helps in maintaining a couple focus and in understanding the nature of the couple's relationship. As with some of the ideas above, they can be thought of as on a spectrum from more mature to more disturbed or dysfunctional relating.

Not all of these aspects will come to mind or even be discernible in a consultation, but some of them might and can be helpful in the process of assessment. It can provide a framework for the therapist in understanding something of what is happening in this relationship and thereby help contain the couple.

- What kind of shared unconscious phantasies are operating in the relationship? For example, couples often relate as if the partner doesn't understand them, is deliberately misunderstanding them, should understand them, or is the same as them or completely different/alien, is attacking them, is not interested in them, is rejecting them, the list could go on. They are not conscious that they are relating in ways coloured by these unconscious phantasies and even part of creating the expected response. Can they be made more conscious and brought into contact with reality? Is the couple gripped by deeper and more rigid unconscious beliefs, perhaps particularly about the meaning of being a couple? Are there more conscious fantasies about the relationship that the couple assume to be shared, but in fact are not shared and thus are leading to conflict. What does it feel like in the room for the therapist? Is there, for example, an atmosphere of defensive certainty or more openness to exploring perceptions (see Chapter 4)?
- What is the transference dimension of the couple's relationship, are they working through, maintaining and repeating unresolved earlier

relationships which interferes with their perception of each other and stops the relationship developing. How do the therapist's counter-transference and the couple's transference to her elaborate this picture (see Chapter 5)?
- What is the nature of the couple's projective system – to what extent does it function to contain the couple and have some flexibility, or does it constrict the couple in positions they cannot free themselves from and is stopping the relationship developing? Does the therapist find herself caught up in the couple's projective system and unable to get out of it, or does she feel she can think about the pressure towards enactment (see Chapter 6)?
- How much can the couple bear the difference and otherness of the other, or is the relationship very narcissistic? Is there room in the relationship for two (or three/four) separate and different minds? If it is very narcissistic – does this take the form of a very fused relationship, or does it have a more sado-masochistic dimension in which one or each partner is required to fit in with the other? Can the couple engage with the difference and otherness of the therapist or is this experienced as a threat (see Chapter 7)?
- What kind of couple are they in terms of psychic development? Is the couple fearful of becoming an adult intimate sexual couple? Has their psychic development towards this stage been halted at an earlier stage of psychic development; for example, are they more like a mother–baby couple or like two adolescents? How resistant are they to growth as a couple? How does the transference and countertransference inform the therapist of this (see Chapter 8)?

These are broader questions about the relationship and provide a context for the presenting problem. For example, if the couple presents with a problem of 'no sex', this could be thought about in terms of a shared belief that intimacy is dangerous; or that the transference to the partner – for example, towards father or mother – interferes with their capacity to relate to each other as adults with the freedom to have the sexual relationship they want to have; or has the projective system become rather fixed, with one partner carrying the sexual desire, the other with no desire because, between them, they share a fear of sex; or is the relationship too fused or too sado-masochistic to want to have sex or to have consensual sex, or is the 'no sex' a symptom of the couple's difficulty in feeling themselves to be a grown-up sexual couple?

A 'couple state of mind' is also a diagnostic tool in formulating the couple problem. In an assessment, I am always interested in the extent to which this exists in the couple, if at all. Sometimes it has existed and trauma has disabled it. When this function develops in the couple, I see it as a sign of development in the couple and if it can be sustained, as the earliest stage in the process of withdrawing from the therapy and ending. Although when a couple asks how long the therapy will take, it is almost impossible to answer, an assessment of the couple's 'couple state of mind' does give the therapist some idea. On a few occasions, I have said to a couple coming for an initial consultation that I don't think they need therapy. I may offer them a few consultations, but it becomes clear that the couple, through encountering the therapist's couple state of mind, can access their own couple state of mind, talk about their relationship, are interested in it and can think quite creatively together about their current difficulties.

What makes a couple suitable for psychoanalytic treatment?

At Tavistock Relationships, although the main form of treatment offered is open-ended psychoanalytic psychotherapy, or psychodynamic therapy (the latter for individuals and couples with relationship problems), there is also a range of other services, psychosexual therapy (a model that combines psychodynamic therapy and cognitive behavioural therapy), a divorce and separation consultation service, time-limited mentalisation therapy, and the other services for parents, currently Parents as Partners, and Adopting Together.

Assessing in the context of a clinic such as Tavistock Relationships means that there is a range of options, other than offering or not offering therapy, while in some settings the options may be different (individual, family, group) or more limited. What does it mean to be suitable for psychoanalytic couple therapy? There are differences in views about how to determine suitability, some people looking at it on the basis of inclusion, i.e., that certain criteria have to be met; others on exclusion, i.e., as long as any reason to think that the patient will be harmed by the treatment can be excluded, then they should have the opportunity for therapy (Garelick, 1994; Milton, 1997). Sometimes a couple who seem very psychologically minded and considered very suitable for therapy hit a deep resistance as the therapy proceeds that cannot easily be reached. In contrast, other couples in which one or both partners seem quite concrete, wanting a quick fix with instructions about what to do, can make extraordinarily good use of psychoanalytic therapy in a way that neither they nor their therapist would have imagined.

There is some debate about why to offer couple therapy rather than individual therapy or analysis. Aznar-Martínez et al. (2016), drawing on the work of Links and Stockwell (2002) who consider couple therapy in the case of narcissistic personality disorder, suggest a number of indications and contraindications for couple therapy: (1) the couple's "capacity for dealing openly with feelings of anger or rage must be assessed", but "if one member of the couple is unable to deal with or express feelings that might be humiliating or that could prompt an attack on the other partner" (2016, p. 3), individual treatment would be more appropriate; (2) "the aim of treatment is shared by both parties" (2016, p. 3), particularly that there is a shared wish to continue the relationship or an agreement to separate; and (3) that the couple accepts the complementarity of the dynamics in their relationship. They suggest that if these three criteria can be met there is a good basis for couple treatment.

The couple's difficulty in managing their dysregulated anger and aggression is an important consideration. If this is extreme, then it will be very difficult for the work to proceed and the therapist does not want to be put in the position of being an impotent witness to either partner's abusive behaviour towards the other. In this situation, individual therapy may be indicated first or there may be a modification in technique towards a mentalising approach, or in the case of Tavistock Relationships, a referral for mentalisation-based couple therapy.

It is very frequently the case that couples come into therapy with different agendas about staying together or separating; sometimes this is in the open, sometimes hidden. But because we know about the powerful nature of the projective system, we know that this uncertainty and ambivalence can be in both partners but unconsciously divided up between them, one expressing the need to separate, the other the longing to be together. We might also need to consider that the wish to separate by ending the relationship may be an unconscious expression of the need for more psychic space *in* the relationship. However, there is the danger, which these authors may be drawing attention to, that one partner has already psychically left the relationship and is bringing the partner to leave him or her with the therapist.

I also used to consider that one criterion for taking a couple into therapy would be that there is some acknowledgement of a shared problem (Morgan, 1994), but I think that sometimes we are in the situation as therapists in which we are aware of a shared problem, but the couple may not consciously recognise anything as shared, except perhaps sharing the view that the other is the problem. So as part of the assessment process we may be looking to see what is shared, but actually agreeing to see a couple for therapy where there is no conscious agreement between them that there is a shared problem. One might even say that it would be premature to expect a couple, at this point, to recognise the shared or interlocking nature of their difficulties. This is something that emerges in the course of treatment and may take some time. Being able to acknowledge that they are both involved in creating the problem that exists between them, and move away from a position of accusation and blame of the other, is a major psychic shift for some couples and not easily achieved.

Assessing for risk

Exploring areas of risk – concerns about children, violence and other dangerous acting out, mental health concerns, addiction – so that these concerns are in the open, and can be thought about is important, including considering if any action should be taken. However, it is important that the therapist does not come across as a police-like figure who causes the couple to close down. The therapist's anxiety, including that about the influence of her own superego, can contribute to this, but also, fear of being a police-like figure and shutting the couple down can also lead to a failure to address concerns.

Violence

Where there is violence in the relationship, it is important for the assessor to understand the kind of violence, its severity and whether it can be safely worked with in the context of couple analytic therapy. Humphries and McCann (2015), in an important paper on psychoanalytic therapy with violent couples, argue that, contrary to the approach of some agencies, with certain kinds of violence it is more useful to work with the couple together than separately. They draw on Kelly and Johnson's (2008) distinction between four types of intimate partner violence: coercive controlling violence, violent resistance, situational couple violence and separation instigated violence. Coercive controlling violence is defined by Kelly and Johnson as "emotionally abusive intimidation, coercion and control coupled with physical violence used against partners" (2008, p. 478) and this usually occurs in the context of other controlling behaviours. Violent resistance is a violent response to coercive controlling violence, and separation instigated violence is a violent response to separation, usually without previous violent behaviour. Humphries and McCann found that

> at TCCR, we are much more likely to encounter situational couple violence. This type of violence is not part of an ongoing state of coercion and control, but arises from a current event, as may occur, for example, when a row escalates. Both parties are involved in these fights. Usually there is no presentation at assessment of fear or control; the violence is not accompanied by other intimidating behaviour, and is not injurious.
> (Humphries & McCann, 2015, p. 151)

They note that situational couple violence can escalate into more severe assaults and injury, but distinguish this from "coercive controlling violence" in which one partner abusively controls the other through threats of violence, fear and actual physical harm.

An understanding of these different kinds of violence is helpful for the assessor. In terms of assessing for risk and a contra-indication for couple therapy,

> the assessor is looking for the presence of coercive controlling violence and abuse, as well as the more problematic kind of situational couple

> violence, where the degree of dysregulation and attempts to control the agenda limit the capacity for thinking and so prevent the therapeutic container from operating effectively.
>
> (Humphries & McCann, 2015, p. 159)

Humphries and McCann advise that in order to avoid the police-like dynamic, it helps to use language that opens up the experience of violence in the relationship rather than making the couple feel pinned down. For example, when the couple is talking about a row or fight they have had, asking them how bad the fights get. If they talk about a violent episode, the assessor might ask them if this happens often, and if it does, if they can recognise the kind of situation that triggers it. The assessor will get a sense of more coercive controlling violence from the way the partners in the couple relate in the consultation, when she should be able to pick up very controlling behaviour in one partner, fear in the other, and a counter-transference experience of fear or being controlled. If this is the situation, the assessor has a dilemma. It might feel important to arrange to see the couple separately; on the other hand, the loss of control the perpetrator of violence may feel could escalate the violence. The fact that the couple has come together for the assessment may or may not indicate that they both want some help with this dynamic. If it can be addressed to the couple together it may, despite considerable anxiety, be more containing.

Mental health, alcohol and addiction

The therapeutic approach to couples where there is an addiction, mood disorder or psychiatric illness needs a particular therapeutic stance.

> For the therapist, treating these couples is complex and challenging. The therapist must maintain a dual focus, examining the couple dynamic while keeping in mind the individual meaning and management of the illness. To lose track of either focal point compromises the treatment, as a destructive couple dynamic will exacerbate the illness or the illness itself can defeat the couple treatment.
>
> (Wanless, 2014, p. 311)

Many couples come for therapy where there has been, in one or both partners, a history of mental health problems, sometimes a psychotic illness or an acute or chronic depression. It is not uncommon for one or both partners to be depressed and on anti-depressant medication. In this situation, the therapist will be interested in exploring the meaning of the depression for the couple. Hewison et al. (2014, p. 73) advise exploring "the number and severity of previous depressive episodes" ... and "the circumstances prevailing at the time", and "whether a partner was depressed prior to starting their relationship, or whether onset of the first episode succeeded the formation of the partnership". Consideration of these factors helps the therapist understand what one partner's depression might mean for the relationship, and even if it has been part of their unconscious contract.

Quite a high number of couples coming for help at Tavistock Relationships indicate being at risk in one of the questionnaires they are given (CORE [Clinical Outcomes in Routine Evaluation]; see Evans et al., 2000) – thoughts about self-harm or suicidal thoughts, or a fear of harming others. Quite frequently couples are seen where one or both partners are borderline, such that they become very easily emotionally dysregulated, unable to think and find the other's separate existence a threat and unbearable. In the assessment, the question is: can this couple benefit from couple therapy now, is there sufficient health in the relationship to support the inevitable demands of analytic therapy? If there is a current drug or alcohol problem, it is important that this is not so severe that the couple or one partner arrives intoxicated or is continually managing emotional pain by using drugs or alcohol. With such couples, if taken into therapy, the therapist will be more alert than usual to the ongoing viability of therapy. If analytic couple therapy does not feel viable, other forms of couple treatment might be considered, as well as other non-couple interventions that might be indicated before couple therapy could proceed.

Concern about the children

It is common in couples presenting for help that there will be some concern about the children. Couples who are frequently fighting or conversely are remote and distant have an adverse effect on the children. One of the most important outcomes of couple therapy is the long-term benefit for the children. Harold and Leve (2012), drawing on the research by Cowan, Cowan and Heming (2005) state that

> children living in households marked by high levels of inter-parental conflict and discord are at elevated risk for a variety of negative psychological outcomes including increased anxiety, depression, aggression, conduct problems, lower levels of social competence, reduced academic attainment, and poor physical health related outcome.
> (Harold & Leve, 2012, p. 46)

Thus, parents' concern about the impact of their relating on the children is a valid rationale for offering the couple help with their relationship. Couple therapists, as part of the couple's treatment, often have to manage an ongoing concern about the negative impact of the couple's relationship on the children. What is important here is the state of mind of the couple – are they distressed and concerned about what is happening and wanting help, or do they try and minimise, rationalise or deny the concerning behaviour and is this a one-off event or an ongoing damaging or abusive situation? If the assessing therapist makes the judgement that the children are not safe, then she needs to link up with other professionals involved or make a referral to the relevant agency, hopefully, though not necessarily, with the couple's agreement. There may be hints or reports of physical, sexual or emotional abuse from the parents or sibling abuse, as well as reports of children's disturbance – self-harm, anorexia, violence, school problems. These kinds of worrying situations are sometimes part of the ongoing work and the therapist has to decide, with the help of consultation, how to intervene. In all these situations, it is important that the therapist does not have to manage this alone, but has colleagues or supervisors to liaise with.

Sometimes the symptoms in the children can be understood as problematic aspects of the couple projected into them – as Hewison (2014a) describes in the Doll's House marriage. The couple may be appropriately concerned about the children, but perhaps don't recognise what the child may be carrying for them, often anxiety because of the uncontained nature of the parents' relationship. Here the assessor has to think about these symptoms in the children as indicators of what is not contained in the couple; and clearly an aim of ongoing therapy would be to help the couple to contain their anxieties so that they cease to be projected into the children.

Technique in relation to risk

Areas of risk are often difficult for the couple and the therapist to talk about. Sometimes they can be avoided as the partners in the couple feel themselves to be too destructive and have to conceal the level of their disturbance in order to get help. If there was a row that erupted into unexpected violence, or concern about fighting in front of the children or hurting the children, the couple can feel deeply ashamed and fear any action the therapist might take. Therefore, when the therapist is alerted to areas of risk, it is important to acknowledge the seriousness of the situation alongside conveying a genuine wish to join the couple in trying to understand and think together with them about how to prevent further incidents. If this can be done in a way that is not too persecuting, although difficult for the couple, it can also feel containing. This process helps the therapist make a judgement about how amenable the couple will be to psychoanalytic treatment. Are there concerns about damage to the partner, the self, the children? Do they want to understand it and try to find ways of mitigating it? As stated earlier, one of the contraindications for therapy would be denial of the problem by minimising it or rationalisation.

Assessment as part of an ongoing process

Assessment is also part of the ongoing process of therapy. In a well-functioning therapy, this process, though remaining in the background most of the time, stays alive between the couple and the therapist. The couple can let the therapist know when and if the therapy, a particular session, an interpretation, is feeling helpful or unhelpful. The therapist too has this assessing function inside her, monitoring the progress of the therapy, including if it is appearing not to be helpful, or feeling stuck or drifting. There may also come a point in the therapy where the therapist feels the treatment is not helping and may even be making things worse. In couple therapy, there can be quite a pressure to keep the couple together, coming from the couple and sometimes evoked in the therapist. Certainly, being in therapy can enable the couple to stay together when otherwise they would have separated. But sometimes the therapist becomes aware of keeping a destructive relationship going which is having an adverse impact on the couple and their children. This can be a painful moment of realisation for the therapist. While the therapist is not in a position to tell the couple to stay together or separate, she might notice that she is avoiding helping the couple face their destructiveness fully and perhaps begin to mourn what cannot be.

There are factors that arise in the course of therapy – the continuance of an affair, an untreated alcohol, drug or sex addiction – that impair the therapy and may need addressing in order for the therapy to continue. Sometimes in couple therapy, the therapist becomes installed in the couple's relationship, the therapist providing a couple state of mind that is containing in the sessions, but there is little evidence of this being internalised by the couple into their relationship, and hence the therapy drifts (see Chapter 10). The therapist might discover a limitation in herself with a particular couple and feel that the work with her cannot progress beyond a certain point. Having said all of this, it is also important to note progress and development in the couple therapy. This assessing function helps the therapist and the couple recognise when the therapy has done its job and the couple can end. But that is a topic to be explored later.

Chapter 3

Engaging a couple in treatment and establishing a couple analytic setting

In this chapter I explore what it feels like for a couple coming into therapy; their unconscious phantasies as well as their more conscious fantasies about what couple psychotherapy is, and typical early transference and countertransference. I will describe how the therapist's couple state of mind is part of establishing a couple analytic space which helps contain the couple in this early stage and is part of the therapist's internal setting. I will also discuss the frame, that is in part the practical arrangements for the therapy, but which also carries meaning for the couple, both conscious and unconscious, as well as supporting the therapist in being able to do the work.

The decision to seek therapy

The decision to seek therapy is usually a difficult step for a couple to take and brings its own complexities, different to individual therapy. When they do make contact, the approach is often tentative. As described in Chapter Two, it might be that one partner wants to come and the other doesn't and the ambivalence between them acts to delay the couple. Sometimes one partner is 'brought' to therapy, their partner threatening 'break up' unless he or she comes. This can mean that, in the initial stages of therapy, one of the partners is reluctant to be present. In contrast, sometimes there has been an explosive event that leads the couple to seek help immediately and in a highly anxious emotional state. In these states of mind, they may not have been able to think about what therapy is or what it might mean for each of them or their relationship.

Anxieties and phantasies about couple psychotherapy

There are often preconceived ideas and unconscious phantasies about what couple psychotherapy is. More consciously, there might be an idea that couple psychotherapy is a kind of 'marriage guidance' in which the couple will have their problem diagnosed and be given advice about what to do and how to do it. They may hope this can be achieved without too much interference or turmoil. Behind this there might be a less conscious phantasy or belief that the couple therapist, being a 'couple therapist', will have special, privileged, knowledge about what a healthy functioning relationship is, and from this position she will be able to 'show them the way'.

Often the relationship and family life, as a whole, feel at stake and perhaps one of the most common hopes is that couple psychotherapy will help the couple stay together. At the same time, there may be a fear that therapy will lead to the relationship breaking up which can feel catastrophic. Sometimes there is a wish to separate, at least in one partner, and the hope that the therapist will make this possible. There can also be the fantasy, conscious or not, of being able to leave the partner safely with the therapist while extracting oneself.

At this early stage, it is important to recognise and allow room for the anxiety and the ambivalence that are often present both between the couple and also in relation to the therapist. These feelings will be present in the initial meetings and if the therapist is attuned to them, she can help the couple with them – for example, the feeling of both wanting and not wanting to come, fears about what will happen in couple psychotherapy, the fact that the couple may want very different things from the therapeutic encounter. The couple therapist will expect this ambivalence and anxiety and can communicate to the couple that these are ordinary anxieties for them to be experiencing without giving them false reassurance. She also knows that no one knows the outcome of the therapy at this stage and it is not possible to give the couple assurances about that. What she can offer is containment in the process of the couple working through their difficulties. The therapist's presence, confidence and the process of making a commitment to the couple are important in containing the couple at this early stage.

Early transference

The transference to the therapist can be quite saturated at this point. Enormous hope can be invested in the therapist because so much is at stake, especially if she is the 'expert' who knows what a 'good' couple relationship is. The couple can also become quickly dependent as they are often highly anxious and may feel things are unravelling between them in frightening ways.

At the same time at this beginning stage, the couple is very sensitive to the presence and the approach of the therapist. In the assessment meeting, the couple was probably holding some distance from the therapist as they observed her and wondered whether analytic couple psychotherapy was for them. Now they are embarking on a process with her. It can feel very exposing inviting a third into the privacy of one's relationship and the couple might fear they will no longer feel in control of the relationship. Although all therapies have a life of their own and are not under the control of either party, patient or analyst, undertaking therapy as a couple, more than in individual therapy, may mean the therapy takes a direction that either one of the partners may not want. Each partner may fear what the other partner will reveal of the relationship or him- or herself, aspects they would not choose to bring now or ever. The idea of the therapist being invited into the couple's relationship may sound odd, as clearly there is a boundary around it and the therapist supports and respects this. And yet the emotional experience for the couple and the therapist is of inviting the therapist into their relationship as they share the intimacy of very private moments, their shameful rows and loss of control, their bad moments with the children, the intimate details of their sexual relationship and often, with time, difficult things they have never even shared with each other. So, despite the couple coming and asking for help, at another level, the therapist may be an unwanted, even a hated (because needed), third – the 'uninvited guest' as Fisher describes (1999).

As well as experiencing the therapist as unwanted or intrusive into their relationship, she can also easily be felt to be one-sided or feared as judgemental. There can be enormous shame in coming for help and the therapist may be experienced as a disapproving parent, horrified child or internal persecutory superego. The couple's conscious and unconscious hostility can get into the therapist who may find it hard to hold the couple at this stage. This negative transference may be avoided by the therapist and yet it is always a relief to the couple to have this acknowledged and understood.

The couple may shift between the hope that the therapist will help the relationship and such persecuted states in which they suspect she will support the other and not them, and even damage the relationship. This is particularly the case if one of the partners is being 'brought' by the other and identified by both as the problem – for example, the partner who has been physically violent in a row, or has had an affair or has an alcohol or drug problem. There may be an anxiety that if the partner is heard and understood by the therapist, there will not be room for oneself. But there may also be a wish in either partner to establish their own emotional reality as the 'truth' and to enlist the therapist's support in establishing this. One couple was so anxious about this that for the first few weeks of therapy they came with their separate written accounts of the preceding week's difficulties and insisted in taking turns to speak without any interruption from the other or the therapist.

It is also possible that the couple may not really want help; Ludlam points out:

> [O]ne of the first errors a couple therapist can make is to assume that a request for help constitutes a desire to be helped. On the contrary, a couple may be seeking the confirmation that, in spite of everything, nothing can be done.
>
> (Ludlam, 2014, p. 66)

The couple may feel they have to come, have to be seen by their partner and family to come for help and to satisfy their own superego and sense of moral rightness, but actually consciously or unconsciously, in one or both of their minds, the relationship is over, or they want things to stay as they are. Thus, they may be very resistant to the therapist's attempts to explore the relationship.

Early countertransference

If the transference to the therapist is saturated at this point, so too can be the countertransference. The couple's anxieties can lodge in the therapist and be difficult to think about. Instead there can be enactments; for example, the therapist can be pushed into telling the couple what to do, telling them what a couple relationship is, taking sides, reassuring them and making assurances that she cannot realistically make or fulfil and so on. The couple's ambivalence, nearly always there, even in the consciously 'keen' couple or partner, instead of being contained, can result in the therapist trying to persuade the couple to come into therapy. This in turn can make the couple anxious, particularly if they are feeling tentative and unsure. The therapist may be idealised, the couple's 'last hope' and therefore feel under enormous pressure to 'save the marriage'.

Holding a couple state of mind is not so easy at this stage. We cannot avoid difficult and unsettling feelings of judgement, liking one partner more than the other, really disliking a couple, feeling useless, dismissed, attacked, bored or idealised. It is not always easy for the therapist to maintain an evenly balanced view of the couple. The therapist may feel at a loss to understand why these two people are together when one seems quite reasonable and likeable and the other so irrational and unlikeable. She might feel more identified with one partner than the other, warm to one partner more than the other. This is where a couple state of mind is an anchor to the therapist, helping her analyse these feelings and use them to understand more about the relationship.

Clinical example: Julia and Rob
I felt this uneven response strongly with a young couple who came to see me. The female partner, Julia, was a professional woman, appealing and easy to talk to, while the male partner, Rob, was independently wealthy and presented as a kind of 'drop out' with no apparent personal ambition. Rob was uncommunicative and

dismissive of me, making it clear that he felt coming to see someone like me was a waste of time. It was fairly obvious to me that I might be more identified with her, but still I struggled in the first meeting to understand how these two people could be together. I thought about my antipathy and rather judgemental internal response. I felt that if they came into therapy, I would in time understand more about this. This helped me survive a very difficult first session. I did come to understand a projective system in which much of Julia's disturbance, behind her capable professional self, was projected and contained in Rob. Over time I saw that Rob possessed great warmth and responsiveness which I came to witness in relation to both her and me. He was able to let me know from the beginning about this more disturbed, anti-relating part of their relationship which it emerged was preventing the expression of more loving feelings between them.

The therapist can have particular anxieties at this early stage. One of these is about whether she feels she is going to be able to contain the couple and whether she is going to be able to help them. This can be very difficult with a couple where unconsciously there is a wish to disturb us, to evacuate what feels unbearable and at the same time to invite us into what is their sometimes disturbing world. The therapist feels anxious about what she is going to have to bear. There can be other anxieties too, especially for therapists who are newly qualified or still in training, about whether the couple will engage and stay. For example, if the couple is very acrimonious, it can be hard to find a way to create a thinking space; or with a depressed couple, there can be anxieties about reaching the couple.

There are some things that help the therapist at this stage. One of these is having an established analytic setting which supports the work. The consistent, reliable structure of the setting is helpful to the couple contemplating beginning therapy and also provides a structure within which the therapist is supported to think about and contain the couple. This might include regular supervision or in some settings, institutional support. The therapist also needs to establish what might be called a therapeutic alliance with the couple. This involves a level of trust in the therapist and the process because coming into therapy is a big step for any couple to make. The couple needs to feel some confidence in the therapist – that she will be able to contain them, take care of the setting and commit to their therapy.

It also helps the process if the therapist enlists her curiosity about the relationship, a wish to know more and get her mind inside it. Developing an interest and curiosity helps both with her own survival (Fisher, 2006; Morgan & Stokoe, 2014), but also helps the couple become interested themselves in their own relationship. Without this, the therapist can easily feel defeated by the couple, witness to destructive or sado-masochistic relating, from which she might want to withdraw. The couple may not even have thought about the fact of their relationship as something that exists and that they co-create and could think about. The very act of the therapist talking about and being interested in the couple's relationship starts to bring the realisation that they are part of a relationship into existence.

The therapist's use of a couple state of mind at the beginning

Holding a couple state of mind is important so that without having to spell it out, the couple has an experience of there being room for both of them, their conflictual internal feelings and the way these manifest in the relationship. When we say that the 'relationship is the patient', we do not simply mean what is happening between the members of the couple – for example, the couple's problems in understanding each other or communicating effectively; we also mean what aspects of each partner are lodged in the other and also what the couple unconsciously creates together. Because of the way the couple manages things between them – for example, in their projective system, often one partner is bringing the other or the relationship to therapy. It can be difficult for the couple therapist to hold a couple state of mind and to understand that the different, even opposite ways that the partners in the couple present are part of the picture of the couple and their shared anxieties and defences. Also as Fisher describes (1999, p. 143), drawing on the work of Rey (1988) and Riviere (1936), damaged inner objects are often split off, but in a couple relationship can be kept alive, and be available for help, *in the other*. "Not only do couples bring internal objects to therapy for repair, they do so in a very concrete way. Through complex and interlocking processes of mutual projective identification, they bring the damaged internal objects concretely located in the partner". So, although as couple therapists we are wary of going along with the idea that one partner is the patient brought for treatment by the other, even when the couple agrees on this as sometimes happens, in another sense through this kind of presentation, the couple is unconsciously describing an accurate psychic reality. One of them, as with Rob and Julia, carries a split-off part of the other, alongside that damaged or disturbed part of themselves which is being brought to therapy for repair.

The therapist's couple state of mind is intrinsic to couple analytic psychotherapy, it is part of the setting, containment, interpretation and eventually becomes introjected by the couple into their relationship. But this takes time, and at the beginning of therapy, the therapist's couple state of mind functions in a modified way. It is strongly present in the way the therapist approaches the referral and sets up the initial consultation and in the way the therapist establishes the setting. But in terms of interpretation, the therapist may initially have to use her couple state of mind with a light touch. This is because while it is the therapist's state of mind, at this stage it will mostly not be the couple's. They may not be ready for a couple interpretation. The couple may not be ready to make a shift from seeing the other as the problem, to recognising there is a shared problem. They may each need to blame the other, or hold onto to a belief that the other is wrong and so on. Even if the therapist at this early stage has some understanding of what is often a complex unconscious interplay between the couple, she has to judge how much to say. For some couples, a strong couple interpretation at the beginning is absolutely what they need. They can take it and it can have a powerful effect in reconfiguring their perception of each other and the relationship and lead to a real engagement. But other couples will resist such an interpretation, not hear it or understand it, or feel that such a perspective, which is about what is happening in the relationship, leaves them feeling misunderstood as individuals at this stage.

However, even without explicit interpretations about the relationship, the couple is often very affected by the *therapist's* couple state of mind. This is a part of her internal setting but it is also expressed in the external setting; for example, the physical arrangements of the consulting room and the practical arrangements. The couple coming for help is often in a persecuted and persecuting state of mind and, as described earlier, each partner may seek validation from the therapist that he or she is the one who is right and therefore wronged by the other, or in other ways attempt to get the therapist on their side. The couple therapist who can take into account their different experience and make proper contact with each of them, with curiosity and without judgement, creates a different kind of space for the couple. The most important thing in this early stage is that the couple therapist creates a setting in which both partners can properly exist and she will have to judge when to make interpretations about what the couple is creating together.

Managing the setting – internally and externally

The couple needs to be given space to settle into therapy, to get used to it and to have ambivalent feelings about it. The therapist also has to settle into the therapy with this particular couple. Couple psychotherapy sessions can be complicated, confusing and even chaotic. Meltzer, in discussing how to establish the setting, states:

> The secret is stability, and the key to stability is simplicity. Every analyst must work out for himself a simple *style* of analytical work, in time arrangements, financial agreement, room, clothing, modes of expression, demeanour. He must work well within the limits of his physical capacity and his mental tolerance. But also, in the process of discovery with a patient, he must find through his sensitivity the means

of modulation required by that individual within the framework of his technique. In a word, he must preside over the setting in a way which permits the evolution of the patient's transference.

(Meltzer, 1967, p. xiii)

The frame is important in another way too; it supports and contains the therapist. The boundary of the session makes the work possible. The regularity of the sessions enables the therapist to take difficult things up, or hold something that comes right at the end of the session, knowing there will be a session at the same time next week. It also helps the therapist feel contained and take a third position in relation to the couple and the session. The stability of the setting is externally represented by the physical and practical arrangements of the therapy – particularly maintaining the consistency of the sessions, which represent a different kind of space in which the couple is held. This in turn supports the therapist's internal setting and couple state of mind, underpinning her capacity to make emotional contact with the couple and become properly attuned to the interior of their relationship. Having said this, although the therapist takes care of the setting and this is crucial to the work, it is never a perfect process, either internally or externally. As Churcher says:

> In practice, we all have to cope every day with the fact that the setting we maintain is not ideal. It is constantly being compromised, infringed upon, and modified. Patients may attack it; colleagues undermine it; we ourselves neglect it. Like the house you live in, it only survives because you also care for it and try to repair the damage as you go along.
>
> (Churcher, 2005, p. 9)

The work of Jose Bleger on the setting, translated and elaborated by Churcher and Bleger (1967/2013) is interesting to comment on here, because of his insight into the meaning of the analytic setting for the patient, which I feel may elucidate an aspect of analytic couple psychotherapy. Bleger defines the psychoanalytic situation as comprised of the 'process'; i.e., the analytic process and a 'non-process' – something held constant within which the analytic process occurs, which he calls the frame, or setting. If the setting is kept constant, we don't notice it, it's constructed to provide the conditions for the analytic work. Sometimes, some aspect of the setting, perhaps a disruption to it, or imperfections in it, as Churcher points out above, needs analysing, but mainly it stays in the background. However, Bleger argues that the primitive, symbiotic meaning of the setting itself eventually needs to be understood and analysed.

> The normal, silent, continuous, presence of the setting thus furnishes the patient with an opportunity for repeating the original symbiosis of

the infant with the mother. The psychotic part of the patient's personality, the undifferentiated and unresolved part of the primitive symbiotic relationship, is deposited in the setting, where it silently persists as a 'phantom world', undetected but nonetheless psychically real.

(Churcher & Bleger, 1967/2013, pp. xxix–xxx)

The patient's symbiosis can only be analysed within the analytic setting, "the psychoanalyst's setting must serve to establish the original symbiosis, but only in order to change it" (Bleger, 1967/2013, p. 240).

The couple analytic setting, while enabling the couple analytic process, might also itself need analysing. The couple can develop a primitive fusion with the therapist who becomes psychically installed in their relationship and they fear relinquishing her. I will return to these ideas in Chapter 10 (on endings) as I think it may help us understand why this, sometimes unanalysed, part of the couple psychotherapy makes it hard for some couples to separate from the therapist and end the therapy. At some point, the therapist needs to step out of the couple's relationship and the couple needs to let her, but there may be resistance to this, an 'invisible bastion' as Bleger describes, because the setting contains this primitive part of the self and the couple's relationship.

The Tavistock Relationships frame

In the Tavistock Relationships model of psychoanalytic therapy, the usual frame consists of weekly sessions for the couple. If there are two therapists working together in co-therapy with the couple, each session lasts an hour. If there is one therapist, the sessions are 50 minutes. The amount of time given to the session has been worked out over time and there are no rights or wrongs about this, but with regular weekly sessions, 50 minutes or an hour feels a reasonable amount of time for the couple to be able to communicate something and the therapist to have an opportunity to think with them about it and to reach some understanding, especially regarding their unconscious relating. Unlike some other approaches to couple psychotherapy, if one partner can't attend, the session will usually go ahead unless it feels unhelpful for a particular couple, or unless this becomes so frequent as to jeopardise the couple psychotherapy. I shall explore this more fully later in this chapter. Also unlike other therapies, there isn't a movement from couple to family, child or individual therapy, it remains couple psychotherapy.

Assuming that the couple are at the point of beginning therapy, I think it is really helpful somewhere in the first session, often at the end, after the therapist and the couple have had a chance to begin to engage with each other, to state or restate the frame in simple terms. What the frame is varies from practice to practice and within different clinical settings, but for example, at Tavistock Relationships, the couple will probably have had a prior consultation with a 'therapist in assessment', so now the new therapist might state that she is the ongoing therapist who is available to see them each week, at a particular time except for holiday breaks. There may be a discussion about when breaks usually are, that good notice will be given, that there is an agreed fee and the couple will be financially responsible for sessions missed, that the therapy is open-ended. It is also helpful at this stage to discuss what would happen if one partner were unable to attend.

Couples sometimes ask how long will the therapy take. One couple said in the initial consultation that I needed to know they "were not coming forever". When I commented that I wasn't actually offering to see them forever, I felt they were both relieved and disappointed. There can be anxiety at this point that the therapy will be too long, too painful to endure, and at the same time, an anxiety (often, but not always, less conscious) that it will not be long enough. They might want things fixed quickly because their emotional state feels unbearable. The therapist tries to convey a commitment to be present and available without making the couple feel trapped into something they fear they will find too difficult. Perhaps the couple needs to hear that they can end at any time, but it is usually better that this comes out of a discussion between them and the therapist. The couple can be supported in giving themselves some time, as their relationship, however troubled, may be important enough to them both to warrant that.

The continuity of the frame – session or couple?

The question as to what happens if one partner can't attend the session relates to the question of what constitutes the frame. Are both partners of the couple being present an essential part of the frame and therefore, unless they are, the session cannot take place? This is the position taken by some couple psychotherapists and we might consider for good reasons; the therapy is 'couple psychotherapy' and can any work take place if there is no couple present? It avoids the problem of one partner coming and all the feelings this arouses for the present and absent partner, and the risk that information will be shared with the therapist that they do not want shared with their partner. If this information is crucial to the couple psychotherapy – for example, the revelation of an ongoing affair – unless this can be shared with the partner, the therapist is left with a secret that undermines the therapy to such a degree that it may not be possible to continue. If the therapist holds the secret, the partner who was absent feels betrayed; if she refuses to hold the secret and shares the information, the other feels betrayed.

The problem, though, with this approach is that it is harder for the therapist to maintain the regularity and rhythm of the therapy if she has to cancel sessions due to one partner's unavailability. Of course, a missed session, agreed to because only one partner can come that week, is still a session, but it can create a lack of continuity. In this sense, the therapist cannot take care of and manage the setting so well through her presence – it can start to feel like it is in the hands of the couple's availability, not the therapist's availability which is hopefully more regular and consistent. Of course, this can be worked with, and the couple having to pay for the missed session is an acknowledgement that there was a session available and, in that sense, there is continuity. But it can also be very hard for the partner who could come, maybe badly wants to come to the sessions, which are paid for but unavailable. Sometimes if that partner is seen, the therapist can be tempted out of a sense of fairness, to offer the other partner a session on their own. While this may make sense and in fact helps the therapist re-establish a couple state of mind if she feels she is losing it, I think I would be wary of doing this as a matter of course rather than holding the frame and analysing the way the couple are using it.

The alternative is to make the session the frame and while having an expectation that both partners attend, accepting that sometimes this is the way the couple is presenting. The couple still exists in the separate minds of the individuals and the therapist analyses the material in front of her; in this case, the couple has presented one individual and withheld the other. By insisting on a session with both partners, the therapist defines the way the couple needs to present. The session has to take account of the absent partner, the experience of the present partner, and the experience of both, once the couple is in the room together again. These experiences may illuminate important aspects of the relationship, how the couple deals with separation, how it feels when one of them gets their needs met and the other doesn't, whether it feels to the present partner that they have too much responsibility for the problem, issues of trust and what can be shared, issues of avoidance. It also creates a frame in which the therapist can take care of the regularity and rhythm of the work, by being available at a regular weekly time. It might be argued that this provides a more consistent and containing frame for the couple and for the therapist to be able to do the work. In this situation, the onus is on the therapist to maintain continuity and she does this by holding a couple state of mind. This model does carry the risk that information may be shared with the therapist that the present partner does not want shared with their partner. For this reason, it is important, when discussing the frame and one partner missing a session, that it is clear that it is couple psychotherapy and that what is discussed by either one should be shared. One might even go further and say that if a partner brings important information they don't want shared, this could jeopardise the psychotherapy.

There are some caveats to this. Sometimes one partner will use the absence of the other partner to discuss something with the therapist that they want to share with their partner, but only feel they can do so having discussed it first with the therapist and getting the therapist's help to bring this into the relationship. There are also times when one partner is too frightened to speak of something with their partner; for example, exposing the extent or severity of domestic violence which is revealed to the therapist and does lead to the couple separating.

Whichever version of the frame one adopts, it is important to be consistent. Having said that, there will be times, working in either frame, that the therapist might make a clinical decision to depart from usual practice. The therapist, who meets only with the couple, may decide on clinical grounds, that she needs to have a session with each partner separately. The therapist holding the session as the frame may decide that with this particular couple, it is always more containing to meet them together. Or if one partner is missing too many sessions such that it starts to feel impossible to hold a couple state of mind. But even this can be diagnostic. A colleague described this situation with one of her couples, in which the partners seemed to take turns to attend. There were always practical reasons given to do with work or child care, but the therapist started to feel it was actually very difficult for the couple to be in the room together. As she started to become fully aware of this and take it up with them, they were able to recognise that in using the sessions in this way, they were bringing to her a central aspect of their couple difficulty in which they found it very hard to share psychic space and continually avoided it. This led to some productive work, including eventually the couple getting back into the room together.

The beginning stage of therapy

Freud (1913), "On Beginning the Treatment", wrote:

> The next question with which we are faced raises a matter of principle. It is this: When are we to begin making our communications to the patient? When is the moment for disclosing to him the hidden meaning of the ideas that occur to him, and for initiating him into the postulates and technical procedures of analysis? The answer to this can only be: Not until an effective transference has been established in the patient, a proper rapport with him. It remains the first aim of the treatment to attach him to it and to the person of the doctor. To ensure this, nothing need be done but to give him time. If one exhibits a serious interest in him, carefully clears away the resistances that crop up at the beginning and avoids making certain mistakes, he will of himself form such an attachment and link the doctor up with one of the imagos

of the people by whom he was accustomed to be treated with affection. It is certainly possible to forfeit this first success if from the start one takes up any standpoint other than one of sympathetic understanding, such as a moralising one, or if one behaves like a representative or advocate of some contending party—of the other member of a married couple, for instance.

(Freud, 1913, pp. 139–140)

Here Freud is talking about allowing a positive transference to develop. He is also, although not calling it that, referring to potential difficulties arising in the countertransference. Whether or not we think exactly as Freud did, there is something in this statement that is very important about a capacity to both hold an analytic stance while also allowing rapport and a warm enough response from the therapist. We don't want to behave like the partner, but equally we don't want to create a cold and alien analytic setting. It is hard enough for some couples to get to grips with the therapist not responding as one would in a more social encounter, such as answering personal questions, but if the therapist is too 'clinical', it can be too unsettling.

In the early stages of the work, there can also be a tension between wanting to 'give' the couple a formulation, which the couple might expect and put pressure on the therapist to provide, and also allowing space for the couple to be. This could be seen as a tension between 'containment' and 'holding' (Brookes, 1991). Bianchini and Dallanegra thoughtfully raise the question of the needs of couples who have little experience of containment in their relationship, whereby the request for therapy "can also be read as an implicit request for a mind into which to evacuate, a container that can serve its primary function, that of containment" (Bianchini & Dallanegra, 2008, p. 76). In such cases, before considering a transformational therapeutic relationship, they suggest we think of "a preliminary phase of constituting a container which can meet the couple's needs of evacuation and which can tolerate containing tension and excesses, allowing above all the experience of a receptive space" (Bolognini, 2008, p. 174; translated and cited by Bianchini & Dallanegra, 2011, p. 76). At this stage in the therapy, even though the couple may want a formulation from the therapist, the kind of formulation they want would not be very helpful, as it would be to validate one partner's position against the other's or to accept one partner's view that the other is the problem. In this state of mind, a couple interpretation, which might require them to take back a projection, could leave them each feeling misunderstood. As described earlier, the couple might want to project into and blame the other, and in this early stage, it can be important for the therapist to also hold the projections without giving them back, or as the couple might perceive it, pushing them back.

Co-therapy as a way of working

At Tavistock Relationships, co-therapy has played an important part in the development of the model. Starting along the lines of each partner having their own therapist and the therapists meeting to discuss the couple, there was a natural move to see the couple together with both therapists.

> With the development of the concepts of countertransference and the reflection process, the foursome setting was also seen to offer the opportunity for the co-therapist pair to be a therapeutically useful area, both for the projections emanating from the couple and for the processing and understanding of the purpose and meaning of the use of this mechanism.
>
> (Ruszczynski, 1993b, p. 21)

Co-therapy remains an important part of the Tavistock Relationships model and is a crucial component of the couple psychoanalytic psychotherapy training. Not all couple psychotherapists have the opportunity to work in co-therapy, and in most settings, therapy with one therapist is the more usual form of couple psychotherapy.

There are different ways of utilising the co-therapist relationship, both in the session with the couple and in reflecting on the session afterwards. Some are aspects that naturally occur, others can be a more conscious approach and part of technique. For example, it may happen as part of the process that one therapist becomes much more engaged with the couple, while the other co-therapist takes more of a third, observing position. This can be immensely helpful if the engagement moves towards enactment – one of the therapists getting very caught up with the couple or one partner and unable to think. The co-therapist can then reintroduce some thinking space, perhaps by commenting on what she or he is observing in the room. For example, the 'observing' co-therapist may comment on the atmosphere in the room – perhaps things are becoming very combative between the couple and the therapists, or very fused, with endless agreement that doesn't feel real, or any other dynamic. This can move between the co-therapists within a session. It can help create the kind of space in the session in which either co-therapist can feel contained by the other so that, for example, difficult things can be said or sensitive areas explored, knowing that if this gets the therapist into deep water, his or her colleague can help out.

Couples can feel very contained by having a therapeutic couple working with them. The co-therapists talking together in the session can also create more psychic space, allowing difference and more thinking. The couple can experience two therapists, another couple, thinking together in their presence, which many may never have witnessed their parents doing. It

The co-therapy relationship and the reflection process

Following Searles's conceptualisation of the reflection process, Mattinson (1975) developed this idea at Tavistock Relationships and the reflection process has been thought about as occurring in case group discussions and the co-therapy relationship. As Searles understood, "the processes at work currently in the *relationship between* patient and therapist are often reflected in the *relationship between* therapist and supervisor" (Searles, 1955/1965, p. 157; emphasis in original). In relation to co-therapy, Ruszczynski suggests, "the co-therapist couple may need to make sense of something between themselves – put there unconsciously by the patient couple through projective identification – before the patient couple are able to do likewise" (1993b, p. 13). In this way, co-therapy can function as a therapeutic tool, giving us information about the couple's relationship, particularly aspects that are unconscious in the couple and hidden from the therapists until they make discoveries based on what is happening to them and between them. Aspects of the couple's shared unconscious are projected into the therapists: either the unconscious relationship itself is projected, or one or both partners project separately into one or both of the therapists. It can be very useful and often essential to try and understand this. It is useful in furthering the work and essential if something is getting into the co-therapy relationship that is disabling it. For example, sometimes the co-therapists find themselves unconsciously enacting something for the couple.

Vincent, a former colleague at Tavistock Relationships, describes an occasion when he was due to present a case in a clinical seminar with his student co-therapist. He had been feeling hopeless about the case and the couple was talking about ending the therapy, which would in fact solve a timetabling problem for him as he was going to be running a new course at that time with another colleague.

> On the morning of the presentation I looked at my notes and, quite convinced that we had already presented them, tore them in half and put them in my waste paper basket. Worse was to follow because at the time of the presentation I had double booked and met up with the colleague with whom I was planning the course that would directly compete with their time in the spring.
>
> (Vincent, 1995b, p. 5)

Of course, this was interesting material for the seminar group to explore and we could imagine many possible meanings. Was there something about the couple in which one of the partners or each of them obliterates the other (that was how the student felt)? Was it about something valuable (the notes) which got destroyed? Was there a real difficulty about a couple coming together in a creative way? Exploring what this acting out meant did help the co-therapists connect more deeply with the experience of this couple and possible enactment in the therapy. They felt that the destruction of the creative work of the notes obliterated something good, which resonated deeply with the couple's relating, but also interestingly the fact that the previous session had, in fact, been much more hopeful. The turning to the 'new love' of the 'new course', away from the couple, also spoke of how easily the couple devalued their own good experience and felt this was something others had, which they envied. The split between the co-therapists was a kind of wake-up call, as they then became acutely aware of the containment of the therapy breaking down. "Acting out on the fringe of therapy had proved creative because it had been possible to reflect on the meaning of the enactment and through that learning gain an understanding of the emotional depth of what was happening" (Vincent, 1995b, p. 6).

Allowing ourselves to be available to be affected by the couple is of course central to the work, but when this involves our relationship with a co-therapist colleague, it can be quite difficult. Perhaps the co-therapists have the row the couple can't have or perhaps they are picking up, through their feelings and interaction, something the couple can't bear to know about, but that becomes projected into the co-therapy relationship. The problem with countertransference is that it feels real and personal, just as transference does. For this reason, a co-therapist might hold back from talking about it, particularly if it involves negative or overly positive feelings about the co-therapist. But it is important to start from the position that the feelings evoked are to do with unconscious dynamics in the couple and explore this first – rather than that it is to do with the co-therapist's personality. Sometimes it *is* to do with the therapist and one of the advantages of working with the same co-therapist and with different couples over time is that it reveals what Bion (1961) called our valencies, the personal hooks or vulnerabilities we have to particular projections.

For these kinds of reasons, it is important that boundaries around the co-therapy relationship are as well held as the session. The therapists should commit to have an agreed amount of time to meet after the session and stick to it, even when it feels there is not enough to talk about or too much to talk about. The therapists can then monitor what happens in these meetings; for example, if it becomes difficult to meet, or if the time becomes misused, they can think about what is being avoided. The co-therapist dynamic might be reflecting something the therapists and the couple are aware of in their relationship, which both elucidates something about the couple relationship, but also, if not understood, can get in the way of the co-therapist couple working creatively together. Furthermore, there are difficulties intrinsic to co-therapy because central to psychoanalytic work is the countertransference process and it is not possible in the moment to know what the co-therapist is experiencing. It can mean that the co-therapist interprets in a direction the other therapist doesn't comprehend or agree with. It can mean that the session feels discordant. In this situation, the co-therapy discussion becomes vital to the therapists understanding each other and being able to work together.

Another interesting area which is made more available by seeing two therapists is the ideas the couple has about the therapists as a couple, often conscious fantasies as well as unconscious phantasies or beliefs. One couple I saw when I was a student at Tavistock Relationships told my co-therapist and me that they imagined that when they left the room at the end of a session, we turned to each other like television news readers and carried on talking. I think this couple felt we were interested in them and felt quite contained by us, but we also wondered what other unconscious phantasies they had about us. Did they feel that we were too distanced and dispassionate? Did they feel we carried on talking about them because we were so fascinated by them? Or did they fear we stopped talking about them as soon as they left because they were unimportant to us and dropped out of our mind the minute the door closed? These phantasies might relate both to aspects of their relationship projected into us as well as their experience of being held by their own parental couples.

Over the years at Tavistock Relationships we have often thought about the question at allocation of what does this couple need in terms of one or two therapists and the gender of the therapist/s. The most usual combination tends to be a male/female or female/female pair. Two men together seemed to be felt as the most difficult option, at least for a heterosexual or lesbian couple and it's interesting to think why this should be the case. If there is a history of sexual abuse or violence from a male, two men may feel overwhelming. We know that there have been cases that have been successfully treated by a male co-therapy pair. In a review of the impact of the therapist gender on analytic patients that I wrote some years ago, the conclusion that most analysts of individual patients came to was that the gender of the therapist might be a factor in engaging patients in treatment, but less so in continuing treatment, the gender of the therapist being transference blind. However, for couples who come for treatment, the gender of the therapist might feel a more 'real' factor. This is partly because the treatment is conducted sitting up facing the therapist or therapists, but also perhaps more crucially because the issues of gender, sex and sexuality, including sexual orientation, might more often be at the heart of couple psychotherapy.

Do some couples need two therapists?

While this is not always possible, there may be certain kinds of couples who benefit from the experience of working with two therapists. In my experience, these are couples with whom it is difficult to think and therefore they are hard to contain. It might be where there is a lot of acting out in the therapy – for example, walking out of sessions – or where there is risk-taking behaviour in the individual or in the relationship. Co-therapy can also be helpful with very conflictual or dysregulated couples, where the couple needs a lot of containment. Each therapist may feel supported and contained by the other and perhaps the couple feels less afraid of destroying the therapist when there are two. Co-therapy can also be helpful with very stuck couples in which it can feel hard to survive the session and know if any work is being done. The couple's defensive system is so impermeable, because of the fear of change and an unconscious wish not to change, that the therapist needs another thinking mind in the room. In this situation, a lot of the work, for a while, may be done in the co-therapy discussion after the session.

The couple analytic space

The analytic couple therapist provides a setting that is confidential and non-judgemental. That which might be censored in the context of relationships with family or friends can be brought and thought about. It takes time to build a relationship like this in which irrational and disturbing thoughts and feelings can be brought and an attempt made to understand them, not judge them. In couple psychotherapy, the therapist has the added task of establishing this kind of safe environment, when for each partner, it may not feel safe in the presence of the other who is experienced as critical and judging or finds the other's feelings too painful or feels attacked by them. So what the therapist may be attempting to provide may feel undermined.

However, over time, the therapist not responding with judgement or criticism may help the partner listen in a different way too, not simply as a reflection on them or an attack on them, but as something going on inside the other and between them which can be thought about, with the therapist's help. But sometimes for many sessions, sometimes all of them, it can't be. As the wife in one couple in therapy tried to articulate what she thought, and how she felt, her husband became more and more disturbed, saying, "You don't think that, that's not how you feel, you're lying". This response from the partner that closes down communication is the opposite of what the therapist is trying to do.

If the therapy goes well, the couple psychotherapy as a regular, reliable, bounded space becomes established as a different space from that outside it. As well as a safe, non-judgemental place, the therapist tries to create a different kind of space for the couple to the one that the couple normally inhabits. This is a place in which they can both exist as fully as possible, where they can talk about things that they can't when alone with each other; an environment in which their unconscious relationship can be understood. Being 'in' the couple analytic space is different from being 'outside' it. As this develops, it becomes more possible to bring what is inside the relationship into the therapy, and hopefully more possible to bring insight developed in the therapy into the couple's ongoing relationship. The couple analytic space is a special kind of space securely bounded by a time frame that is managed by the therapist, but also by the ongoing regularity of the sessions. What the couple talks about is treated differently – not as social communication, but as thoughts and feelings to be understood, however trivial, however disturbing. As Ogden states,

> Everything the analyst does in the first face-to-face analytic session is intended as an invitation to the patient to consider the meaning of his experience. All that has been most obvious to the patient will no longer be treated as self-evident; rather, the familiar is to be wondered about, to be puzzled over, to be newly created in the analytic setting.
>
> (Ogden, 1992, p. 226)

What cannot be said fully enough can be said again or elaborated on in the next session. Or it can be held onto with the hope that given time, it might be talked about. New aspects of the couple's relationship with each other and emerging feelings in relation to the therapist need to be talked about and understood.

With a couple state of mind, in which there is space for each partner and attention to relationship, the couple can be helped to move away from the idea of who is to blame to consider what they are creating together. This is not always possible, sometimes it is not emotionally possible to come together in this way. Then the couple interpretation may address how as a couple they have to maintain the position of blame, it might feel safer than looking at what they create together.

The couple analytic space also provides a particular kind of triangular space (Britton, 1989; Ruszczynski, 1998; Morgan, 2001, 2005; Balfour, 2016) in which the couple can experience the therapist as a third relating to them and their relationship. When in the position of observer, they can see the partner and therapist interacting which can provide a window from which to observe and think about themselves interacting with their partner, or they see their partner from a more outside/third position place (see Chapter 7 for a fuller discussion of this). As the couple state of mind develops, the partners in the couple are much less likely to bring something to a session in which the partner is absent that they don't want shared, because they know (unconsciously) that this is an attack on the capacity to think about them as a couple and an attack on their relationship.

It has often been said that everything an analyst will discover about a patient has been brought to the beginning of therapy, if only she could see it. That may or may not be true, but the point about this chapter is that the beginning is the opportunity to provide the best chance of a reflective and ultimately therapeutic process. By finding a way to maintain a couple state of mind, which includes holding onto a capacity to be curious and interested in the couple in the room, we can establish an experience of a thoughtful container in which anxieties, hopes and pain can be expressed and explored safely.

Chapter 4

Unconscious phantasy, shared unconscious phantasy and shared defence, unconscious beliefs and fantasy

Unconscious phantasy, shared unconscious phantasy, shared defence and unconscious beliefs are all ways of understanding the unconscious life of the couple. The concept of fantasy while conscious is also of interest as couples often have conscious fantasies about their relationship which they are invested in but that aren't known about or shared by both partners. These concepts are related and sometimes overlap but do have some differences, including how they are experienced and worked with in couple therapy. Shared unconscious phantasy and shared defence are concepts created in the early pioneering work of Tavistock Relationships and have been central in clinical practice for many years. In this chapter, I will elaborate these key concepts and the ways in which they help the therapist deepen her understanding of the couple.

Unconscious phantasy

Like many psychoanalytic concepts, unconscious phantasy has not evolved in a straightforward way and how it is understood varies between different analytic schools of thought. Freud used the term in at least two different ways: as a wish-fulfilling activity when instinctual impulses are frustrated (Freud, 1911); and later the idea of primal phantasies, scenes commonly imagined by children – parental sexual intercourse (the primal scene), seduction by an adult and castration which are elaborated around actual hints coming from external reality (Freud, 1916–1917). The idea of innate phantasies has been put forward by others, notably in Bion's idea of innate preconceptions (Bion 1963) and Money-Kyrle's idea of innately known 'facts of life' – dependence, the parent's coitus as a creative act and death (Money- Kyrle, 1971).

For Klein, unconscious phantasy was a much broader and central concept, seen as ever present, accompanying all conscious activity. This was expressed by Isaacs in her seminal paper: "Phantasy is (in the first instance) the mental corollary, the psychic representative, of instinct. There is no impulse, no instinctual urge or response which is not experienced as unconscious phantasy" (Isaacs, 1948, p. 81). From the beginning of life, as we experience both internal states and the impact of the external world, we begin to form ideas about what the world is like. These are rather like stories built around our experience of relating internally and externally. The explanation provides a way of making sense of what is happening to us. Spillius probably speaks for contemporary Kleinian writers when she says,

> Essentially, I think that Klein viewed unconscious phantasy as synonymous with unconscious thought and feeling, and that she may have used the term phantasy rather than thought because the thoughts of her child patients were more imaginative and less rational than ordinary adult thought is supposed to be.
>
> (Spillius, 2001, p. 364)

And *The New Dictionary of Kleinian Thought* states, "Much of the therapeutic activity of psychoanalysis can be described as an attempt to convert unconscious phantasy into conscious thought" (Spillius et al., 2011, p. 3).

Unconscious phantasy and reality

It is important for psychic health to bring phantasies into contact with reality so that there can be reality testing. Unconscious phantasy is constantly influencing and altering our perception or interpretation of reality. The converse also holds true: reality has an effect on unconscious phantasy. For example, an infant when he feels hungry might build up a picture of a mother who will usually be there to satisfy his hunger, or he might feel he is left too long and has the phantasy he won't survive. These unconscious stories or unconscious phantasies build up layer upon layer, though along the way, some dissolve, some are modified and new versions come into being. Later, as part of a couple, the phantasy may be: 'usually, when I need something basic to my emotional survival, I can turn to a partner for help' or there may be the phantasy that there won't be anyone to meet my need.

As a consequence of the distorting effect of unconscious phantasy on one's conscious view of the world, it is wise not to take a patient's reported history as a collection of facts. Perceptions of events can change as particular unconscious phantasies change. And because unconscious phantasy is present all the time, influencing the perception and experience of the outside world, it affects how each partner perceives and experiences the other in a couple relationship. As couple therapists, we can see that each partner is relating to the other in particular ways. This is something the couple therapist is tuning into all the time, particularly when engaged in helping the partners understand how they are perceiving and misperceiving each other. Unconscious phantasy helps us understand how one partner experiences the other, or the therapist, in a particular way. Each partner's communication is affected by unconscious phantasy – it is like another conversation going on between the couple which they are not aware of.

Working with couples, we can see a clear manifestation of this when they argue about an event, which they see in sometimes entirely different ways and there is hardly any agreement about what occurred. In this situation, as Fisher states, "it is important to keep in mind that, when we talk about the capacity to acknowledge the truth of our experience, we are talking about the truth of our emotional experience, the meaning, the emotional meaning, of our experience" (Fisher, 1999, p. 53).

Or when the therapist makes an interpretation, what she meant to convey may be experienced differently by the couple or each partner. This is why seeing how an interpretation lands and following it through is so important. For example, the therapist may have a countertransference experience of her comments and interpretations being blocked by the couple; they don't seem to find anything she says helpful, and after a while, that experience intensifies as they seem to push what she says away. She eventually interprets to the couple that they are both fearful of taking in what she is saying, as if she is making an assault rather than trying to understand and (if it is the case), that she feels something similar is happening between them. One of the partners feels very understood by this interpretation, as she recognises that feeling of pushing people away and notes that she often talks over her husband before he can finish what he's saying. Several sessions later, she connects this to an experience of a very intrusive father whom she had to try and deflect in various ways. So the therapist picking up this slightly paranoid atmosphere in the room leads to this partner making a link to an internal, and external father object, and its influence on her relationship to her partner. The other partner, with a critical maternal object very alive in him, needs to feel that he is behaving in an exemplary way and he hears the therapist's interpretation as criticising him. At that moment, she becomes the critical maternal introject telling him that once again, he has got it wrong. It takes some working through and understanding of their respective unconscious phantasies to understand that his response to the therapist of feeling criticised is why he too finds it difficult to take in what she and his partner are saying. By understanding the lens through which couples experience their partners, themselves, the therapist and their relationship to the outside world, we build up a picture of their unconscious inner world.

Another important aspect of unconscious phantasy, seen clearly in couple relationships, is that it can create the expected response in the other. In other words, the way we experience the external world and the way we relate to others often generates in them the response we expect, therefore confirming our phantasies. One partner delaying coming up to bed at the time the other does can be experienced by that other as sexual rejection, loss of love or anger. Sometimes these are transient unconscious phantasies having their roots in an earlier experience in the relationship and experiences before the relationship. They could take a grip, but if the other partner then does arrive in the bedroom, the phantasy might recede, reality has an influence, and another unconscious phantasy might present of a couple who do sometimes have sex and still feel sexually attracted to each other. However, as Symington shows, the other can be induced to play a part or confirm one's unconscious phantasy (Symington, 1985). Thus, the partner who arrives in the bedroom is perceived not just as late, but too late, the lateness confirming a lack of love or sexual desire. The waiting partner then rejects or misses the other's sexual overture as his unconscious phantasy holds sway over reality. Unconscious phantasy feels real and it *is* real in the sense of being psychic reality. However, where psychic development occurs, inner psychic reality is modified when it does not correspond with external reality.

This understanding about unconscious phantasy is central in the work of couple therapists, because couple relationships are full of misperceptions and misunderstandings. The partners often do not experience the same events in the same ways. Although, in many ways, this is an ordinary fact of life, it can lead to conflict. Some of the worst rows couples have are when they get in a state of mind in which each feels they have the hold on the reality of the event they are describing and the other does not. The concept of unconscious phantasy, that can have such a strong influence on the perception of reality, helps us understand how a couple can experience things so entirely differently.

Shared unconscious phantasy

The development of the concept of shared phantasy

In a couple relationship, some of the unconscious phantasies of one partner come together with unconscious phantasies of the other, and the couple play out particular unconscious stories together. The effect of unconscious phantasies coming together may strengthen them and, if this provokes too much anxiety, the couple will set up defences against them. This was at the heart of some of the thinking of early pioneers of Tavistock Relationships. Hewison, in an historical overview of the concept of shared unconscious phantasy, traces the development of this concept in Tavistock Relationships. He notes that it was Bannister and Pincus who grasped the idea of unconscious phantasy as properly 'shared' (Bannister & Pincus, 1965; Hewison, 2014b). The important shift that was made with the concept of 'shared' phantasy was the understanding that an unconscious system was created in which the members of the couple act on each other and shape a shared unconscious relationship.

Bannister and Pincus describe the need for this conceptual shift in approaching a couple relationship:

> In dynamic psychology, the traditional tendency has been to think in terms of the relationship of the subject to its objects. Concepts are centred on a 'person' or 'subject' and one thinks primarily in terms of the existence and function of that person. This is essentially a 'one-person psychology', each person being thought of as the centre of the world consisting of himself and his objects, to whom he relates by complicated processes and manipulations of the objects in his world. When dealing with a disturbed marriage, both the individuals and the relationship between them must be the object of study. We have to be aware that each is both subject and object. Each is a subject in his own right, but has taken the other, in some measure, as his object and is also the object of the other's attachment. There is a complicated interaction going on between the two, a mutual psycho-biological system in which the adaptive and defensive processes of each are geared in with those of the other and have to function in relation to the other.
> (Bannister & Pincus, 1965, p. 61)

Shared unconscious phantasy and reality

As with unconscious phantasy, the relationship between shared phantasy and reality was seen as central. Bannister and Pincus observed the kinds of relationships in which shared unconscious phantasies could change, and also those that were overly collusive and entrenched. "Shared phantasies and illusions exist in all marriages – but in those with less anxiety and more flexibility, the collusive interaction between the partners will be modified by the changing demands of life experiences" (Bannister & Pincus, 1965, p. 62). However, as Pincus noted:

> [T]he unconscious residues in the personality of earlier conflicts, phantasies which are charged with anxiety or guilt, may 'match up' so that each partner reacts to the other in ways which perpetuate rather than resolve the conflicts and intensify the phantasies which they dare not risk putting to the test of reality.
> (Pincus, 1962, pp. 14–15)

Part of external reality is the other partner and the partners in the couple might act on each other to keep these phantasies alive or might act on each other to dissolve them. As Symington describes, "phantasy creates a response in the social environment and this is a constituent part of it. When the social environment ceases behaving in a particular defined and familiar way then the phantasy is no more" (Symington, 1985, p. 349). In this sense, unconscious phantasies become shared because the other is induced to play a part in them. On the other hand, it can be that the otherness of the other that does not succumb to the pressure to partake in the phantasy can stop its proliferation. This is part of the efficacy of psychoanalytic work in which the analyst tries to detect the pressure to participate in the patient's phantasy and by avoiding it, or in part succumbing to it but interpreting it, creates a new experience for the patient. But this might not be possible for the couple, who share phantasies and are in it together. In a healthy development, the phantasies can gradually change as they are tested out by each partner against the reality of the other and the external world. Alternatively, they may be reinforced by the other partner and become part of the couple's *modus operandi*, being played out in many aspects of their relationship.

A review of shared unconscious phantasy

Rather like unconscious phantasy, tracing shared unconscious phantasy in the couple literature reveals that it has become synonymous with the unconscious life of the couple. Hewison, for example, states: "Shared unconscious phantasy is part of the couple's ordinary life, underlying mutual attraction and enabling them to bind together" (Hewison, 2014b, p. 33). I will illustrate some of the ways it has been described.

Shared phantasy and the projective system

One of the early case studies, the 'Smiths', shows the way that shared phantasy is embedded in the couple's projective system (Bannister & Pincus, 1965, pp. 9–22). The shared phantasy was that

> [W]omen damage men by asserting the opposite: the man had to be strong, the woman weak. Mr Smith projected onto his wife the weak irrational aspects which he could not tolerate in himself, as he feared to become like father and brother Stephen, unless he was governed by logic and reason. Mrs Smith re-lived, in relation to her husband, her anxieties about competing with mother for father's love, which had made her hang onto many of the weaker aspects of her personality, and her feelings of exclusion and sexual rejection.
>
> (Bannister & Pincus, 1965, p. 66)

Witnessing the other's capacity to manage feared aspects of the self enables the projector to reintroject aspects of the self, as they become less feared. In this sense, the unconscious phantasy is modified by being lived out in the couple relationship. As Ruszczynski describes, "the exploration of shared phantasies in couple psychotherapy may allow the projected attributes to be found less terrifying and eventually felt to be capable of being taken back" (Ruszczynski, 1993b, p. 9). For example, the shared phantasy that separateness means abandonment may be worked through together by the couple who unconsciously recognise a shared difficulty, or it might be that the other partner's way of managing separateness may be different enough to bring about another perspective, more thought and a shift in the shared phantasy. Alternatively, the shared phantasy may be further reinforced through the experience with the other. In the idea of a 'defensive' or 'developmental' relationship, shared phantasies can be something the couple defend against or are able to work through together.

Shared phantasy and shared defence

Shared phantasy also tends to be linked explicitly or implicitly with a shared anxiety. To manage the shared anxiety, the couple sets up a shared defence. Thus, simply put, if a couple shares an anxiety about separateness, a shared phantasy may be that separateness leads to, or is experienced as, abandonment (perhaps having roots in an emotionally or physically absent primary object), then a shared defence may be that the couple clings together. The couple therapist might see that the couple always has a row after a separation when one of them or the therapist goes away.

In his discussion of 'Mr and Mrs Avon', Ruszczynski describes the dynamic relationship between shared phantasy, shared anxiety and shared defence, drawing on Ezriel's interrelated three kinds of object relations between patient and analyst. "This concept of a *shared defence*, used by both partners to ward off a *shared fear or phantasy*, is central to the theory and practice of psychoanalytic couple psychotherapy" (Ruszczynski, 1993a, p. 208; emphasis in original). In Ezriel's formulation,

> first, one which the patient tries to establish with the analyst and which I call the *required* relationship, since he requires it in order to avoid the second, which I accordingly call the *avoided* relationship; this he feels he has to avoid in external reality because he is convinced that if he gave in to his secret desire of entering into it this would inevitably lead to the third relationship, a *calamity*.
>
> (Ezriel, 1972, p. 235; emphasis in original)

In relation to Ruszczynski's couple, the 'Avons',

> "the required relationship or shared defensive behaviour was that of a non-sexual relationship. The avoided relationship was that of procreative sexuality. And the shared fantasy or feared calamity was that if they were to produce a child, the other would leave them, either physically

or emotionally. Paradoxically, it was as if, in phantasy, procreative sexuality was life-threatening rather than life-creating.

(Ruszczynski,1993a, p. 209)

Shared phantasy, unconscious choice and couple fit

Shared unconscious phantasies can also be seen as what unconsciously draw a couple together. A couple's unconscious choice of partner will also be influenced by other unconscious elements, transference – the choice of someone who will fit with one's expectations; and projective identification – the choice of someone who will hold and contain split-off aspects of the self. How the partner responds to the transference expectation or projection is crucial. To take Symington's first example in his paper, "Phantasy Effects that which it Represents", in which he describes a female patient who had the phantasy that men just use women for their own sexual gratification, he says, "The phantasy was destructive of her own potential for love, emotional closeness and feminine creative capacity. At the same time it fostered in the man the idea that women are just sex objects" (Symington, 1985, p. 350). In a couple relationship, this woman might choose a man who fitted with this phantasy and it might become a destructive, even abusive relationship. The woman may find, however, that over time, the reality of her experience in the relationship is that she doesn't feel, at least not all of the time, that her partner is using her to meet his own sexual needs. The relationship becomes more mutually satisfying, or one might say that, through the process of taking back her projection of her own unacknowledged aggression towards her own sexuality, she finds herself feeling more empowered in their sexual relationship and less the victim of someone else's desires. Here we have unconscious phantasy coming into contact with reality and changing. This is the developmental potential of the couple relationship. However, the central point of Symington's paper is that sometimes we create a response in the environment that confirms our phantasy, either by subtly manipulating the other to meet our expectations or by ignoring any aspect of external reality that doesn't fit.

New shared unconscious phantasies

Shared unconscious phantasies are created by what each partner unconsciously brings to the relationship, having roots in the myriad of their internal and external experiences; the couple creates a shared unconscious phantasy life. However, the couple's present and live relationship is one of those experiences and a significant one. Some shared phantasies get created newly in the couple as a product of their coming together. Thus, the unconscious phantasy as expressed in the couple's unconscious fit or projective system may change as they react on each other. Things might not go according to the 'unconscious plan'. The partner chosen because they seemed to be a 'rock' may crumble in the presence of the other's unexpected growing confidence; the partner who carries the depression in the relationship may not contain the split-off depression of the other, but be overwhelmed by the 'double dose' (Pincus, 1962, p. 18) causing anxiety and depression to feel uncontainable in the relationship; or one partner's sexual proclivity which seemed exciting to the other initially doesn't map out at all in the way imagined and challenges the couple relationship.

Object relations theory perhaps emphasises the shared phantasy determined by the past, but psychoanalytic couple theory encompasses the shared phantasy, created in the present, as a product of the couple coming together. Both are part of shared unconscious phantasy; it is not just what they share from before, but what is created and changed by their conjunction now. South American writers and others (see, for example, Bleger, 1967/2013; Baranger & Baranger, 2008; Berenstein, 2012; Losso et al., 2018) emphasise the newly created from the unconscious psyches of the two; for example, as Baranger and Baranger state about the two members of the patient–analyst couple coming together, "The basic phantasy of the session is not the mere understanding of the patient's phantasy by the analyst, but something that is constructed in a couple relationship" (2008, p. 806); and Novakovic, from an couple object relations perspective, observes, "both partners impact upon and effect changes in the unconscious phantasies of the other" (2016, p. 98).

Shared unconscious phantasy – the couple's ordinary unconscious relating

Over time, shared unconscious phantasy in the Tavistock Relationships literature has become an overarching concept. It is summarised by Hewison as follows,

> [S]hared unconscious phantasy has many facets and has many layers. It acts intrapsychically and interpersonally. It bridges or encompasses "marital fit" and "shared defence". It is affected by external events. It is recreated in the transference relationship and is mainly known clinically through the countertransference. We work with it by focussing on the relationship, not the individual. We keep the couple in mind. We note how the partners relate to each other and to their marriage, and how a couple relates to us.
>
> (Hewison, 2014b, p. 32)

In thinking about how we access unconscious phantasy in clinical work, he says we need to answer the question, "which version of unconscious phantasy is at play at this moment, what is its content, in what way is it shared, what are the psychic processes that make it shared, and why are we seeing it now?" (2014b, p. 33). Fisher also points out that shared phantasy in couple therapy is ever present. "Sometimes I think we look too hard for shared unconscious phantasies because we have not learned to listen to the stories that are right there before us" (Fisher, 1999, p. 162).

Colman, discussing unconscious phantasy and individuation, says:

> [T]hey should not be regarded merely as an impediment to the relationship but, rather, as its basic substratum, even its driving force. The question, as with Jung's archetypes, is whether the marriage is in the grip of its phantasies, to the extent of being lived by them, or is able to act as a developmental vehicle for them.
> (Colman, 1993b, p. 128)

Thus, some shared unconscious phantasies may grip a relationship and be anti-developmental for the couple, but others may be constantly tested out and reworked between the couple and lead to development.

While some writers talk about 'the' shared unconscious phantasy, others might think of there being many shared unconscious phantasies and in that sense, as with unconscious phantasy, going on all the time between a couple, with perhaps some that are central to their relationship and repeat in many guises. For example, Novakovic, describing a detailed case study says,

> This couple enacted not only one particular unconscious relationship, but different couple unconscious relations that derived from their unconscious phantasies about themselves, the other, and the couple relationship, and their enactments, in turn impacted on their conscious and unconscious experience of themselves and the other.
> (Novakovic, 2016, p. 105)

Specific, central, primitive and dominating shared unconscious phantasy

As well as this broader definition, shared unconscious phantasy has often, and perhaps most often, been talked about as something more specific, a dominant unconscious phantasy that shapes the relationship. The therapist should aim to understand and reveal this phantasy because it will lead to psychic change in the couple. For example, in Clulow et al.'s paper on shared phantasy (1986), Mrs Frazer believed she could only separate from Mr Frazer at his expense. Mr Frazer believed he could only have the marriage at her expense.

> Their inability either to live together or live apart, and the paralysis induced by the double-bind they had created for themselves, reflected a

> powerful unconscious shared phantasy: that life for self, risked death for others; life for others implied the death of self. It was this, concluded the therapists, which exerted its vice-like grip on their marriage.
>
> (Clulow et al., p. 128)

Tarsh and Bollinghaus capture this idea in their comment that, "the concept of shared unconscious phantasy is the heart and soul of psychoanalytical marital psychotherapy". They suggest, "the very attraction of one for the other is to the unconscious phantasy which they share" (Tarsh & Bollinghaus, 1999, p. 125). Therefore,

> it is the Holy Grail – the Holy Grail for which marital psychotherapists search, believing that once found all the defences will fall away, and the couple can go waltzing off into the sunshine to live happily ever after.
>
> (Tarsh & Bollinghaus, 1999, p. 123)

Although they acknowledge that that is a rather romantic view, they are describing a notion of shared phantasy that is more about a particular dominating phantasy about relating which grips the relationship. They suggest that phantasy "is more in the nature of an absolute conviction or belief system than the rather ephemeral-sounding word 'phantasy' would suggest. At bottom it is a belief about what being in a relationship with an *other* means" (Tarsh & Bollinghaus, 1999, p. 126; emphasis in original).

In couple therapy, the couple's beliefs about the meaning of being a couple or being two or of relating to another, are of great interest. Chris Vincent and I, many years ago, shared some thoughts about this. He suggested that there was a limited lexicon of (what we were then calling) shared phantasies: "Most formulations of shared phantasies are expressed in terms of primitive anxieties about the survival of the self" (Vincent, 1992, personal communication). He thought most shared phantasies are concerned with two-person interactions wherein the self is described as being under threat from experiences with another; for example, experiences like separation/fusion, dependence/independence, rejection/incorporation, idealisation/denigration, love/hate, etc.

Because of the way the concept of shared unconscious phantasy has evolved into an overarching concept describing many different aspects of the couple's shared relating, I think these more specific, central, primitive and dominating shared unconscious phantasies identified early in the Tavistock Relationships literature and in other key publications can now be more usefully conceptualised as a particular kind of unconscious phantasy, which Britton has termed an 'unconscious belief', which I discuss below.

In summary, the way I think of shared unconscious phantasies is that they are part of the couple's ordinary relationship and functioning – "stories that are right there before us" – and that they express the unconscious world of a couple in an ongoing way. I don't consider there to be just one shared unconscious phantasy but many, although there may be some key ones. Shared phantasies are often part of the couple's unconscious choice and couple fit enacted by the couple in their projective system, and shared defences are developed by the couple to manage shared phantasies which may be anxiety provoking. While shared phantasies are created out of what each partner brings to the relationship, they are also what are newly created in the relationship. In couple therapy, shared unconscious phantasy informs the ongoing interpretive work of the couple therapist, particularly in a couple interpretation.

Unconscious beliefs

In his book, *Belief and Imagination*, Britton takes the view that not all unconscious phantasies are what he terms unconscious beliefs. He proposes that first, "phantasies are generated and persist unconsciously from infancy onwards". And second, "the status of a belief is conferred on some pre-existing phantasies, which then have emotional and behavioural consequences which otherwise they do not" (Britton, 1998c, p. 9). Following Klein's idea that some unreconstructed infantile phantasies remain in the deep layers of the unconscious in their unchanged original form (Klein, 1958), he describes the way in which a defence system builds up around the phantasy and the phantasy becomes a belief and part of the personality. A challenge to the belief is felt as threatening as this feels a challenge to the self.

The concept of unconscious beliefs elucidates how some unconscious phantasies are felt simply as a fact about life. They remain as unchanged from their primitive form deep in the unconscious, affecting the structure of the personality. Pre-dating Britton's conceptualisation, some of the early Tavistock Relationships case studies described unconscious delusions and phantasies in this way. For example, in the case of the 'Donovans', the therapist identified that

> in order to keep alive the joint illusion (or rather, disillusion) that both could remain what they were, if only they could find the perfect partner, the marriage had to be kept utterly bad, to avoid the possibility of settling for it, making it acceptable.
> (Bannister & Pincus, 1965, p. 65)

These authors refer to Storr's understanding of the way that the emotional strength of a delusion can hold the personality together. Storr's distinction between a hypothesis and a delusion speaks to the distinction between unconscious phantasy and an unconscious belief.

> A hypothesis is, by definition, provisional; a notion which can be modified at any time by the discovery of new facts which do not support it. A belief is more emotionally toned, and requires a change, not only of thought, but of heart, to alter it. A delusion cannot be modified – for the whole personality is attacked if the delusion is undermined – and, whatever facts may be adduced against it, it remains unshaken. It is the emotional strength with which a delusion is held that is its chief characteristic – not its falsity. Every one of us has false beliefs; but these do not amount to delusions because they can be modified if necessity demands it. But delusions may be the only things which render life tolerable. And, as such, are jealously defended against all the assaults of reason.
>
> (Storr, 1960, pp. 14–15)

Whereas shared unconscious phantasies may be revealed in the way each partner relates to the other and to the therapist, and in the shared defences they create, unconscious beliefs are harder to access. There is often a difficult or elusive countertransference. Tarsh and Bollinghaus capture very well this dynamic in relation to what they call shared phantasy when they suggest that

> the deeper and more entrenched the phantasy, the more it suffuses the surface of the couples' interaction; yet the more elusive it will be to grasp, precisely because it is deeply unconscious and heavily defended against. In the consulting room it will be all around like the air that we breathe, but like the air it cannot be seen.
>
> (Tarsh & Bollinghaus, 1999, p. 126)

Similarly, Symington's description of unconscious phantasy has this same fixed and pervasive quality that is so much a feature of an unconscious belief.

> It is like a photograph which sits on the mantelpiece and never changes. It is not a living changing reality. There is an analogy between such a phantasy and a fanatical belief. It resides in the personality but creates the social environment to conform to its stasis. Its capacity to mould the social environment to a static image or representation is an essential part of phantasy. If it loses that capacity the phantasy crumbles and vanishes. This fixed static phantasy screens the ego from change. It throttles what lies in potency within the individual.
>
> (Symington, 1985, p. 350)

Whereas shared unconscious phantasies do not necessarily stop the relationship developing, unconscious beliefs, in one or other partner or gripping the relationship as a whole, do. As I described in a previous paper,

> The relationship is required to fit into the unconscious belief about what a couple is. Therefore, instead of curiosity about the other and discovery of the other leading to something potentially creative, the feelings or behaviour of the other that oppose the belief are experienced as problems. As well as this, they do not feel like problems that can be engaged with or thought about. Unconscious beliefs are like a fundamentalist state of mind – you don't have to find out about the other because you already know what is true.
>
> (Morgan, 2010, p. 52)

Unconscious beliefs, described here, are unconscious phantasies that don't shift in response to an external reality that doesn't confirm them. They are "shutting out of the new, so that increasingly one must limit internal and external experience" (Schaefer, 2010, p. 59). Those aspects of reality that don't confirm the belief may be ignored or experienced as a contrary belief threatening the self. Julie Humphries (2015, p. 38) writes, "Couples in the grip of beliefs can find it hard to distinguish fact from reality, and internal from external reality". The couple Ruth and Chris whom Humphries describes "became muddled about what was reality and what was not" (2015, p. 38). Citing Fisher, she notes that "the reality of the(ir) emotional experience (was) confused with the reality of the external world" (Fisher, 2009, p. 50), their belief manifesting as "couple relationships didn't just feel dangerous, they were dangerous" (2015, p. 38). Fisher, in his thinking about the 'proleptic imagination', which helps us see how unconscious beliefs get lived out in the mind and in the interaction between a couple, describes the way in which each partner has a story about what will happen which does not wait for reality: "In the proleptic imagination, whatever it is that is pictured, there is no space between the image or the idea and the fact or the reality" (Fisher, 2009, p. 35).

When unconscious beliefs are dominating reality, there is often a particular kind of atmosphere in the session. The emotional tone of a session is often one of certainty and it feels difficult for the therapist to offer another view and make an interpretation. If the therapist tries to do this, she can be experienced as completely missing the point, not understanding or trying to impose another reality, experienced by the couple as her own belief. The presence of unconscious beliefs can evoke disturbing countertransference, from feeling annihilated and helpless or aggressive towards the couple, wanting to forcibly stop them. Nathans, in describing the proleptic imagination in action, says:

> This is also what gives many couple interactions a scripted quality. They know where this story is heading and where it will end. And as we, as therapists watch the couple over time, we too can know exactly where the disinterested look on someone's face, the interruption, the

late arrival, the rolling of the eyes, will lead. We can predict each partner's response and the subsequent back and forth, because we have witnessed it many, many times over. Once a couple is caught up in such a dynamic, it can feel like there is no getting out of it; they are trapped and we are trapped in the consulting room with them.

(Nathans, 2009, p. 59)

In this situation, the therapist is also vulnerable to enactments as it becomes difficult to think. Interpretations can take on a lecturing quality or be rather repetitive as the therapist struggles to maintain a separate position.

Fantasy, assumptions and illusions

Before leaving the topic of phantasy, I want to say something about 'fantasy' as a conscious phenomenon in couple relationships. By this I mean the way couples consciously fantasise about their relationship, their more conscious ideas about what the relationship is or should be. Often these ideas are assumed to be shared when in fact they are not, but the partners act as if they are. Sometimes there is an awareness that these fantasies are not shared and there is an attempt to manipulate the other into sharing them. These fantasies, expectations or assumptions can cause considerable conflict as if there really is agreement about them when there isn't. For example, the idea that as parents, the couple should present 'a united front' to the children, the idea that all arguments are destructive and should be avoided, the idea that each partner should always feel sexually attracted to the other, the idea that they have to have sex at least once a week or something is wrong, the idea that the couple should agree with each other, the idea that the other really is responsible for one's happiness. Some of these ideas might be more unconscious phantasies, shared unconscious phantasies or beliefs, but all couples also have a range of conscious fantasies, taken as given, some not thought about, some assumed to be shared but in fact not shared.

Clinical example: Jake and Simone

The couple was arguing about the fact that Jake was often late home from work and missed doing bath time at 6.00 pm with their young children. Jake was very defensive, coming up with various reasons why he couldn't leave work early. The therapist noticed this was an argument that came up regularly between them and then never got resolved. Jake usually promised to try harder the following week, as if somehow the reasons he had given were not to be taken seriously by either of them. Jake's 'excuses' made Simone feel unheard and rather despairing. The therapist realised that the couple was arguing, based on the idea that 'this was how the relationship should be'. Simone was outraged when the therapist said this as, in her mind, there was an agreement about being together as a family in the early evening and she experienced the therapist as undermining this. She then felt just as unheard and despairing towards the therapist. The therapist nonetheless pursued this thought, and Jake said that actually they had never discussed it, but he had gone along with the idea that this was what he should be doing, even if he couldn't actually do it. He then admitted it was rarely possible for him to be home by 6.00 pm. In his mind he wanted to do it when he could, but he did not want Simone to rely on him as he could not guarantee being able to. He realised he had not said this clearly to Simone, or even to himself, but had gone along with this idea, even though this was not really possible. It seemed they had a fantasy about their relationship, the relationship they wanted to have, even though this could not be supported by reality. There is disappointment when the fantasy of the relationship cannot be maintained, but trying to maintain it can lead to fruitless conflict and also get in the way of more creative thinking between the couple.

Disillusionment

"Love, at the very heart of couple relationships, is a state that is often far from realistic – it can be full of idealisation, blurred boundaries, fantasy and illusion" (Friend, 2013, p. 5). As the relationship develops, the couple moves out of permanent residence in this 'in love' state of mind. It doesn't mean that it isn't re-inhabited joyfully, excitedly and passionately at times, but there is a process of disillusionment as the reality of the other as he or she really is, with good and bad aspects, is faced. But for some couples, this becomes a real stumbling block because the other never lives up to or embodies the partner's fantasy of what they need them to be and the disappointment about this becomes a paralysing force in the relationship. The wish for a particular, fantasy object is so strong that new and unanticipated aspects of the other that could be satisfying, even exciting, are not seen or, if glimpsed, not engaged with. For others, there is a capacity to bear the disillusionment of the 'fantasy couple' and for the relationship to develop in unexpected ways.

Alain de Botton, in an article titled "Why you Will Marry the Wrong Person" (2016) writes:

> We marry to make a nice feeling permanent. We imagine that marriage will help us to bottle the joy we felt when the thought of proposing first came to us: Perhaps we were in Venice, on the lagoon, in a motorboat, with the evening sun throwing glitter across the sea, chatting about aspects of our souls no one ever seemed to have grasped before, with the prospect of dinner in a risotto place a little later. We married to make such sensations permanent but failed to see that there was no solid connection between these feelings and the institution of marriage. Indeed, marriage tends decisively to move us onto another, very different and more administrative plane, which perhaps unfolds in a suburban house, with a long commute and maddening children who

kill the passion from which they emerged. The only ingredient in common is the partner. And that might have been the wrong ingredient to bottle. The good news is that it doesn't matter if we find we have married the wrong person. We mustn't abandon him or her, only the founding Romantic idea upon which the Western understanding of marriage has been based the last 250 years: that a perfect being exists who can meet all our needs and satisfy our every yearning. We need to swap the Romantic view for a tragic (and at points comedic) awareness that every human will frustrate, anger, annoy, madden and disappoint us — and we will (without any malice) do the same to them.

(de Botton, 2016, n.p.)

This romantic view, as de Botton puts it, is deep in our psyche. Being part of an adult couple is the first opportunity since being part of the young baby–mother dyad, to re-find that special intimacy. There can be the wish to recreate an exclusive, magical relationship in which all our needs were met – at least temporarily, until we had to face more of reality and the outside world, including mother's adult partner. Even if it wasn't at all like this, one might yearn even more for it to be like this, once one finds the 'perfect other'. While these feelings are likely to be unconscious, their outward conscious manifestations about the other meeting all our needs, a perfect harmony, agreement, someone who takes care of our unhappiness are often there. The cultural manifestation of this fantasy is seen in many aspects of the media which promotes this idea of perfect relationships.

Some couples report that they were never really in love, but many do feel they were in love, and some would describe being in love throughout their relationship. Often couples describe a change from the 'in love' state to a different kind of love, sometimes described as a deeper and more enduring love. This might still include some 'in love' aspects. But, however couples describe it, there is usually a change to something more reality based in which the other is freed a bit from one's fantasies and allowed to be more of their real self. However, this is not always an easy process because it does involve loss and disappointment, and finding out who the other really is can bring surprises – some challenging to the couple, some deeply gratifying.

The clinical picture

To take a simple example:

Danek and Milena

Danek: You are so critical of me, I don't think you realise that nearly everything you say to me is an assault.

Milena: I'm not critical, I don't know how I can talk to you about anything without you feeling criticised, I have to learn how to say nothing (slumps in despair).

This is an ordinary kind of exchange in couple therapy and the only way out of this for the couple is an understanding of what is occurring internally as well as externally in each partner. What is the correlating internal unconscious phantasy and shared unconscious phantasy and possibly unconscious belief?

Danek does feel demands from his wife Milena as critical. The therapist might have an idea why Danek experiences his partner's comments as so critical. Perhaps by now in the therapy she has seen this critical internal object in relation to herself or heard about an experience of a critical and demanding father which is manifesting in the present relationship. And if she hasn't heard of it, she might wonder about it.

Perhaps the couple may make the link themselves, Danek saying to Milena, "You're just like my father". If these links can be made, then I think we are in the area of unconscious phantasy. Something a bit different happens if we are in the presence of unconscious beliefs. It may be that the therapist wonders if there is a link, but feels too afraid to make it; it may be that she can't think at all, it may be that she makes the link with an interpretation and this is experienced as an assault, as if she is trying to distort reality or impose her own belief.

Also, the fact that Danek says, "Everything you say to me is an assault", is very different to "Everything you say to me feels like an assault". The former indicates more of a belief, the latter more of an unconscious phantasy that could be brought into contact with reality – 'that's how I experience it, but it may not be real'.

Milena does come across to the therapist as critical at times, but not all the time and not always like an assault, but nonetheless the therapist can see that sometimes she does come across like that. Milena does always deny her criticism and the therapist wondered if she is frightened about these critical negative feelings and has to disown them. Perhaps there is a shared unconscious phantasy that differences are destructive, particularly where there is an active dislike about something of the other.

Perhaps the therapist might have this thought and put it to the couple – that they seem to share an anxiety about difference and particular things they don't like about the other being very destructive (shared unconscious phantasy), and they manage this between them by Milena being experienced as overly critical and Danek experienced as assaulted, and they seem to keep repeating this between them. Or, possibly, the therapist might say to the couple, "I wonder if it is ever the other way around, are you, Danek, ever critical of Milena?" Then Danek responds with vehemence that, "I could never be critical of her – all hell would break loose!" This would suggest to the therapist that this is their shared unconscious defence. However unhappy they are with the arrangement whereby Milena is critical of Danek, it is better than "all hell breaking loose". But the couple expressing it in this way leads to a greater depth of understanding. What does it mean that "all hell would break loose"? What is the nature of the catastrophe – another layer of shared unconscious phantasy?

It's not that in working with unconscious phantasy there is no resistance; after all, unconscious phantasy does influence our perception of reality. However, with unconscious phantasy, there is a gap, where some light can get in, in the form of the therapist's view, a third position and reality that does not confirm expectations but shifts them. With an unconscious belief, there isn't this gap. Becoming aware of an unconscious belief usually comes through being unconsciously affected by the belief and struggling with an elusive countertransference which may need to be enacted before it can be seen.

Chapter 5

Transference and countertransference and the living inner world of the couple

The ubiquitous nature of transference

In "Remembering, Repeating and Working-Through", Freud wrote that the patient does not *remember* anything of what he has forgotten and repressed, but *acts* it out. He reproduces it not as a memory but as an action; he *repeats* it, without, of course, knowing that he is repeating it (Freud, 1914, p. 150). He saw that people didn't always deal with their neuroses by producing symptoms, but by recreating and repeating the past in the relationships they made. He also pointed out that, "It is not a fact that transference emerges with greater intensity and lack of restraint during psycho-analysis than outside it" (Freud, 1912a, p. 101).

Relationships, and particularly the intimate adult couple relationship, are one of the arenas in which unresolved aspects of the past, alive in the present, are unconsciously brought and repeated with intensity. Thus, in psychoanalytic couple therapy, we see transference dynamics occurring not only in the couple/therapist relationship, but in the couple relationship itself, a relationship that has a life outside the therapy, but which is brought into, and becomes a focus in the couple analytic setting. Each partner is a transference object for the other, transference being an element in unconscious choice and couple fit, part of the bond between the couple and sometimes a cause of tension, particularly if the transference is very unresolved and can't be worked through.

Working with couples also introduces some interesting new questions about transference and countertransference; particularly, what is a couple transference? What is countertransference to a couple? In couple therapy, the couple enacts the living inner world of their relationship in the therapeutic setting. The therapist is temporarily invited into the couple's inner world and their emotional experience of relating. One could think of this as the couple's inner world transferred or projected and enacted in the couple analytic setting, and the therapist's response to this a couple countertransference. Before elaborating this further, I will discuss the development of the concepts of transference and countertransference and the way in which I think of them.

The concepts of transference and countertransference

Transference and countertransference are psychoanalytic concepts that have evolved significantly in the development of psychoanalysis. What began as problems to be overcome in psychoanalytic treatment have since been discovered to be essential aspects in understanding the patient and of psychoanalytic technique.

Transference can now usefully be conceptualised as the projection of a *living inner world* into current situations. This idea of a living inner world has been an important development in psychoanalysis and adds complexity to all relating, internal and external and the relation between the two. Freud understood the way in which objects in the external world were identified with and taken into the ego, becoming part of an internal world, writing in "The Ego and the Id", that "the character of the ego is a precipitate of abandoned object-cathexis ... that contains the history of those object-choices" (Freud, 1923, pp. 29–30). Klein's understanding of splitting and projective identification (1946) was crucial in elaborating this idea, as an interchange between the internal and the external world, each influencing the other, each feeling as real as the other. This process is continuous throughout life so that the inner world is affected by the experience of the outside world, just as the outside world is experienced in unconscious phantasy through the lens of the inner world. Although there is usually a reasonably stable inner world built up over time, it is also, in health, capable of being modified by new experience. This idea is at the heart of therapeutic change.

Freud's understanding of countertransference, as the analyst's unresolved conflicts or pathology that interfered with the analytic work, came to be seen later as an important "instrument of research into the patient's unconscious" (Heimann, 1950, p. 81). In this way, as Heimann stated in her classic 1950 paper, "the analyst's counter-transference is not only part and parcel of the analytic relationship, but it is the patient's *creation*, it is a part of the patient's personality" (Heimann, 1950, p. 83). The analyst's countertransference can be seen as an unconscious response to the patient's transference of an internal relationship projected into the analytic situation. This understanding has been developed by others; for example, Sandler (1976) who suggests that the patient casts himself in a role and his object in a complementary role, which represents the externalisation of an internal object relationship. The other is then subtly manipulated to accept the role into which he or she has been cast. Joseph describes something similar in the wish in all of us to maintain what she calls a 'psychic equilibrium' or balance (Joseph, 1989a). Having established an expectation about relationships and objects in the external world, we tend to see others conforming to these expectations. In her clinical papers, she demonstrates the subtle unconscious attempts that patients make to manipulate or to provoke situations with the analyst, which are a recreation of earlier experiences and relationships, or the externalisation of an internal object relationship.

> Much of our understanding of the transference comes through our understanding of how our patients act on us to feel things for many varied reasons; how they try to draw us into their defensive systems; how they unconsciously act out with us in the transference, trying to get us to act out with them; how they convey aspects of their inner world built up from infancy—elaborated in childhood and adulthood, experiences often beyond the use of words, which we can often only capture through the feelings aroused in us, through our countertransference, used in the broad sense of the word.
> (Joseph, 1985, p. 447)

Ogden in writing about transference and countertransference takes this a stage further in describing the 'intersubjective analytic third' as "a product of a unique dialectic generated by (between) the separate subjectivities of analyst and analysand within the analytic setting" (Ogden, 1994b, p. 4).

The field of transference and countertransference in couple therapy

In couple therapy, it is possible to conceptualise two different *fields* of transference relationships: on the one hand, the 'therapeutic transference relationship'; and on the other, the 'couple's transference relationship'. Clinically, these two areas of transference are experienced somewhat differently for the therapist. The transferences to the therapist and her countertransference are experienced directly, while she can observe in a very live way the transference relationship between the couple, and also have a conscious and unconscious response to it. The therapist might either address what is happening between the couple or address the transference and pressure for enactment in relation to her. But whatever aspect of the transference is attended to, it is part of the same clinical picture. Nonetheless this introduces specific new challenges to technique, as in clinical work with couples there is considerable fluidity, the therapist moving between these different areas of the transference. So, for example, when the therapist is observing the couple talking and she is thinking about the way they are relating, one or both partners inviting the other to recreate with them an aspect of their internal world, the couple, at the same time, is relating to the therapist in a certain way, also unconsciously inviting her to play a particular part. Sometimes it is possible to capture what is going on between everyone in the room. At other times, the therapist focuses on one aspect of the transference and countertransference and it adds to a developing picture in her mind which may come together and be addressed at a later point. And in fact, if one includes the transference and countertransference between the individual partners and the therapist, the field expands further. If there is a co-therapist, it has yet another dimension. While this adds some complexity, the co-therapist relationship can be an important source of understanding the couple, since aspects of the couple's relationship are projected into and reflected in the therapeutic couple. (For a further discussion of co-therapy, see Chapter 3). How the therapist understands and works with this expanded arena of transference and countertransference will be explored throughout this chapter.

The living inner world of the couple

The partners in an intimate couple relationship act on each other, unconsciously forming a specific link unique to the two of them. They bring separate aspects of each of their living inner worlds, their internal objects created through past and present influences and the kinds of unconscious phantasies that operate, and sometimes unconscious beliefs that grip them. The partner becomes a new influence shaping the subject's inner world, and between them they create their own couple inner world.

Because there are two people coming for therapy who bring their relationship, not just as a problem to be discussed but as an alive phenomenon in the present, the therapist does not only observe the couple, think about their relationship and process the ways in which they experience and relate to her. She also has an alive and immediate experience of that relationship, an experience that conveys what it is like actually to be in it. The therapist is affected by the way the couple interacts, speaks, the tone of voice each of them uses, the silences, the aggression and fear, or warmth and connectedness. In other words, alongside the transference and countertransference relationship between the therapist and the couple, there is an enacted dynamic between the couple that the therapist is witness to, and experiences consciously and unconsciously.

For example, a couple recreates the unresolved argument they had earlier in the week, in the session. The therapist can feel the pressure on her to take sides as each partner seeks to make an alliance with her and show the other to be at fault. Together they relate to her as judge or arbiter of the 'truth' and the therapist in her countertransference can feel manipulated, bullied, idealised or denigrated as she fails to respond in the way they want. At the same time, through their enactment of the argument, the therapist is invited into the couple's living inner world, she feels what it is like for this couple when things break down, how frightened and out of control they feel, how despairing of their relationship. This might tell her about unmanageable aspects of their projective system, but also about the nature of their shared internal objects and relating, how one partner becomes the bullying father, the other the helpless victim-like mother, and in transference and countertransference these object relationships can move around between all three. As Ruszczynski and others have pointed out, this is particularly true when the countertransference becomes enacted (Ruszczynski, 1994).

The more the couple is unable to have a couple state of mind in which they can think, with the therapist, about what is happening in their relationship, the more there will be a tendency to act out their relationship. For example, the couple may be engaged in a conversation that feels impossible to follow, and the therapist becomes progressively more and more lost and confused, or it takes on a momentum in which it will follow a predictable pattern with no room for anything new. Nathans (2009) describes this in relation to Fisher's concept of 'proleptic imagination', picking up the 'scripted quality' that is sometimes witnessed in couples' interaction (see Chapter 4).

A note about relationships that repeat

Although transference enters into all relationships, there are some relationships which seem to have a very fixed transference dimension of a narcissistic nature. There are some patients seen either individually or as part of a couple who do seem continually to make the same kind of object choice and, having made it, will not allow the other to break free of these transference requirements. These kinds of couples can be very defeating for the couple therapist, as the wish to repeat overrides working through.

Although our understanding of transference has developed further since Freud's discovery, this kind of fixed transference is reminiscent of the kinds of individuals that he described in "Beyond the Pleasure Principle" (1920). He gives examples of individuals whose relationships all seem to have the same outcome which demonstrates the influence of unresolved transference, something we might describe today as a 'defensive choice of partner' in which a similar object is repeatedly chosen, but nothing is worked through. He describes

> the benefactor who is abandoned in anger after a time by each of his protégés, however much they may otherwise differ from one another, and who thus seems doomed to taste all the bitterness of ingratitude; or the man whose friendships all end in betrayal by his friend; or the man who time after time in the course of his life raises someone else into a position of great private or public authority and then, after a certain interval, himself upsets that authority and replaces him by a new one; or, again, the lover each of whose love affairs with a woman passes through the same phases and reaches the same conclusion.
>
> (Freud, 1920, p. 22)

And later,

> if we take into account observations such as these, based upon behaviour in the transference and upon the life-histories of men and women, we shall find courage to assume that there really does exist in the mind a compulsion to repeat which overrides the pleasure principle.
>
> (Freud, 1920, p. 22)

Some couple relationships have this quality of repeating the past, particularly a conflictual or traumatic object relationship. Those working in social work or health professions will have witnessed many such relationships in which the choice of partner, as abandoning, abusive or controlling, or as a relationship in which the partner will be abandoned, abused or controlled, will repeat an earlier troubled relationship. Sometimes these are violent relationships in which both partners feel caught up in something they cannot escape from. In such couples, there seems to exist an unconscious belief that this is what a relationship is. Even though very restrictive and often very destructive, it is also an attractor and perhaps holds a hope for resolution (because of the certainty it provides). This may be partly because, in more traumatic early experience, uncertainty and hopeful feelings about something better feel even more unpredictable and potentially dangerous.

The therapist's countertransference

So far, I have been talking about transference and countertransference together, but here I will discuss some aspects pertaining specifically to countertransference. It is axiomatic that to practise as a psychoanalytic psychotherapist, one also needs to be analysed. We need to understand the analytic process from the inside out as it is not an experience that can just be taught, it has also to have been had. In addition, we do all need help to understand and work through, to the extent that we can, our own difficulties and to know about areas in our own psyches that are susceptible to enactment or even acting out. Psychoanalytic work is dependent on the use of self and to be able to work this way, we need regular support from colleagues and supervisors.

Working with couples can stir up unresolved areas for the therapist, as it takes the therapist inside a couple relationship. Many therapists will have experienced parents who separated and divorced or had conflictual relationships. Others may have suffered trauma in the family. All of us will have had to struggle with Oedipal conflicts, feelings of exclusion from the parental relationship or inappropriate inclusion. Working with a couple, we are back inside a triangular situation. It may be difficult for the therapist to feel on the outside of the couple or she may feel overly anxious about being drawn into their relationship. She may struggle as to where to locate herself. If the couple wants to separate, her own feeling about her parents' separation (if this occurred), may propel her to try and keep them together as an unconscious attempt to repair her parents' relationship. These difficulties may of course be part of what has unconsciously drawn the therapist to this field of work.

It is not possible to work effectively or responsibly using the tool of the countertransference without this personal analytic work. It is not that, having had an analysis, we are not still vulnerable to being stirred up by patients in ways that relate to unresolved issues of our own, what has been described as 'real countertransference', but as much as possible, we need to be aware of these ways in which we are susceptible and to find ways of monitoring this, through consultation with colleagues and our own self-analytic function.

Gathering the transference

Sometimes it can feel in a therapy session with a couple that there is not much going on in the transference, and it is hard to hold in mind that what the couple is talking about 'out there' (out of all the possible things they could be talking about) are unconscious expressions of what might be happening 'in here'. With some couples, the therapist can be made to feel a passive observer in the face of the couple describing or arguing about events that occurred between them during the preceding week. But there is always the question of why these particular events are brought now into the couple therapy setting. While it is not useful to interpret everything the couple brings as a transference to the therapist, it is useful to have this in mind and to interpret it when the therapist feels the transference connection to her is strong enough or accessible enough, as this enables an emotionally closer understanding of what is going on. In fact, as Hobson (2016) suggests, discussing self-representing events, sometimes what is being talked about out there is happening at that moment in the session. So, when a couple is talking about events that have occurred during the week, the therapist is thinking about this as not only a description of something that *has* occurred and their emotional experience of it, but as an unconscious communication of something in the present relationships in the room, both between the couple now or between her and the couple. I shall give an example to illustrate this.

Clinical example: Eva and John

Eva and John were a couple who seemed to share the absence of any secure internal object. Although they were an insightful couple and recognised that they shared this experience, painful experiences of rejection were often recreated in the relationship despite a conscious wish for closeness and both seeking a containment from the other. They had a 6-year-old son, Robbie, and John had a teenage son, Max, from a previous relationship, who lived with them some of the time.

In one session, Eva and John arrived a little late. Eva was upset that another parent in the school playground seemed to ignore her when she was trying to get her attention. It left her feeling rather embarrassed. She imagined other parents had noticed.

There are several ways this material could be thought about and interpreted. For example, this upsetting experience could be a communication about how Eva can feel in the session, ignored by me. It could also be, as in a self-representing event, how she actually feels now about what is happening in the session. It could be understood as how Eva feels in the relationship with John, at times feeling left on her own with the children, waving to John for some help and feeling ignored. Perhaps the childlike feeling that Eva often expresses – not being enough of an adult, shamed and humiliated in the playground – are also feelings John has. In couples therapy, the therapist might explore any of these aspects, depending on what she feels is most important to attend to at that point in the session. At some point, links may be made to history and the way the couple recreate between them a shared internal object relationship between a child who cannot get through to and make contact with her object.

In another session, the couple were coming into the consulting room when John's phone rang and he went back to the waiting area to take the call. The door was open and Eva and I were left waiting for John and hearing snippets of his conversation. He returned to the room smiling, saying he thought the call might be important, but it wasn't really. Clearly Eva felt annoyed and I had a similar reaction that I tried to think about. I was aware that I could think about this in several ways in relation to me, the therapy, his partner Eva or the relationship. When John came into the room, I wondered about his reticence in coming into the session and his feeling that he might want to leave it again, as I noticed he hadn't turned his phone off.

Later in the session, following more material about how John felt he had to fit in with various colleagues, I interpreted how he didn't want to fit in with me, he felt the couple therapy was imposed on him and I wondered if the phone call had felt welcome to him. I wasn't sure about this interpretation, but John responded positively to it and described how difficult he found it to be in the session, with me observing how difficult things were between them, which he found humiliating. At this point I began to understand my countertransference at the beginning of being disregarded by John, waiting and rejected as he talked on the phone. I felt he had given me (and possibly Eva) a direct experience of what it was like for him in the relationship. What had felt like annoyance (an unprocessed countertransference) I now felt grateful for, as although consciously rejecting of me, John had through projective identification given me a taste of what he experienced with Eva, being rejected and humiliated. I elaborated on this with John, aware that Eva was now observer. I was mindful that now John and I were getting together 'on the phone' and Eva might feel left out.

Reflecting on this, I spoke to the couple about how easily this experience of someone being left out could happen in their relationship. They were telling me about it with friends, other parents, and colleagues and it was recreated so easily here in the therapy with me. Eva said she felt angry with John at the beginning; left with me and waiting for the session to start, she wanted to go ahead without him. I said, "Exactly, he rejects you and me, you want to reject him, and I very easily find myself leaving one of you out ...". In the last part of the session, Eva talked about how she felt John wasn't confident as a parent to their young son, and that he did not engage much with his teenage son when he stayed with them. She felt resentful and left by him with all the responsibility. At this point, the work in the earlier part of the session seemed to bear some fruit as they both realised that these mutual feelings of rejection kept them from connecting together as parents.

It is through the feelings aroused in the therapist – in other words, the countertransference – that much of the couple's internal world is communicated and can be understood. This might be from either partner or the couple. The transference and countertransference does not always occur between the couple and the therapist, it can also happen with either individual in relation to the therapist. Some couple therapists may feel wary of thinking about and interpreting the transference and countertransference in relation to one partner, but as long as the therapist maintains a couple state of mind, which holds the couple, this can be a helpful part of the picture. As described with Eva and John, the transference to me, and the feelings evoked in me, which developed in the course of the session, were also able to be thought about in relation to the couple. By attending to the individual transference, I was able to understand more about not only Eva's internal experience, but ultimately John's as well, as aspects of the lived experience of their relationship.

In psychoanalytic therapy with couples, there is usually one therapist and the couple – three people in the room. In the moment to moment of the session, the therapist turns her attention to the different arenas of the transference, the transference between the couple, the transference between the couple and her, individually or together. An important tool that the therapist can use to explore her countertransference is her couple state of mind, which is always leaning towards understanding the couple's relationship and so allows the therapist to move between these different positions in a creative way. In trying to understand the transference of one partner to her, she is also thinking about how this manifests in the couple relationship. In addition, she is mindful of the 'observer' partner and will include his or her experience at some point. In fact, being the observer member of the couple in this situation can lead to insight.

The triangular nature of the couple therapy

One of the concerns the couple therapist can have if she is interpreting to one of the partners is the exclusion of the other. It is unlikely that the couple therapist will spend too long talking to just one of the partners, but she needs to monitor and attend to the experience of the temporarily observing partner. That partner can feel excluded, but they can also have a useful experience in the observer/third position role, more usually the position of the therapist. In this observer position, they can witness something happening between the therapist and their partner, perhaps what the therapist interprets to the partner or the particular way the partner relates to the therapist. It might even be some sort of subtle enactment between the therapist and partner. What is observed might also be recognised as something occurring in that partner's own relationship, but more easily seen as it is now potentially from a more 'third position' perspective. Of course, this might not be happening, the partner may feel neglected and switch off, or feel in some kind of alliance with the therapist against the partner, or in an identification with the partner against the therapist, but, as the therapy progresses, it can happen. Often couples are so gripped by powerful transference dynamics between them that they cannot get any kind of objective/third position. However, this triangular situation in couples therapy can provide a different viewpoint and help create some objectivity.

Balfour describes exactly this phenomenon in relation to a clinical example.

> From this perspective, they began to be able to see that it was no longer just the two of them enacting the dynamic in a linear way, but a three-way affair, where within the "triangular configuration" in the room, each had experienced the other playing out an aspect of this object relationship with me. For each partner, witnessing the same thing that they were familiar with in their battles with each other now happening with me was important — perhaps for a moment giving a perspective on something that normally they were just "in" together.
> (Balfour, 2016, p. 69)

Transferences that can be difficult to address

Sometimes there are transferences to the therapist that are not only part of the work, but will impede the work unless addressed. This is particularly true of negative transference, but also in couples work, there are often other kinds of transference; for example, idealisation or erotic transference. Although this might be connected to dynamics between the couple, the emotional intensity is in relation to the therapist and may therefore threaten the therapy if not brought into the work. The therapist may be experienced as threatening the relationship, perhaps because there is pressure from one of the partners to keep the relationship intact and the therapist is not offering a quick fix or even taking the position of saving the marriage. Or perhaps one of the partners feels that the therapist is on the other partner's side (something the couple therapist has to continually monitor in herself), and because of this belief, is left feeling misunderstood (or not agreed with) and wants to end the therapy. This dynamic is common in couples in which one partner has had an affair and the other partner tries to elicit support from the therapist to interrogate the partner. There can also be fantasies of the partner having a metaphorical affair with the therapist, and sometimes there is an erotic transference from one partner to the therapist, or the couple together, in talking about their sexual relationship, get too excited and try to recruit the therapist as voyeur which might then feel frightening. The therapist might also be experienced as a critical superego figure as Strachey (1934) described and, unless this transference is understood and interpreted, whatever the therapist says and does will be experienced in this particular light.

How interpreting the transference can bring change

Although both the therapist and the partner are going to be subject to similar projections and enactments of the transference, they are in different positions in relation to it. The couple therapist tries to take a third position in relation to the feelings evoked in her and the pressure to enact, to analyse them in order to understand the patient's inner world. Although she is not a neutral object and aspects of her own internal world and objects will be evoked and she may enact these dynamics, hopefully the enactments will not be gross and she can recover from them and use this experience to understand the couple. In recognising the pressure to respond to the couple in a particular way and resisting this, she provides a different object for the couple, and in doing so, enables them to become aware of an expectation which doesn't necessarily have to be realised. For example, the couple may come into the room with one of them blaming the other for some misdemeanour. They might both agree that the blamed partner is to blame and expect the therapist to join in with this. But the therapist (unless caught up in the countertransference) doesn't blame that partner. And then two things occur. One is that in that moment, there is an experience of a different object that does not fit in with the transference expectation from the couple. The other is that more space is created for the couple to think about what has happened between them.

However, the partner as well as the therapist can be a force for change. Although the partner is not a neutral object in the way the therapist attempts to be, the way the partner modifies or changes his or her response to the other partner's transference expectations can also bring about change.

Sometimes the partner has fitted the transference expectation, this has formed part of the couple's unconscious fit, but the dynamics of the relationship have stretched it beyond its capacity and the recipient partner feels trapped in being perceived in a particularly fixed way. Here the therapist can have an important role in pointing out that while the partner might be like this (transference object) in some respects, in other respects, he or she is a different (new) object.

The therapist as a particular kind of third: familiar themes

There are some transference and countertransference dynamics that seem to come to the fore in couple therapy and can lead to countertransference enactment on the part of the therapist.

Dependency

Couples coming for therapy can sometimes become intensely dependent on the therapist, sometimes in a child-like way. The couple relates to the therapist as if she has psychically taken up residence in the marriage and she becomes thought about, referred to and talked about by the couple during the interval between the sessions. This can evoke a countertransference response in the therapist which is very parental, or even grandparental, and the therapist feels aware of being given an inappropriate and unrealistic responsibility for, or authority by, the couple and might find herself lecturing the couple or giving advice.

Idealisation

Similar to the above is an idealising transference in which the couple looks to the therapist as a kind of saviour (Freud, 1923). The therapist can feel it is up to her to 'save' the marriage and it becomes very hard to stay with the possibility that the marriage may not succeed and the couple may have to separate. Where one partner wants to leave the relationship, there is often an unconscious hope that separation could happen without turmoil and pain and that the therapist would provide the magic formula for this to be achieved.

This dynamic often reflects the search for a similarly idealised relationship between the couple. Couples sometimes feel they have got 'the' therapist who can save them. One couple insisted after their assessment meeting that they continue with the assessing therapist even though this meant waiting for an indefinite period before they could be seen. When she met with them after a period of time to try and help them again to accept a referral, they had developed a very fixed idea about her which included aspects such as the way her voice sounded. They had previously seen various counsellors and therapists who had been unable to help them and she felt that she was set up as some kind of Messiah with magical capacities. When she was eventually able to offer them therapy, they were able to maintain the idealisation for a while, but as the therapist became more real to them, they unsurprisingly became crushingly disappointed. Then they would try and revive what they described as their "great white hope". Both partners in this couple had suffered early traumatic losses which they had been unable to come to terms with. For many years, they managed to maintain a very idealised relationship until the wife had a breakdown and the husband had an affair. The therapy was an extremely painful process for them, but working with the transference to the therapist as the disappointing object seemed a way forward in beginning to come to terms with the loss of the idealised object in each other.

Vincent (1995a) describes the enormous pressure the couple therapist can come under with divorcing or separating couples to act as a judge, magician or servant. Where the pressure is to act as judge or magician, the consultant is turned to, to act as a "rescuer who might provide either a decision or a solution which would release one or more of the participants from intolerable stress" (1995a, p. 679). Where one partner wants to leave the relationship, there is often an "unconscious hope that separation could happen without turmoil and pain and that the consultant would provide the magic formula for this to be achieved" (1995a, p. 680). The third wish for a servant is a rather different kind of pressure in which the consultant is treated disrespectfully and made to feel subject to the ceaseless demands of the couple or one of the partners, which Vincent suggests is a way of dealing with tremendous anxiety about being out of control and a victim to the whims of others (1995a, p. 680).

The pressure to take sides

This is a frequent pressure in couple psychotherapy, as very often the individuals in the couple try to make an alliance with the therapist. This happens both in and out of the session. Couples often report that during an argument at home, one of them cites something the therapist had said, or was imagined to have said, or would say if she were there, and uses it to support his or her view. The therapist herself is subject to her own internal pressures in which she may often have a more positive affective response to one partner or the other. The tendency to take sides, or the couple's perception that the therapist has taken sides, is a good example of a dynamic between the couple and therapist that has to be interpreted. The therapist can be under a lot of pressure to enact something for either partner; for example, by challenging an intellectually defended husband for the wife who becomes silenced by his clever, precise and closed statements. Or by pursuing or interrogating an emotionally unavailable partner on behalf of the other spouse. In this situation, either one of the partners may not experience the therapist as separate, but as a part of the partner – his or her voice, a part object transference. Even when the therapist can remain more separate by interpreting these unconscious pressures rather than enacting them, the couple may perceive the therapist in a distorted way; for example, the couple may both maintain the phantasy that she is in agreement with each of them.

Oneness

In this situation, the couple's narcissistic way of relating gets into the transference and countertransference relationship, something I have described as 'projective gridlock' (Morgan, 1995). The therapist's countertransference can be that she perfectly understands the couple, as all her interpretations seem to be well received and agreed with. Usually after a while there is a more deadly feeling in the countertransference in which the therapist may start to wonder whether in fact anything much is going on in the therapy. It may then become apparent that agreement is not the same thing as understanding; in fact, as Britton has pointed out, writing about narcissistic patients, there is an inverse relationship between agreement and understanding. The higher the need is for agreement, the lower is the expectation of understanding (Britton, 2003b, p. 176). When the therapist has recognised this dynamic, she has to find a way of creating more psychic space so that she can exist for the couple as a separate person.

The oneness dynamic is also seen in another common kind of presentation, which is more sado-masochistic. This can lead to the therapist becoming pulled into one side or the other, so that it can look like there is the pressure to take sides. The more unpleasant this sort of relationship appears to be, the more likely the therapist is to be drawn in as a protector. It then becomes very hard to see how much real power the masochist has in this relationship because the sadist is so dependent on having a willing victim. Once this happens, it will be impossible to understand the way that this is a relationship and that there is an agreement, albeit unconscious.

It is striking, as Stokoe (personal communication) has pointed out, that these themes of dependency, idealisation, pressure to take sides, and oneness relate directly to descriptions of relationships and group behaviour in a paranoid schizoid state of mind. Bion (1961) described the defensive strategies adopted by groups in the face of anxiety which he called basic assumption modes: 'dependency', 'pairing' and 'fight flight'. He described these in terms of the unconscious phantasy that the group appears to share. Subsequently Turquet (1985) added a fourth – 'basic assumption oneness' – to the three Bion had described. Although idealisation has some of the features of basic assumption dependence, it might in fact be more closely linked to basic assumption pairing in the form described by Bion. He believed that the group unconscious phantasy was that if only the right two members could get together to make a baby, they would create a Messiah who would lead the group out of difficulties. This sort of magic is central to the image of the therapist created by such a couple.

Erotic transference and countertransference

Erotic transference and countertransference may arise in any therapy, but there are particular dynamics in couple therapy. It is unusual for both partners to have an erotic transference to the therapist but that can happen. Some couples are reticent in talking about their sexual relationship, unless that is the presenting problem, but there are couples who get quite excited talking about it, inviting the therapist as a voyeur. More often, one of the partners has an eroticised transference or the other partner imagines that they do, and this can range from different intensities of loving feelings towards the therapist to sexual feelings. This isn't always easy to address, but it is an important aspect that needs understanding, whether it relates to infantile or more adult sexuality in the patient.

Working creatively with transference and countertransference and couples: differences, challenges and opportunities

As in other psychoanalytic work, understanding and working with transference and countertransference are just as central to psychoanalytic couple therapy. But in this arena, there are some differences, some challenges and some opportunities. The fact that a 'relationship' is being brought to therapy and enacted in the couple analytic setting allows the therapist access to the couple's inner world in a live, immediate and often powerful way. The triangular nature of the therapeutic relationship allows each participant to, at different times, take a third position and observe a relationship which might in fact be their own. The therapist holding a couple state of mind can work creatively with all the relationships in the room, attending to the different manifestations of the transference and bringing together a richer understanding of the couple's relationship.

Chapter 6

Projective identification and the couple projective system[1]

The concept of projective identification is a psychoanalytic gift to those trying to understand the unconscious dynamics of a couple relationship. It is a clinically and theoretically rich concept that has been elaborated extensively since it was first articulated by Melanie Klein in 1946. We now understand projective identification as an intrapsychic and an interpersonal process, as a defence, and a mode of communication and way of relating. In couples and other relationships, projective identification can also be part of creating a narcissistic relationship in phantasy and in the way a couple functions together, such as that seen in a 'projective gridlock' (Morgan, 1995).

Projective identification is central to the couple analytic concept of the 'couple projective system'. This concept has been crucial in shedding light on why some couples who are apparently so unhappy together nonetheless cannot separate. The nature of the couple projective system, how communicative and flexible, or defensive, rigid and intrusive it is, rests on the way that projective identification is being used by the projector and experienced by the recipient. The couple's projective system can be containing for the couple, or result in something very narcissistic and anti-developmental. The projective system is also an overarching concept that includes an understanding of the couple's 'unconscious choice of partner' and the 'unconscious couple fit', two other important couple analytic concepts.

The concept of projective identification

Melanie Klein first described the process of projective identification in 1946 in her paper, "Notes on Some Schizoid Mechanisms", although she did not use the actual term "projective identification" until a later version in 1952. She understood projective identification as a primitive phantasy of splitting off and projecting parts of the self and internal objects, and identifying with them as if located in another person. For Klein, projective identification was a defence, an unconscious phantasy, and an intrapsychic process.

> Together with these harmful excrements, expelled in hatred, split off parts of the ego are also projected on to the mother or, as I would rather call it, into the mother. These excrements and bad parts of the self are meant not only to injure the object but also to control it and take possession of it. In so far as the mother comes to contain the bad parts of the self, she is not felt to be a separate individual but is felt to be the bad self. Much of the hatred against the parts of the self is now directed towards the mother. This leads to a particular kind of identification which establishes the prototype of an aggressive object relation.
>
> (Klein, 1946, p. 102)

And later,

> It is, however, not only the bad parts of the self which are expelled and projected, but also good parts of the self. Excrements then have the significance of gifts; and parts of the ego which, together with excrements, are expelled and projected into the other person, represent the good, i.e. the loving parts of the self.
>
> (Klein, 1946, p. 102)

For Klein, the infant functions in this way to manage unbearable bodily and mental states. Bad parts of the self that were experienced as threatening to the self are projected, as are sometimes good parts of the self for safekeeping, if felt to be threatened by the bad inside. In Klein's picture of early development, a paranoid schizoid universe, there were also aggressive and controlling impulses towards the object that threatened the subject. She was describing a complex primitive internal world in which the object is at times experienced as threatening, partly because the infant has projected bad and threatening aspects of the self into it.

Since Klein's first description of this process, the concept of projective identification has been developed by many others, not only as describing processes in early development, but in describing processes between patient and analyst and in other relationships.

Bion – container/contained

The person who has made the most significant development of the concept is Bion (1959, 1962, 1967a). Following Klein, he understood that, as well as being a defence, projective identification could be a primitive mode of communication. He described it as the most primitive pre-verbal way in which the infant not only gets rid of, in unconscious phantasy, unbearable feelings, physical and emotional, into the mother, but in which the mother receives this as a communication of the infant's psychic/physical state. If the mother can digest and process these inchoate states, which he terms 'beta elements', the mother, through her reverie, performing a function that he calls 'alpha function', transforms these into 'alpha elements', which can be given back to the infant in this processed, manageable form. Eventually, 'alpha function', the apparatus for thinking, is itself introjected, which helps equip the developing infant in processing his own emotional states.

This process of containment is what the ordinary mother provides for her infant, and what the ordinary infant seeks from the mother, though many things can go wrong in this exchange between mother and infant, the factors depending on mother, infant or both. In offering containment, the mother allows herself to be affected by her infant's emotional state; for example, to feel the infant's primitive states of terror and falling apart. Some mothers will be overwhelmed by their infant's anxiety, which may make them feel they are falling apart and, consequently, they may try to force the anxiety back into the infant, unprocessed and amplified by their own anxiety. And some infants, it seems, may not be able to make use of a containing object; for example, being too affected by envy of the mother's capacities which they do not yet possess themselves. Thus, it is easy to see how a vicious circle can be created – the overwhelmed mother quickly becoming an untrustworthy object for the infant. Many mothers and babies struggle in the early stages of being a parent and being a new born, but mainly they learn from each other and the relationship develops. This struggle is normal and provides the infant with living evidence of an object committed to him.

In some cases, there is very limited containment:

> Normal development follows if the relationship between infant and breast permits the infant to project a feeling, say, that it is dying, into the mother and to reintroject it after its sojourn in the breast has made it tolerable to the infant psyche. If the projection is not accepted by the mother the infant feels that its feeling that it is dying is stripped of such meaning as it has. It therefore reintrojects, not a fear of dying made tolerable, but a nameless dread.
>
> (Bion, 1967a, p. 116)

If the mother is very disturbed or psychotic, not only are the infant's anxieties not contained, but the mother may project her own disturbance into the infant. This description of early development is relevant in thinking about couple relationships, not only because of the elucidation of the concept of projective identification, but because the difficulties experienced in this early relationship will always manifest in some form in the adult couple relationship.

Some writers, following Bion, now consider the process of projective identification to always include the impact on the object who has been projected into and the potential for the projected feelings to be contained by that object; for example, Ogden states,

> In a schematic way, one can think of projective identification as a process involving the following sequence: first, there is the fantasy of projecting a part of oneself into another person and of that part taking over the person from within; then there is pressure exerted via the interpersonal interaction such that the "recipient" of the projection experiences pressure to think, feel and behave in a manner congruent with the projection; finally, the projected feelings, after being "psychologically processed" by the recipient, are re-internalised by the projector.
>
> (Ogden, 1979, p. 358)

For British Kleinian writers, this is not always part of the process, as the "projective phantasies may or may not be accompanied by evocative behaviour unconsciously intended to induce the recipient of the projection to feel and act in accordance with the projective phantasy" (Bott Spillius et al., 2011, p. 126). This view emphasises projective identification as an unconscious phantasy and an intrapsychic process, which may or may not include these other stages. In fact, I think it is useful, even in couple therapy that has at its centre an interpersonal dimension, to keep an understanding of projective identification as both intrapsychic and interpersonal. This is because in relating to another and particularly in more narcissistic relating, each partner's intrapsychic projective identification affects their perception of the other, and they relate to the other distorted by this projection. However, the recipient might not accept the projection and so can feel trapped and misunderstood by the other's distorted perception.

Acquisitive and attributive projective identification

Another way in which projective identification has been elaborated is by considering that phantasies of the identification part of the process are sometimes felt to have 'acquisitive' as well as 'attributive' properties, meaning that the phantasy might involve not only getting rid of aspects of one's own psyche but also entering the mind of the other in phantasy, to acquire desired aspects of the other's psyche. "In acquisitive identification, the phantasy is *I am you*; in attributive identification, it is *You are me*" (Britton, 2003b, p. 167; emphasis in original). In other words, in attributive identification, as in the usual sense of projective identification, some aspect of the subject is attributed to the object, and in acquisitive identification, the projective phantasy involves entering the object to acquire some attribute that the object is thought to possess. The more omnipotently this is done, the more delusional the result. This is similar to Bollas's idea of "extractive introjection", "a procedure in which one person invades another person's mind and appropriates certain elements of mental life" (1987, p. 163), or in a couple relationship, a partner recognises something in the other that they themselves don't possess and takes it over. Both ideas indicate the close relationship between projective and introjective processes. Bollas gives an interesting example of extractive introjection in a couple, which I quote here.

> *A and B have recently decided to live together. A is actually quite ambivalent about this because he does not like to share his space with anyone else and, although he quite likes B and is sexually attracted to her, she also infuriates him. A self-styled moralist, A is not comfortable with his irritations over B's existence. He aims to transcend this. One of the most irksome irritations in A's life are B's pets, which B has brought into their shared life together because she loves animals and is a very caring person. Indeed we can say that one of the reasons why A has persuaded himself to live with B is that she is loving and nurturing. In a short time, A can no longer bear the pets and discovers a device for their removal. He is affectionate and shows intense interest in them, but, after a while and with apparent heavy heart, he tells B that he finds it personally unbearable that such lovely pets should have to be confined to the small flat. Both A and B work during the day, and the pets are alone. This has bothered B. A suggests that if one really loves one's pets this kind of treatment cannot be allowed, and he tells B that he cannot stand it any longer: the pets must be sent to someone who has the time to look after them. As A assumes the function of loving concern, B, who has loved the animals very much now feels guilt (not love) and anxiety (as she knows something will happen to them). She gives up the animals, now believing that all along she has been cruel, when in fact she has been loving. A has extractively introjected the elements of love and care and appropriated them into himself, leaving B to feel dreadful.*
> (Bollas, 1987, p. 162; emphasis added)

If this was a couple in treatment, the therapist would extend these observations to the dynamic between the couple and be interested in, and concerned about, what appears to be very sado-masochistic relating. B, only too willingly, seems to give up good aspects of herself to the envious attack of A, and then identifies with A's split-off and projected cruelty. The example is given in a way that suggests conscious intent on A's behalf, and thus an abusive relationship with a partner, B, who has a limited capacity to hold on to herself and her true feelings. But in some couple relationships, this dynamic is more unconscious but no less powerful, in which one partner takes over or destroys sometimes quite fundamental aspects of the other, as seen in the example of Mario and Lula below. In this situation, extractive introjection or acquisitive identification is a way of dealing with the separateness or otherness of the other which generates too much anxiety or envy.

It is also interesting to note that in couple relationships, a projected aspect that was originally attributive can become acquisitive, as the projected-into partner accepts the projection and takes over this aspect. That partner then carries what has been described as a "double dose" (Pincus, 1962, p. 18; Cleavely, 1993, p. 65), but not always unwillingly. A typical example of this is when partners in a couple with young children temporarily attribute to the other aspects of themselves that are in fact useful to the other. The parent at home attributes her 'outgoing competence' to the partner out working, while that partner attributes his 'nurturing caregiving capacities' to the partner at home. When the children are older and the partner who has been at home wants to return to outside work, she may feel denuded of the capacities she needs. Her partner who has relied on the 'double dose' of these capacities may be reluctant or unwilling to give them back. The opposite is also just as likely to occur – the partner who is out at work and after a while wants to play a more nurturing role with the young children may feel completely inept and be kept this way by his partner.

Intrusive identification and the claustrum

Although many writers, following Bion, have fruitfully elaborated the communicative aspects of projective identification, Meltzer returned to Klein's more defensive use of projective identification and elaborated this. He suggested making a distinction between Klein's original use of the term 'projective identification' and Bion's development of it. For Bion's development of the concept, he suggested retaining the term projective identification as a process describing "the unconscious phantasy implementing the non-lexical aspects of language and behaviour, aimed at communication rather than action". For Klein's original use of projective identification, he suggested the term 'intrusive identification' to describe the "unconscious omnipotent phantasy, mechanism of defence" (Meltzer, 1986, p. 69). In this formulation, Meltzer draws attention to the experience of the kind of object in unconscious phantasy that is being projected into; the former being a container, the latter a claustrum. In thinking about couple relationships, the unconscious phantasy the couple has of their relationship is important. Do they conceive of it as a container – "feeling that they exist within it – are contained by it" (Colman, 1993a, p. 90); or do they experience it as a claustrum, in which "the unconscious experience of being entombed inside one's partner leads to feeling suffocated, as there is no air inside the claustrum and little hope of reclaiming what is hermetically sealed" (Feldman, 2014, p. 145). Fisher describes this as the interlocking adhesive and intrusive dynamics that function in a particularly narcissistic way.

The adhesive dynamics exacerbate masochistic tendencies and the intrusive dynamics exacerbate sadistic tendencies, mutually reinforcing each other in the couple relationship, as each partner feels increasingly locked into intensifying spirals of retaliation. The couple's *folie à deux* offers no way out.

(Fisher, 1999, p. 243)

I will return to this latter kind of phantasy in discussing the nature of the couple's projective system.

Clinical example – a projective system with intrusive projective identification: Mario and Lula

Mario and Lula came for a consultation as they felt their relationship, which had started off promisingly, was starting to unravel and both were very distressed. One issue they brought to the session was a disagreement about a holiday plan to stay with Mario's parents. Mario was keen on the plan, but Lula said she wanted time for the two of them without the intrusion of Mario's parents. As the session proceeded, Mario insisted more and more forcefully that this was not really what Lula wanted, they had agreed to join his parents, this is what they often did and both wanted. Lula started capitulating and I noticed that as she lost the position she started with, it felt like she was losing her own mind. As I put it to the couple that it might be difficult for them to have different views, Mario spoke over me, telling me that Lula really didn't know what she thought and relied on him. I felt at that moment in the session that he was right, he had taken over this capacity in her, and it was a very disturbing experience.

In this example, we see intrusive projective identification in the couple's relating. It is not about communicating an unprocessed feeling, but about dealing with the anxiety that separateness and difference bring, and controlling and taking possession of the object. Mario could not bear Lula's separateness and when she did something which highlighted that she did have a separate mind, he became very controlling. As is often the case in this kind of couple relationship, Lula had a very fragile sense of self and was attracted to Mario's seeming certainty, which she easily gave way to.

When projective identification occurs in this intrusive way, the process of reintrojection is very difficult. One of the reasons is that taking back the projection shifts the perception of the other from one who is part of the self to a separate other, and this feels threatening to the self. There is also anxiety about retaliation by the object who has been forcefully projected into. Klein describes this in her 1946 paper:

> Another aspect of projective processes, as we have seen, implies the forceful entry into the object and control of the object by parts of the

self. As a consequence, introjection may then be felt as a forceful entry from the outside into the inside, in retribution for violent projection. This may lead to the fear that not only the body but also the mind is controlled by other people in a hostile way.

(Klein, 1946, p. 103)

Projective identification in the couple: the couple's projective system, unconscious partner choice, and couple fit

The early pioneers of Tavistock Relationships set out from 1948 onwards to try to understand couple relationships using concepts drawn from the psychoanalysis of individuals. From quite early on, however, they realised that these concepts needed modifying and extending and that new concepts that specifically addressed the unconscious relationship between a couple needed to be found. The 'couple's projective system' is a key couple psychoanalytic concept, referred to in many clinical discussions and supervisions at Tavistock Relationships. It describes a way that couples relate through projective identification, creating a flexible, semi-permanent or more or less fixed unconscious system. At its centre is the concept of projective identification, particularly the way that projective identification can be seen to function interpersonally and reciprocally through mutual projective identifications and counter projective identifications.

Bannister and Pincus described a couple's projective system in the following way:

> Into marriage each partner brings conscious and unconscious drives, attitudes and needs which are partly acceptable and partly unacceptable to himself. Those attitudes or drives which each has difficulty in accepting in himself, each might try to attribute to a partner. The more at war with himself an individual is, the more of himself he may project, and the more dependent he may become on the container of his projections. In marriage, the relationship with the partner who is thus invaded then partly becomes a relationship with oneself, and the partner ceases to exist as an individual in his own right.
>
> (Bannister & Pincus, 1965, pp. 61–62)

Alongside this kind of defensive projective system was also the idea of a projective system as an unconscious attempt to find a solution to internal conflicts and unresolved earlier relationships. Through projective identification, unwanted aspects of the self could be attributed to the other but not lost, as the other into whom these aspects were projected was also one with whom one had an intimate relationship. One could both disown and also stay in contact with projected parts of the self, keeping open the possibility of containment, reintrojection and thus growth and development.

Unconscious choice of partner and couple fit

Theoretically, the projective system can also be thought about as an overarching concept that includes other key couple concepts, particularly 'unconscious choice of partner' and 'couple fit' – though these concepts themselves include, as well as projective identification, other elements such as transference and shared unconscious phantasy. One of the questions that caught the imagination of the early Tavistock Relationships clinicians was why couples who seemed so unhappy together chose each other and stayed together. Alongside the conscious choice of adult partner, sexual attraction, finding 'the one', falling in love, choosing someone with whom one feels a deep connection, or however one might describe this process consciously, there are many unconscious factors at play. These arrangements are like an unconscious version of a marriage contract. In this way, a particular kind of intimacy is created in the couple relationship, in which they come to share a psychic life for good or ill.

Klein saw projective identification as a way in which the infant in its most primitive state first establishes object relations, even though early on this is a part-object relationship and the distinction between self and other is not clear. Following this, Rosenfeld thought that projective identification was the process involved in recognising objects and identifying with them, sometimes with the aim of making essential links with them (1983). In the early stages of a relationship, unconsciously 'recognising' in another lost or denied aspects of the self can be a very powerful experience. We might be intrigued by these aspects, even though ill at ease with them, and wish to re-experience these parts of ourselves through contact with the other. The potential of being able to reintegrate these aspects into the ego, thereby enriching it, may feel risky but also creates a sense of possibility. The other is experienced as psychically, if not one's 'other half', as an object with whom, by having a relationship, one can feel more whole. Projective identification is often at play in unconscious partner choice for these kinds of developmental reasons but also for defensive reasons. Sometimes we recognise parts of ourselves that we want to keep lodged in the other, so that we only have to experience that part of our self at one remove. In conflictual relationships, these unwanted aspects of the self are often still feared and, when brought to life by the partner, may be attacked in them.

Couple fit, in the earlier literature referred to as 'marital fit', refers to the projective system as a whole; that is, the projections of both partners as these dovetail and then interact around core issues or shared unconscious phantasies within a couple. The partners in the relationship carry aspects for each other, aspects of the self that are projected into the other or aspects acquired from the other. Unconsciously, there may be a recognition in the other of the representation of some aspect of one's internal world that one wants to make closer contact with, an internal object with which one wants to work something through, or unwanted aspects that can be located in the other and controlled there. Dicks described it as

> unconscious complementariness, a kind of division of function by which each partner supplied part of a set of qualities, the sum of which created a complete dyadic unit. This joint personality or integrate, enabled each half to rediscover lost aspects of their primary object relations, which they had split off or repressed, and which they were, in their involvement with the spouse, re-experiencing by projective identification.
> (Dicks, 1967, p. 69)

Willi (1984) found that couples could collude together to avoid areas that make them anxious and become polarised, each carrying opposite aspects of a shared theme or issue. He described this polarisation of behaviour patterns in relation to the couple's level of psychic development:

> Partners may feel attracted by a mutually fascinating yet at the same time disturbing theme. ... Often unconsciously, these central themes constitute the common basis of marital relations. Similar fears may cause the build-up of a reciprocally organised defensive system helping both partners to neutralize these fears, to compensate for offenses, and to avoid or master threatening situations. The consequence may be a collusion, an unconscious, neurotic interplay of two partners that is based on similar, unresolved, central conflicts and acted out in polarized roles.
> (Willi, 1984, p. 179)

The nature of the couple's projective system: developmental and defensive aspects

In thinking about the projective system in a couple, it is important to consider not just the content projected and introjected by each partner, but the *nature* of the projective system itself, how evacuative, intrusive, controlling, flexible or containing it is. Different writers, in different ways, draw attention to the nature of the projective system and the couple's unconscious relating. Novakovic (2016, p. 97) in describing the "couple's unconscious relations", emphasises 'process' as well as 'content': "What 'connects' the partners in a 'couple' are unconscious objects, internal figures, *contents* of the mind, and the *processes*, functions, or relations between the objects". Fisher, in describing the oscillation in relationships from narcissistic relating to a psychological state of marriage, highlights the inevitable changing nature of relating in a couple, which he sees as "a fundamental human tension" (1999,

p. 1). Ruszczynski argues, if we consider projective identification as part of what links a couple, then

> *{A}ll object relations are in part narcissistic.* The point at issue is the degree, flexibility and forcefulness of the projective identification. If the more primitive defences of splitting and projective processes dominate the nature of the interaction, such object relations will be more narcissistically structured. If there is less splitting and if the projective system is more fluid, so allowing for the projections to be withdrawn, then the nature of the relationship will be based that much more on the reality of the self and other.
> (Ruszczynski, 1995, p. 24; emphasis in original)

Flexible containment

When a couple projective system is working developmentally, we are really talking about containment in the relationship, but not necessarily or only or exactly in the sense that Bion described, in which one person is functioning as a container for the other who is contained. If the relationship is structured with one partner as mother, the other as infant, then the relationship will be functioning in quite a primitive way, be very limited, and under enormous strain. In more mature relating, aspects of the self are not so entirely disowned. As Joseph points out, projective identification occurring in more primitive states of mind functions without concern for the object, though this changes with psychic development.

> As the child moves towards the depressive position, . . . although projective identification is probably never entirely given up, it will no longer involve the complete splitting off and disowning of parts of the self, but will be less absolute, more temporary and more able to be drawn back into the individual's personality – and thus be the basis of empathy.
> (Joseph, 1989b, pp. 169–170)

In more flexible relationships, aspects of the self are disowned and, at the same time, 'lived with' in the other who is in close proximity.

> Developmental (and therefore therapeutic) potential lies in the fact that what is feared and rejected in the internal world, and is located in the person of the partner, is not lost but it is 'lived with'. It is therefore available experientially and may be assimilated.
> (Woodhouse, 1990, p. 104)

The projection, lived with in the other, and as it becomes less feared by the projector, may increase empathy in the relationship and further the psychic development of each partner. This 'lived with' nature of a couple's projective system is experientially very different in a relationship from the intrusive projective identification described earlier.

For most couples, their projective system contains defensive and developmental elements: at times, it functions more defensively; and at other times, more developmentally. Its defensive functioning can support the couple; as, for example, Cudmore and Judd found in working with couples who had lost a child. They found that while one partner temporarily carried the pain of the overwhelming loss, the other could function and contain. "All the couples we saw who used their relationship to assist them in their mourning, demonstrated this flexibility, an ability to take turns in looking after and being looked after" (Cudmore & Judd, 2001, p. 169).

This can work for the couple if what is projected is not too extreme or representing whole parts of the personality, and, if there is flexibility, these aspects of the self can be given back by the object and taken back by the subject. However, if one of the partners is nearly always the angry one, or the rational one, or the depressed one, or the emotional one, or the only one with a mind, unconsciously caught up in expressing these specific emotions and functions and depriving the other of expressing them, the projective system has become more fixed. For Colman, this flexible capacity in a relationship in which each partner takes turns to contain the other, requires a shift in the image of the relationship to one in which

> the *relationship itself* becomes the container, the creative outcome of the couple's union, to which both partners can relate. It is an image of something the couple are continually in the process of creating, sustaining, and maintaining, while at the same time feeling that they exist within it – are contained by it.
> (Colman, 1993a, pp. 89–90)

Psychic development

Deep in the heart of much of the early writing from Tavistock Relationships is the idea of the couple's relationship itself potentially being therapeutic, or at least one in which each partner can continue his or her psychic growth and development. We cannot always, if ever, function as whole, integrated people, and the couple relationship allows for some regression. Living in intimacy with a partner, who contains unwanted aspects of one's self, is an unconscious arrangement that over time can lead to psychic development in each partner.

This is important, because, as a consequence of projecting, the ego is left depleted, which may result in a weak sense of self. For example, it may be that the capacity to feel and appropriately express angry feelings is disowned because such feelings are felt to be too destructive; consequently, one may live a restricted life, avoiding conflict and confrontations, or become depressed. Alternatively, loving feelings may be disowned, because they are felt to place one at too great a risk of hurt and disappointment: this may lead to living a falsely independent and lonely life. The advantage of projective identification in the context of an intimate relationship is that the disowned parts of the self are not too far away, and seeing these managed differently by the other may render these aspects less frightening. Either there is some kind of psychic balance in the relationship, whereby the other can be relied on to carry this aspect of the self, or it might be possible over time to reintroject this part of the self. As Scharff describes,

> the well-functioning, maturing projective identificatory system enables the person to take back impoverishing projections. It simultaneously enriches the self and maximises concern for the spouse as a separate person, as well as refurbishing the internal object or part of the self to which the spouse corresponds.
>
> (Scharff, 1992, p. 138)

Ogden describes this process in the following way:

> The elicited feelings are the product of a different personality system with different strengths and weaknesses. This fact opens the door to the possibility that the projected feelings (more accurately, the congruent set of feelings elicited in the recipient) will be handled differently from the manner in which the projector has been able to handle them. ... These methods of dealing with feelings contrast with projective identification in that they are not basically efforts to avoid, get rid of, deny, or forget feelings and ideas; rather, they represent different types of attempts to live with, or contain, an aspect of oneself without disavowal. If the recipient of the projection can deal with the feelings projected "into" him in a way that differs from the projector's method, a new set of feelings is generated which can be viewed as a "processed" version of the original projected feelings. The new set of feelings might involve the sense that the projected feelings, thoughts, and representations can be lived with, without damaging other aspects of the self or of one's valued external or internal objects (cf. Little, 1966).
>
> (Ogden, 1979, pp. 360–361)

Conscious container/unconsciously contained

In some couple relationships, it does appear that the arrangement is that one partner is a container for the other. However, this is not always as it appears, as "the obvious and conscious container is sometimes the unconsciously contained and, vice versa, the obviously and consciously contained is unconsciously and emotionally the container" (Lyons & Mattinson, 1993, p. 108). One partner in a same-sex couple described the other as "spineless", unable to take any kind of position in their discussions. She felt she was left to make all the important decisions. The therapist was aware of how fragile this supposedly more self-assured partner was and felt that, were the "spineless" partner not prepared to take this projection, her partner would collapse. This is an example of a couple's unconscious projective system and the way in which the partner who appears on the outside to be the container, is, in fact, in other ways, the unconsciously contained. The way the projective system functions in a couple relationship may be defensive, but in a way, that supports the couple's relationship if it is not too constraining. The couple has an unconscious agreement that one carries a projection for the other, as this benefits their relationship, and thereby each of them within it.

The absence of a container

In order for a projective system to function developmentally for a couple, there needs to be the capacity to take in a projection from the other and hold it temporarily or semi-permanently, until circumstances are such that it can be relinquished. Some couples experience a failure in the use of projective identification. As Lyons and Mattinson observed,

> Marriage partners are in the greatest difficulty when both are desperately seeking to be contained and when such is the pressure of this need that they cannot start to perceive or recognise the equivalent need in the other and provide accordingly. They then become enmeshed in the desperate struggle of "who is to be the baby".
> (Lyons & Mattinson, 1993, p. 108)

The projective identification may have occurred intrapsychically, identified in unconscious phantasy as in the other, but in all but the most narcissistic couples, the projector needs some evidence that the projection has been felt, experienced and identified with by the object. Some relationships are suffused with anxiety. One partner in the relationship is overwhelmed with anxiety and deals with it by projecting it into the partner. But that person's anxiety just makes the other too anxious and they push back the anxiety, increasing the original partner's anxiety. In this situation, instead of the projected anxiety being processed by the recipient and the couple eventually being able to think together, the anxiety escalates.

Clinical example: Matt and Abe
This couple who came for help was very keen to understand what was going wrong in their relationship; they could not understand how easily communication broke

down between them. In one session, Matt told the therapist, "There's another problem with how we communicate. Where I get caught is often when Abe seems anxious, yet may be unaware of this. I have recently realised how anxious I then feel. I then get very anxious that I can't take his anxiety away." Abe responded, "We are both anxious people but sometimes I think I'm handling something fine, you know, like when we lost your house keys but then I find you are filling me with anxiety almost like you're enjoying it!" Matt immediately followed with, "But that's the thing Abe, you don't seem to realise how anxious you really are . . .". As the couple interacted, the therapist could feel the anxiety escalating in the room.

In this situation, conflict between the couple can easily ensue as there is a feeling of being attacked by the other's projection. And of course, there is a dynamic – the more impermeable the object is, the more forceful and aggressive the projections become. Matt and Abe were aware they had a difficulty and wanted to manage things better between them; however, sometimes couples can misuse the relationship in order to deal with internal pain and conflict. In this situation, as Zinner describes it, the relationship becomes "a repository or dumping ground for externalised elements of intrapsychic conflict or expelled unacceptable inner objects. . . . the quality of the marital relationship is sacrificed to the need to minimise inner tension within the individual partner" (Zinner, 1988, p. 2).

Defensive projective processes

In some relationships, the projective system is very defensive. Either the couple may join forces around a shared unconscious belief, expelling from the relationship anything that contradicts it, or they may repeat an unresolved internal relationship that they share and cannot relinquish. Or, as just described, the relationship is a means by which they can disown aspects of the self, projected into the other so completely it is no longer identified with in any sense as belonging to the self. Instead, it is firmly lodged in, and controlled in the other. Couples like this often present in a very polarised way, each partner carrying a double dose of a particular set of feelings.

In trying to understand a couple relationship, we need to think about the experience both of the projector and the recipient of the projection. In intrusive identification, the partner is related to as a narcissistic object, not as a separate other. The projection has a different motivation to that of communication; it is about wanting to lodge oneself inside the other and, in phantasy, to control the object from the inside. In terms of how the partners perceive each other, it is very different imagining what is going on inside the other from the position of being outside, to that of feeling one knows what is going on inside the other from the position of being inside them.

From the point of view of the recipient of the projection, Fisher asks what it is like to be on the receiving end of intrusive projections, "a projection in which someone peremptorily defines both himself or herself *and me* without so much as a by-your-leave?" (1999, p. 239) – another meaning, perhaps, of *The Uninvited Guest*, the title of his book on couple therapy (1999). Here it is not about taking in and containing something, but more like the experience of being taken over. As Meltzer says, "this factor of invitation, and consequently of receptivity, is crucial in object relationships" (1992, p. 70). Without this receptivity, the experience of the intrusive identification is the experience of "being manipulated so as to be playing a part, no matter how difficult to recognize, in somebody else's phantasy" (Bion, 1961, p. 149). Some couples do have a particular kind of narcissistic fit, each with a poor sense of boundaries. One of them functions through the use of intrusive (projective) identification and the other, who has a poor sense of self, is taken over by and identifies with the projections.

Projective gridlock

I described this dynamic in the idea of a couple 'projective gridlock', where projective identification is used to deal with anxiety about separateness and difference (Morgan, 1995). While at a cognitive level, the partners in the couple recognise they are two separate people, at an emotional level, the experience of the other as different, and therefore separate, is experienced as persecutory. In this situation,

> projective identification seems often to be used excessively and intrusively, with the aim, or result, that the other's separate psychic existence is denied. Instead, a comfortable sort of fusion or, feeling of being trapped or imprisoned is created, which stultifies the relationship.
> (Morgan, 1995 p. 35)

As Bannister and Pincus commented, where there is excessive projection of unwanted aspects of the self or even excessive introjection of projected aspects of the other, "too much of the personality may be lost in these processes, with the consequent impoverishment of the individual's emotional life, or at the cost of too great a degree of emotional pressure in maintaining the situation" (Bannister & Pincus, 1965, p. 61).

The experience of being taken over and losing a sense of self was described poignantly by the wife in one couple:

> I have now come to a point – where I feel I want to be more independent – have my own ideas and thoughts. Up to now I have sort of let my life go to one side and taken my husband's. I feel sometimes I haven't been living my own life but his ... I would like to feel my own identity.
> (Morgan, 1995. p. 34)

When projective identification is being used in this way, it has a distorting effect on intimacy. A partner using intrusive identification may feel that they know the other completely, better even than the partner knows him or herself.

> Intrusive projections leave no space for the imagination. This helps us to understand ... the fundamental difference between a genuine intimacy with the other and a "pseudo-intimacy", which is actually a narcissistic form of relating. The former is based on the reality that the other is known *only* from the outside. The latter is based on the phantasy of getting *inside* the other.
>
> (Fisher, 1999, p. 236)

Meltzer invites us to consider the difference between the picture of the inside of the internal mother, which results from the use of imagination, and the one that results from the phantasy of omnipotent intrusion. Seen from the "outside" – that is, through the use of imagination – the primary quality of this region of the internal mother is "richness", having the nuances of "generosity, receptiveness, aesthetic reciprocity; understanding and all possible knowledge; the locus of symbol formation, and thus of art, poetry, imagination" (Meltzer, 1992, p. 72). However, "experienced" from the inside and influenced by the motives of intrusion, Meltzer suggests a very different picture: "generosity becomes quid pro quo, receptiveness becomes inveiglement, reciprocity becomes collusion, understanding becomes penetration of secrets, knowledge becomes information, symbol formation becomes metonymy, art becomes fashion" (Meltzer, 1992, pp. 72–73).

Thus, the couple projective system and the way in which projective identification is used by the subject and experienced by the object can manifest in very different ways. Sometimes, it is important to consider the contents of the projective identification – why one partner disowns important aspects of themselves and why the other partner identifies with the projection. At other times, it is crucial to understand how projective identification is being used in the relationship, its intent, and the nature of the relationship created.

The relationship has a life of its own

The discussion of projective identification in a couple relationship can take on a predetermined slant. We often think about what a couple is bringing to the relationship from their past, what intrapsychic conflicts and anxieties they are seeking resolution of in the relationship. What might have looked like a potentially developmental unconscious choice of partner might not turn out like that. Attempts to recreate an internal object relationship, to work something through in the relationship, or to use the relationship to defend the self against psychic pain may or may not be realised. It may not be possible to keep one's depression at bay projected into the other. Perhaps the depressed partner gets help and gets better; perhaps the pressure of projections leads to increasingly forceful re-projection of one's own split-off aspects, now added to by the partner's. Also, events in the external world, loss and change, will have an impact and might result in unexpected behaviours that could not be predicted, and what the couple does with this cannot be known. Although the aggregate that the couple forms is influenced by what each partner brings to the relationship, the way the partners in the couple then relate together and function takes on a life of its own. This creates the kinds of tensions and difficulties that bring couples for therapy. In a healthy relationship, this is what gives life to the relationship, as the couple finds that together they are creative in ways neither could have known (Morgan, 2005). But the couple may also find that what happens between them is difficult, disturbing and hard for them to process.

Clinical example: Dilan and Radhika
The husband, Dilan, complained that when he wanted to discuss something difficult with his wife Radhika, she gradually became less and less responsive until in the end she withdrew and wouldn't speak to him. He found this infuriating. She said she couldn't help it; she just couldn't talk to him when he pursued her in this way, it reminded her of her domineering father intruding on her and tormenting her. It seemed that an aspect of Radhika's experience of Dilan was of a bullying internal object that she felt unable to stand up against. However, it wasn't a bullying object that Dilan identified with and he didn't see Radhika as a victim to be bullied. His experience of her was of an unavailable internal object, which he could not get through to, which seemed to link with his early experience of his mother.

This example underlines the point that the transference dimension in a couple relationship represents the conjunction between the two separate inner worlds, but also creates its own new dynamic and is therefore not just about working through the past but struggling with the complexity of what is newly created in the present.

More creative functioning in a projective system
While excessive and intrusive projective identification in a couple relationship is clearly destructive of any creativity, there are ways in which projective identification and the couple projective system can help the couple's functioning.

If projective identification is used flexibly and not excessively, each partner can feel contained by the other. But in a functioning relationship, it is not quite as the infant is with the mother, in which contents are entirely split off because unmanageable. It is more that they are not entirely split off, but attributed to the other, where they can be observed as lived with by the other. This can lead to psychic growth in the subject who becomes more interested in and less frightened of their projection.

In some relationships, projective identification is not so flexible, but if not excessive, it can support a couple. There is an unconscious agreement to carry aspects for each other and even an unconscious recognition that this *is* the agreement. In this way, the couple creates a relationship in which they function better together than either partner would alone.

Clinical example: Rick and Sonia

The partners in one couple, as I came to understand it, both had a problem with their anger and aggression. On the face of it, it looked like the problem was the wife, Sonia. When they argued, she could become quite aggressive. But I noticed that when this happened, Rick drew attention to it and, in fact, fanned the flames so Sonia became even more angry. Then he would point out to me how unpleasant she was being and that really there was no point in him saying anything as she didn't listen. It was true that Sonia got very worked up and couldn't listen. I then felt I had a very polarised couple in front of me, Sonia angry and uncontained and Rick becoming increasingly less present and presenting as impotent. Sonia found it particularly unbearable that she was being portrayed by Rick, and probably perceived by me, in such a negative light. At the time, I think Rick also felt quite contemptuous of me for not joining with him against Sonia, though, when I had talked about his perception of her as a 'monster', I detected he too gradually became less comfortable with this portrayal of her.

It was only much later in the therapy, when I had a session with Rick on his own, that he felt able to share and acknowledge his own angry feelings towards Sonia that frightened and disturbed him. Sonia was away on a business trip and he felt very left by her, a feeling that ran deep in him, resonating with a sense of aloneness he had always felt. Rick's previously vehemently denied anger broke through in this session and his strength of feeling surprised us both.

I felt he was able to connect to these feelings now because we had begun to work through his anger located in Sonia. Of particular importance, I thought, was that Rick had seen that I was not frightened by Sonia's aggression – he had put pressure on me to join with him in seeing her as 'monstrous', but I hadn't done this. If I had, I would have been an active participant in maintaining the projective system, and thus not only supporting this defensive arrangement, but more importantly, supporting the phantasy that anger was dangerous and had to be split off. This is such a typical example of a projective system in a couple. It wasn't that Sonia was particularly happy carrying what has been described as a 'double dose' of aggression, hers and Rick's, but it emerged that she was less disturbed by these aspects of herself than Rick, who was truly frightened of them. In

Rick's internal world, the expression of anger risked the destruction of his loved object (his mother who had died when he was 5 years old, following the birth of his brother), which would leave him feeling truly 'monstrous'.

This shift in the projective system is not easy. There is resistance and anxiety about taking back split-off and projected parts of the self. It can be hard to recognise these parts of the self. In this situation, the therapist can work with the projected aspect in one of the partners and, over time, this can have an effect on the other partner because this aspect, projected into the other, becomes less frightening and is therefore gradually more available to be re-owned by the projector. For example, in the case of Sonia and Rick, Sonia was presented as the out-of-control, aggressive one, even though she tried to describe how provoked she was by Rick's denial of anger and his withdrawal. I could feel pressure to go along with this, and to see her as the 'monster', both by identifying with Rick's experience and by seeing myself how emotionally dysregulated she could get in the room. But I could also see that when the couple got into these kinds of arguments, they both felt frightened and disturbed. Without condoning what was happening, it seemed very important that I tried to understand and accept Sonia's anger because in this way, Sonia's conscious anger and Rick's unconscious anger could be contacted.

If I had interpreted at this point that Sonia was carrying the aggression for both of them, Sonia might have felt relieved, but Rick would have felt completely misunderstood. Thus, helping the couple to understand what they have needed to project into each other, and might need to reintroject, isn't always accomplished through interpreting what is being projected or the 'double dose' that one partner carries. It is also accomplished through the therapist containing these projections, so that over time, the couple feels that they can begin to own these aspects. It is only at this stage that interpretations about what has been projected make sense. The couple will make it clear when it is possible directly to address the projection of one into the other. In this case, the couple presented Rick on his own at exactly the right moment for him to be able to open up to the therapist that Sonia was not the only one who was angry

A projective system functioning as a container

Clinical example: Olivia and Jack

Olivia and Jack, a successful middle-aged couple, both worked at a senior level in the same financial corporation. They had moved to London 2 years previously for Olivia to take up an excellent job opportunity and Jack was similarly successful a few months later. The session started with Olivia saying she wanted to pick up from last week's session, and Jack said he had "forgotten" what they had talked about. In the previous session, they had shared something that had been kept from the therapy. Two years ago, when they moved to London, they had "left behind"

Olivia's younger, schizophrenic brother, Al, in their hometown in the north of England. In the early years of their relationship, they had both helped Al through various crises and Jack's willingness to join her in this was one of the things that attracted Olivia to him. Tragically, a month after they arrived in London, Al committed suicide. Having managed to talk about this, Olivia was angry that Jack had forgotten. Jack responded somewhat defensively by saying that he thought Olivia would want to talk about what had upset her over the last day or so. He explained that his sister had been staying with them, and she and Jack had talked about Al. This upset Olivia and she felt angry with Jack and his sister for "raking over it" again. Olivia talked about being angry with them for a while, but I had the sense that this was a diversion away from her feelings of enormous sadness and guilt. When I interpreted this, Olivia responded in a very matter-of-fact way. They had needed to get on with their careers and they couldn't have known that Al would kill himself.

Jack listened, but didn't say anything, and became noticeably quiet. When I commented on this, he responded by asking Olivia if she really wanted to know what he thought about it. She said she did, and he told her that he thought they had done a very bad thing, they had not thought it through properly. She was shocked by his response and then became very upset and started sobbing. Gradually she was able to get in touch with how badly she too felt about "leaving Al behind". As we came to understand it, she had projected her bad feelings into Jack, and because he was more able to live with this feeling of having done something "so bad", these feelings, projected into him, didn't get lost. Now at this point in the therapy and the development of their relationship, she was able to acknowledge that this was her feeling too. Later in the session, I interpreted that just as Jack felt there was a potentially understanding figure in his sister, and perhaps in me, he was also more able than Olivia to live with these "bad feelings" in himself. This helped Olivia to feel that she could now get in touch with her guilt about Al, but also start to work through this and to mourn him.

For this couple, the defensive nature of their projective system was permeable and open to change. In most relationships, there is a defensive and developmental tension – a wish to keep parts of the self located in the other, but also a wish to keep in close proximity to those aspects with the possibility of reintrojection. And sometimes a defensive projective system can support the couple as with Jack and Olivia. But for some time, Jack had to carry a difficult unprocessed experience on behalf of them both, until they could both face it and begin to work through it.

In a more creative couple relationship, communication by projective identification, although inevitable, is less present, as the couple feels able to communicate more through words. Of course, some of what they try to communicate may be the experience of something projected into them by the other. But being able to talk about a double dose of, say, "angry feelings", rather than act out the anger or try to push the anger or other feelings back into the partner, can enable this emotional experience to be thought about. The couple feels able, at least some of the time, to share difficult feelings, unprocessed feelings, differences, hate as well as love, with the belief that the relationship can manage it. With experience, there develops confidence in the relationship, and projective identifications, while being an aspect of the couple's relationship, can be processed and contained within the relationship.

Note

1 A version of this chapter has previously been published in Novakovic, A. & Reid, M. (Eds.) (2018). *Couple Stories: Applications of Psychoanalytic Ideas in Thinking about Couple Interaction*. London: Routledge.

Chapter 7

Narcissism and sharing psychic space

In couple relationships there is what I would describe as 'ordinary narcissism'. There are difficulties in tolerating the otherness of the 'other', and in making space in the relationship for both individuals' different selves and thus sharing psychic space. There is a tension between these ordinary narcissistic struggles and the capacity to relate to the separateness and difference of the other. As several writers have pointed out (Morgan, 1995; Ruszczynski, 1995; Fisher, 1999; Colman, 2005/2014), mostly we move between more ordinary narcissistic states to more object relating states. Fisher, for example, writes that, "Marriage as I am conceptualising it, is the state of object relating that can tolerate the tensions of the oscillation between oneness and separation" (1999, p. 220). In some relationships, we see a more entrenched or destructive narcissism in one or both partners. Fisher describes this as

> a kind of object relating in which there is an intolerance for the reality, the independent existence of the other. Narcissism in this sense is in fact a longing for an other, but a longing for an other who is perfectly attuned and responsive, and thus not a genuine other at all.
> (Fisher, 1999, pp. 1–2)

As discussed in Chapter 6, one of the features of narcissistic relationships is the way that projective identification is used intrusively to deny the other's separateness and difference.

Being oneself and relating to another

In a couple relationship, there is always a tension between our own narcissism and our wish to relate to an 'other', who is a separate and different person. All of us have a degree of narcissism; some of us are deeply narcissistic. There is a part of us that doesn't want to relate and engage with another. We have our own view of the world and being with another who is different and separate from us challenges our beliefs. It is not always easy to take in a new thought, a different view, particularly if it does not reside comfortably with what we already think, know or understand. Our own view can be equated in our mind with 'reality', or the 'truth' and another person seeing and experiencing something differently can be anything from annoying to deeply disturbing.

Colman suggests that there is an anti-relating drive alongside our object-seeking drive. However, he distinguishes anti-relating from non-relating – the latter is just as important as 'relating' is in a relationship; in fact, it would be impossible to be actively relating to another all the time, although one might argue that when we are in solitude, we have moved from the current relationship to relating to our internal objects. For Colman,

> [N]on-relating refers simply to the need for "space" and solitude and is an inherent – and essential – aspect of all relationships. Relating to others is only tolerable within certain limits – beyond these we speak of "intrusion" and "invasion", an abrogation of our autonomy. We need not only to be close to others, but also to be separate from them, not only dependent but also independent. These needs amount to a need for non-relating which, in any successful relationship needs to be held in balance with the need for relating.
> (Colman, 2005/2014, p. 23)

But relating to another is not simply whether we open ourselves to another's experience or whether we maintain our own view, it is whether we can do both at the same time. As Segal states,

> The life instinct includes love of the self, but that love is not in opposition to a loving relationship to an object. Loving life means loving oneself and the life giving object. In narcissism, life giving relationships and healthy self love are equally attacked.
> (Segal, 1983, p. 275)

For some, engaging with another as an 'other' while at the same time holding on to who we ourselves are is difficult. When we do manage this, it can be, as Fisher suggests, quite a psychological task. He puts this in the following way:

> The capacity to pursue the truth of one's own experience and also to tolerate the truth of another's experience, acknowledging and taking the meaning of the other's experience without losing the meaning of one's own, especially when these experiences not only differ but conflict, is a major developmental achievement.
> (Fisher, 1999, p. 56)

In fact, as I shall discuss later, this bringing together of two minds without either being annihilated is also what makes relationships ultimately creative.

The loss of understanding

These ordinary difficulties in relating, in being able to listen to and understand the other are also the way that relationships develop. If there was a perfect attunement, would it really be a relationship? As Cohen writes, "Forget your perfect offering/There is a crack, a crack in everything/ That's how the light gets in" (Cohen, 1992).

Couples often feel they should understand, and be understood by, each other. Working closely with couples, it is immediately apparent that understanding and being understood go horribly wrong a lot of the time. When this happens, the couple can feel that there is something wrong with the relationship or with the partner who doesn't understand. Vorchheimer suggests that the idea that each partner can have a full understanding of the other is illusory and "is the effect of the *narcissistic foundation* of every couple" (Vorchheimer, 2015, p. 12). She says the couple's difficulty in making themselves understandable and understanding each other can be experienced by them not just as an ordinary problem, but as catastrophic. Furthermore, as described earlier, each partner often does feel that they do understand, they have a view of the relationship which is the 'truth', but in fact, the other may have a different view also experienced as the 'truth'. There is a belief in one partner that they are 'right' and it is just that the other doesn't 'get it', as if this is a cognitive problem rather than an alternative view.

Vorchheimer points out that in this situation, the other's different view can be experienced as a deliberate misunderstanding or a lie. She says, "People would not think of themselves as victims of misunderstandings but exchanging lies; they think that misunderstandings are the result of second and hidden intentionalities and they do not conceive of them as unavoidable" (Vorchheimer, 2015, p. 9). In the most disturbed relationships, this experience of the other could be described as malignant. The root of an anxiety about malignant misunderstanding, in which "one's experience of oneself would be eliminated", is linked by Britton to a failure of maternal containment in early infancy which is experienced as an attack rather than a deficiency; "a force is believed to exist that destroys understanding and eliminates meaning" (Britton, 2003b, p. 176).

Words, language and meaning

One aspect of this difficulty in understanding and being understood is that words themselves are polysemic; that is – they often have more than one meaning, as well as being approximations (Vorchheimer, 2015). For example, to 'love' might mean 'being in love' or it might mean 'enjoying' something. Also, when we take an expression like 'being in love', we all have our own definition of what that is or may mean, as Prince Charles famously responded when asked if he and Diana were in love: "whatever *in love* means". History suggests that this couple had very different understandings of what that meant, and possibly this expression was inadequate in describing their conflictual and complex emotional states. Words are only approximations of what we are trying to express so that, in that sense, there are always misunderstandings. A word one partner uses to describe a particular thing is heard by the other to mean something else; in fact, to them it does mean something else. In a healthier relationship, there is an acceptance of this. The couple probably doesn't even think about it, they more or less understand each other, and if something feels not understood or needs understanding more accurately, the couple pursues a better understanding. They sometimes do this through arguing, and later through something shifting and making more sense. But in more disturbed relationships, this difference in understanding can become a persecution and source of extreme conflict, with one partner trying to pin the other down, or insist that their meaning is the real one.

We often don't listen very well

Another difficulty is that we often don't listen very well. Understanding requires a capacity to listen and we are not always good at that. And even if we are quite attentive and good at listening, we might hear the words but not the message. Sometimes we don't want to hear what the other person is saying. We might not like what they are saying and this has an immobilising effect on our curiosity. In more disturbed relationships, listening to the other can feel like having something forced into one, and indeed that might be what the speaker is trying to do. It is not uncommon with distressed couples in therapy to see one partner covering their ears with their hands to try to protect themselves from the other's words, felt as concrete intrusiveness and damaging. On the other hand, the experience of being properly listened to, in therapy or in relationships, as we know, can be quite a powerful emotional experience.

We communicate unconsciously too

Then there is the fact, to complicate things further, that our unconscious is always at work. Often, we are communicating something which is beyond the actual words. It is the way we say something, our affective state and behaviour as well as what we do not say. Much of this we are unaware of, and the partner responds in ways he or she is not aware of. Words are sometimes used to project feelings, not just with the wish for understanding, but with the wish to evacuate a feeling – for example, anxiety – into the other. Couples can find themselves in distressing cycles in which anxiety is passed between them, escalating it rather than containing it between them.

Empathy is complicated

To really understand another, we have to be prepared to question what we think we know and try to understand the other's experience – from their point of view. But empathy is complicated. We might try to understand the other, we might really want to, but it can still go wrong. Our understanding of the other is, of necessity, based on our own experience and it is difficult truly to get oneself into another person's shoes. A typical example here is of one partner, say, a woman who has come home stressed from work to her husband. What she wants is just someone to listen to her and empathise with how she is feeling. Her husband doesn't deal with stress himself in this way and sets about (with good intention) outlining how his wife should deal with the problem – talk to her boss, delegate more, cut her working hours – all of which makes the wife feel completely misunderstood and in fact more stressed because now she also feels she has to deal with her husband's expectations. The husband is also feeling completely misunderstood, as in his mind, he has understood and been genuinely helpful. Being in a relationship is not being 'one', but this primitive idea that we think and experience things the same way is usually present in relationships to some degree.

Curiosity and narcissism

Several writers have contrasted curiosity with narcissism. Colman, for example, states,

> Curiosity is the opposite of narcissism. Where curiosity seeks to know, intrusiveness seeks to possess, to incorporate the unknown of the other into the boundaries of the self and so to abrogate the painful rubbing up against the reality of difference. Alternatively, the narcissistic person may claim to already know the other since what he actually sees and takes for the other is merely the reflection of his own projective identifications.
>
> (Colman, 2005/2014, p. 28)

This idea is also central in Fisher's work; he saw non-intrusive curiosity as fundamental to a deep and enduring love in the intimate couple relationship. Keeping curiosity alive can be challenging in long-term relationships. Following Fisher, in a paper on curiosity, Stokoe and I described this in the following way:

As a couple get to know each other (sometimes over many years) it can feel like they know each other from the inside – although of course they don't. It is years of accumulated experience of the other, empathy, imagination, and love that can feel like this. Even in enduring intimate relationships, it is important to allow space for the other and not to trap one another with a phantasy or belief about what the other is thinking and feeling. Curiosity, if alive, helps with this.

(Morgan & Stokoe, 2014, p. 47)

Britton: sharing psychic space – narcissistic adherence and narcissistic detachment

In discussing sharing psychic space, Britton distinguishes between two kinds of narcissism: narcissistic detachment and narcissistic adherence. "In the first situation, the analyst cannot find a place within the psychic reality of the patient; in the second, the analyst cannot find a place outside it" (Britton, 2003a, p. 171). In a couple relationship, the adherent and detached narcissist can come together and create a particularly difficult dynamic, as the adherent narcissist cannot bear the separateness of the detached, and the detached narcissist is terrified of being drawn into the psychic reality of the adherent. Nyberg describes how this combination can create a defensive and pathological 'fit' between the couple, "characterised by a particular power imbalance where the detached and adherent aspects act as poles meant to repel the other and its defensive purpose is to prevent intimacy" (Nyberg, 2007, p. 146).

Britton (2003a) suggests that the central anxiety for both kinds of patient is that psychic intercourse, bringing two psychic realities together and allowing them to mate, is felt to be catastrophic, a fear of psychic annihilation. One way to deal with this problem in a couple relationship is an unconscious agreement that one person's psychic reality colonises the marriage, and the other's is kept entirely out of the marriage, either split off from consciousness or secretly maintained.

As well as these ideas about detached and adherent narcissism, seen so clearly in some couple relationships, Britton's paper throws light on another difficult couple dynamic, the 'need for agreement'. "When there is a desire for understanding coupled with a dread of misunderstanding there is an insistent, desperate need for agreement in the analysis and annihilation of disagreement" (Britton, 1998b, p. 57). And later,

> {T}he need for agreement is inversely proportional to the expectation of understanding. When expectation of understanding is high, difference of opinion is tolerable; where expectation of understanding is fairly high, difference of option is fairly tolerable; where there is no expectation of understanding the need for agreement is absolute.
>
> (Britton, 1998b, p. 57; emphasis in original)

The following clinical material will illustrate these phenomena in a couple.

Clinical example: Antonio and Camila

This couple, both lawyers in their mid-thirties, with two small children, found it impossible to share psychic space; it was not possible to bring together and integrate the thoughts, feelings or experiences of one of them with those of the other. The way they managed this between them was by an unconscious agreement that Antonio would do what Britton describes as "taking psychic leave of absence" (Britton, 2003a, p. 175) from the marriage, while Camila took possession of it. But at the point of coming for help, the illusion of there only being one mind and set of feelings was breaking down.

The husband, Antonio, who was the more detached partner, had little hope or expectation that psychotherapy would help him; apart from the fact that he considered himself somewhat empty inside, the only problem he felt he had was his inability to alleviate Camila's distress.

The couple could only attend the therapy for a year while he was working in London and she was having a career break to look after the children, after which Antonio's job would take them back to their country of origin. Once they started therapy, Camila dominated the sessions with her complaints and palpable distress, and Antonio seemed bewildered and took on the position of a kind of passive onlooker. He would receive my comments with intellectual interest and I would be invited to enter a debate with him, but I could not make emotional contact with him. The couple described appalling rows which sometimes led to Camila threatening to leave London immediately and return home with the children. On the rare occasions when Antonio took the initiative to describe disturbing arguments between them, he would convey them with a kind of sardonic humour. Camila's complaint was that he didn't understand her, that he was a terrible disappointment to her and that he wasn't there for her. Clearly Antonio found it very difficult to engage with Camila's state of mind, her emotion and volatility threatened him. He did actually find her difficult to understand, but there was also a question in my mind as to whether he wanted to understand her. From her perspective, I think she often felt that there was a malignant misunderstanding, that he deliberately refused to understand her, and at times, it felt like this experience of her object would cause her to fall apart.

On the other hand, what Camila was demanding from Antonio in terms of understanding was not really possible. In the earlier phase of therapy, Camila complained bitterly that Antonio did not understand her and he agreed – he didn't know how to begin to understand her. I was often drawn into making interpretations about what I thought was going on for her. I was becoming part of her phantasy that she was perfectly understood by me. But this was not helpful, as she would then attack her husband, saying that I could understand her, so why couldn't he? The splitting was immense and I felt that Antonio was to be kept as an emotional imbecile, whereas I was not allowed to be other than perfectly attuned.

In one way, Antonio did seem to want to provide what it was that Camila needed, but not by really making contact with her emotional state, but by finding a way of calming her. It was important for him to keep himself in the position of doing the 'right thing' for his wife, as he wanted to be the 'perfect husband'. But, of course, this was completely unbearable for her. He also did not have much hope that he himself could be helped, he felt that all he could do was to try harder to be what his wife needed him to be. I did in the course of time become aware of his anxieties, particularly a well-hidden murderous rage, which occasionally burst out; for example, in road rage situations in which he felt annihilated by the other motorist and wanted to "pulverise them". But it was very hard for him to stay with the meaning of such events for him, nearly always his feelings were split off, evacuated into me or his wife and I am sure that this contributed to her disturbance as well as a difficult countertransference in me.

I have picked out one exchange from one of the sessions; it could have been from any session. In this relationship, there were several themes which were regularly and repetitively brought up by Camila. If Antonio brought something up, it was usually prefaced by "Camila says I need to talk about such and such". One of her themes was his family, which she saw as an extension of him. After years of trying to make them fit her idea of what a family-in-law should be and failing, she had virtually given up on them. However, she wanted Antonio's mother (a widow) to join them in London so that she could help with child care; she believed this is what her mother would do were she able to, and felt it was a quite appropriate expectation of her mother-in-law.

In a session, she reported that she had asked Antonio during the week, "Have you talked to your mother yet about moving?" He had said, "Not yet". She felt driven mad by this – what did he mean, did he do it last week, last year, would he do it tomorrow or what?! In fact, she'd told him to do it by Friday and he hadn't. I said I thought the problem was that he wasn't in agreement with her about this expectation of his mother, they both knew this, but they acted as if they were in agreement. She wanted him to agree with her, related to him as if he did, and then felt driven mad by any behaviour of his that indicated the reality. He, on the other hand, contributed profoundly to her disturbance because he didn't tell her what he actually thought about it.

I recognised this dynamic because of my own countertransference experience referred to earlier, as well as what I could observe between the two of them. He responded to what I said by telling me that if he disagreed with her, she flew into a rage. He then said he had found something on the internet about being "assertive" and he wondered if he needed to do a course – "assertiveness training". He had felt quite excited about this, but then realised he didn't know what he would be assertive about, he didn't know if he could formulate in his mind what he thought. I said I thought that when he tried to work this out, something already in his mind, which he then took to be Camila, stopped his thinking; he then didn't feel he could find his own mental space. But, perhaps what he didn't realise was that although Camila might react to his separate thoughts, she also needed them, as she felt that without them, there was nothing there to come up against, no one to think with.

Although this sounds like a hopeless situation, in fact, there was some progress. This interpretation made to Antonio was also of course indirectly made to Camila. It opened up the possibility that Antonio's different thoughts might not destroy hers if they could be expressed. I don't think she felt anything very creative could happen if the thoughts were brought together, but that at least there might be enough space for both to exist. The problem remained that there was this internal voice that actually interfered with him putting his thoughts together before they were destroyed. But, at the point at which the couple left London (and the therapy), there was the beginning of a change – some light getting into their relationship and opening up just a little psychic space. Antonio's disagreement with Camila was coming more into the open, even though at that moment it did not have much substance; it had more of a feel of some technique he was trying. And even though, at this point, Camila was unsure if she wanted to know what Antonio felt or thought, let alone engage with it, she did seem to begin to recognise (if not accept) that he actually had a different view.

I think that as I was gradually able to find a way of establishing a more separate position in relation to her (as he was beginning to), and at least on occasions get closer to him, there was the beginning of a shift. Camila was gradually able to hear that I did have different thoughts and a mind of my own (as she was becoming aware of this in her husband). Just as in the fragment from the session, amidst the insistence on there being one view, there was a dawning of awareness of different views. At the same time, Antonio seemed to feel that there may have been a little more psychic space for him in the marriage, though this felt a very risky business – he wasn't sure he wanted to occupy it. Before they left, she was pregnant with their third child and I was encouraged that they asked for a referral to be able to continue the work we had started.

Other problems in sharing psychic space

Developmental problems

Some couples present in therapy with uncertainty and anxieties about what a couple is. They fear getting too mixed up psychically. Although presenting as a couple, they haven't yet been able to take the step of becoming psychically 'a couple', as this feels too threatening. Sometimes one or both partners are on the brink of taking this step – from the young adult feeling of being completely independent (even though the adult may be much older in years than a young adult) to making a committed relationship. There can be enormous anxiety about the loss of this hard-won 'independence' and a fear of being engulfed by the partner. Such couples often get together, but find ways to shore up their sense of separateness, through separate bank accounts, friendship groups, etc. Sometimes they are psychically a mother–baby couple and one of them, the 'baby', occupies all of the psychic space, and the other, seen as the carer but with no room for their own needs, takes as Britton puts it, "psychic leave of absence". Or they may be like two siblings, sharing out things between them and arguing about what is fair, as in a babes-in-the-wood couple who walk hand in hand with all the hostile feelings split off from their relationship (Hewison, 2014a).

Clinical example: Adam and Andrea
Adam and Andrea have been going out together for several months and are very much in love. They decide it's time to live together and since Andrea already owns a flat, they agree that Adam will move in with her. The first thing he does when he moves in is to put up extra bookshelves in the living room and to merge his books with hers. Immediately, Andrea feels intruded on, insufficiently consulted, her space invaded, that she is going to be taken over by this man without a by-your-leave. Meanwhile, Adam feels controlled and dominated – he feels he's back with the mother that would not allow him to put pictures on the wall of his bedroom in case it spoiled the wallpaper. So, he too feels there is going to be no space for him in this relationship.

(Colman, 2005/2014, pp. 23–24; emphasis added)

Colman comments:

[W]here previously, the couple felt of one mind, suddenly they are faced with the fact that there is an other here, here within the compass of what they each took to be themselves. That is, they are starting to discover that they cannot simply expand the boundaries of themselves to cover the "relationship"; that somehow a new boundary has to be created around a relationship in which two separate persons exist.

(Colman, 2005/2014, p. 24)

Illusory intimacy

Alternatively, each partner may exist in quite a lot of isolation from the other but create an illusion of a relationship. Anxieties about coming together are dealt with by an imagined relationship around which structures such as home and family may be built, but there is a lack of emotional intimacy. When the couple or one of the partners tries to increase the intimacy, it feels a threat to each partner's separate psychic space and the illusory relationship breaks down. For these kinds of couples, the children growing up and leaving home, or retirement or redundancy is often a threat to the relationship which then opens up like a void. Couples like this tend to see the other as so different from them that they struggle to believe they have any shared areas of interest in which they can engage. When one person tries to initiate something, the other doesn't respond in the hoped-for way.

Vincent, from an attachment perspective, conceptualises the idea of a 'couple void'.

> The hallmark of these voids is a sense of emptiness between the partners that results from an angry emotional engagement which excludes the survival of good experience. It is this angry interaction that I suggest has characteristics of preoccupied attachment. Alternatively, the void can result from a lack of emotional engagement between the couple, and I suggest that this interaction is linked to the dismissing category.
> (Vincent, 2004, p. 134)

Projective gridlock

For some people, engaging with the other as an 'other' feels too much of a threat to the self. They avoid the problem by creating a relationship in which they feel they are, more or less, in total agreement, what we might describe as a merged or fused relationship or, as I have described, a projective gridlock (Morgan, 1995). There may be an unconscious agreement that each partner occupies the same psychic space in an undifferentiated and fused relationship. Some couples exist this way for a while, and it is not too uncomfortable as unconsciously relating in this way serves the needs of both. Projective identification is used to create a sense for the couple of psychically residing inside each other, each partner feeling they know the other or are known by the other from the inside. The ordinary tension and conflict that are unavoidable in a relationship is, in phantasy, removed. Usually this kind of relationship becomes claustrophobic, at least for one of the partners, who loses a sense of who they are. As they withdraw from the gridlock, they create an agoraphobic panic in the other, who loses a sense of who the other is and feels they have nothing known to hold onto. This symbiosis usually eventually breaks down, as it can lead to acute anxiety about loss of self, engulfment or disintegration.

Clinical example: Stan and Frank
This couple came for a consultation because Frank had had a brief sexual relationship with another man, and this threw into question their joint understanding of the nature of their sexual relationship. Frank felt alright about his "fling" and did not feel it mattered in the context of his relationship with Stan. For Frank, his committed relationship was to Stan. Stan felt really upset and angry about Frank's behaviour and attitude now, he felt Frank had attacked and damaged their relationship, perhaps irrevocably. In the consultation, I tried to make room for their different views and experience, but noticed that this was not welcomed by the couple. Stan particularly insisted that what he 'felt' was 'their

agreement'. Frank's dissent from this position was just him lying in order to justify what he had done. When I tried again to help Stan listen to Frank's experience, not simply as an attack on him and the relationship, but perhaps a different view or understanding of the relationship, he reacted to me as if I was doing something quite mad and destructive, even unprofessional. Frank, although less angry in the session, could not engage with Stan's distress.

Although the couple was bringing an important issue about the boundaries of their sexual relationship, I felt their central difficulty was their narcissistic relating. The experience in the room with them was that how each of them 'felt' was equivalent to a factual truth about how things should be. It meant that they could not listen to each other or the therapist, as if another view would annihilate rather than expand their own experience. Although the couple came with a particular issue, their sexual relationship, any other issue that faced them with their separateness and difference could have brought them. I wondered if the narcissistic relating had moved from something more comfortable and merged to something more controlling, and Frank taking sex outside the relationship was a way of breaking free of the control and even potentially a healthy move in opening up some differences between them.

A sado-masochistic dynamic

The relationship can take on an intensely sado-masochistic quality as one or each partner tries to force themselves into the other's psychic space. Any creative space between the couple collapses as only one set of thoughts and feelings is allowed to exist. The existence of otherness in the partner is experienced as an attack, and a counter-attack with more force, or submission, are seen as the only options. There is enormous anxiety in this situation because the other's separate mind is not felt as creative, but as a threat to one's own. This is the intrusive projective identification dynamic described in Chapter Six. As Colman points out,

> [I]t is no joke to be in a relationship which is "not big enough for the both of us". As well as the ubiquitous arguments about space, these couples typically speak in terms of being robbed, cheated, ripped off, wiped out, trampled on, kicked in the teeth, taken over, dominated, controlled, incorporated, invaded, colonised.
> (Colman, 2005/2014, p. 29)

Sometimes at the point of coming to therapy, we see a projective system that is unravelling, one partner is withdrawing their projection into the other and no longer identifying with the projected attribute of the other. This can lead to a dramatic increase in the sado-masochistic dynamics.

Clinical example: Johann and Anna

When I first met Johann and Anna, a young couple in their late twenties, Johann told me categorically that his girlfriend did not understand relationships, she had not had any relationships of substance prior to theirs and did not understand how they worked. It was not clear to me initially to what extent Anna accepted this view of herself, but it felt like it hardly mattered. That was his view and he related to her, and to me about her, accordingly. What soon became clear was how much of a projection this was, as although he had convinced himself he was the expert on relationships, he was clearly very lost, confused and overwhelmed by being in a relationship. Coming for help with their relationship was also a risky endeavour since this potentially set me up as the expert which might threaten Johann's own expert view. However, as we proceeded, it became clear that I could not be allowed to be the expert, or really know very much about relationships. Each move I made towards understanding what was happening between them was met by, at first subtle, then increasingly forceful attempts to silence me. From their account of the beginning of their relationship, I think there was initially a more wholesale acceptance of the projection by Anna and that this was unravelling now. I think Johann was seeking help from me to shore up their previous unconscious arrangement, whereas Anna, very tentatively, wanted to open up a bit more psychic space between them.

I never got as far as hearing very much about their backgrounds other than a few interesting facts. Anna, an only child, was witness to a lot of rows between the parents. Johann grew up in a family in northern Europe, part of a small rural community, where he said, "nothing was hidden". He said that in his family, everyone talked about every intimate detail of everyone else. However, one thing was hidden, which was that as a young adolescent, he had a close sexual liaison with an older man in the village. This secret relationship did not in the end feel a good place for him, he found it hard to break away from something that felt abusive, and so privacy had a dangerous meaning for him, just as openness was experienced as too translucent. It was clear to me that for this couple, being in an intimate relationship with another raised a lot of anxiety. For him, the anxiety was at a near psychotic level, he felt he lost control and didn't know where he was. For her, I felt it was disturbing in a different way. It left her feeling uncertain and vulnerable; in particular, she could not rely on her own judgement about her state of mind.

When Johann reiterated how Anna had a problem with intimacy and had not had any previous successful relationships, she accepted this and indicated that there was one relationship that went on for some time, with an older married man, in which she was badly treated. Johann presented with very clear ideas about the essence of a relationship, and in particular, that there should be "total honesty". He felt this strongly. It seemed that any idea of any kind of separate psychic space in Anna was felt as an utter betrayal. The problem was that when Anna tried to be honest with Johann, to let him into her psychic space, he would fly into a rage – telling her she didn't feel like that, or this was not what they agreed, or she was a liar. As the interchanges between them went on, he became increasingly abusive. There was a very difficult dynamic with me too, verging on the abusive. I was not to have a different view and, if I did, I was not understanding or he was completely contemptuous of my view, or it was because I was a woman and therefore unable to understand him.

Johann tried to take control of each session. He would do so in many ways – coming into the room and walking around and owning the space, plugging in his devices and so on. Anna was more polite and respectful and self-contained, though she could be provoked into extremely distressing states in which it was clear she felt she couldn't hold herself together. I had to interrupt Johann to find a space, but he resisted this strongly. I felt the pressure was on me to stand up to Johann, but in doing so, I felt we only got into a fight and Anna was a helpless witness.

In my countertransference, it was as if I too were fighting for psychic space at a very basic level, to keep ownership of my consulting room, my thoughts and the right to express them and my belief in being able to help them. Anna tried her best to agree with Johann, to be fair, to acknowledge her part in the particular issue he was bringing, but I increasingly felt this was just appeasement and wondered if she was afraid of him. I explored this and they assured me that there had never been any physical violence, and that it was much worse here in the room with me than at home.

With such couples, it is often very hard to see why the seeming masochist endures this. Did Anna need to keep the psychotic level of rage (perhaps her child-view of her parents' rows) in Johann? Was it an identification with the masochistic parent's position? There seemed to be an unconscious agreement between them that Johann would take all the psychic space and Anna would be allowed to stay completely hidden. But sometimes the masochist is the more powerful member of the sado-masochistic couple. Johann was completely dependent on Anna fitting in with his version and any move by her, however small, was a destabilising threat to Johann. Johann could not tolerate this, it disturbed him beyond what he could endure. Just as he wanted to fill the room and the relationship with his psychic contents, he wanted to fill Anna's internal space too. As she started to find this unbearable, he found it increasingly difficult to maintain.

It is important for the therapist to recognise that, for such couples, a couple relationship is a much more primitive thing, akin to the very early relating between mother and infant. As Klein described, in this early stage, projective identification is used defensively to keep unwanted parts of the self in the other and to control them there. In this primitive state of mind, if the other either dis-identifies with the projection or tries to project it back, this will be experienced as extremely threatening to the self. A fear of annihilation leads to an increasingly forceful projection back into the object. This was the dynamic between Johann and Anna, in which Johann's sense of being lost and confused about relationships was projected into Anna. This met with a part of her that accepted the projection, but as she became herself less lost and confused (through her own internal development), the hold of the projection loosened. This sent Johann into an absolute panic because for him to get back in touch with this aspect of himself threatened his very existence. This couple also illustrates the interplay between container/contained in a relationship (see Chapter 6) in which it could appear that Johann was the container, but in fact, Anna's capacity to receive the projection without being destroyed contained Johann at a more fundamental level.

These kinds of couples can be described as borderline/narcissistic and can be very difficult to work with. A problem for the therapist is that working with the projective system and trying to help the individuals to take back their more disturbed projections increases anxiety. One can then get a very agitated couple who become increasingly emotionally dysregulated, and sometimes can't stay in their seats or the room. The therapist can feel anxious, as I did with Johann and Anna, that the therapy is not containing them and may be making things worse. In this situation, it is often more helpful to work with these dynamics primarily in relation to the therapist; in other words, to make analyst-centred interpretations (Steiner, 1993a). Often there is the belief that the therapist's separate view is misunderstanding, even wilful misunderstanding, and there are forceful intrusive projections into the therapist in an attempt to control her. The therapist can often be felt as a dangerous object, on the verge of pushing back some unbearable aspect of the individual or couple.

The therapist will be very reliant on her countertransference to understand what is going on in the transference. But working with the transference is not straightforward, either; the therapist may be felt to be such a useless, denigrated or dangerous object that the couple or one partner breaks off. But some couples can be helped in this way, and I think keeping in mind the very primitive nature of the anxieties behind this controlling defence helps the therapist keep going and helps the couple feel understood in relation to her, if not yet being able to get much understanding of themselves (Steiner, 1993a).

Working with the projective gridlock dynamic in its more comfortable fused manifestation also has its challenges in the countertransference. The therapist can be pulled into the gridlock, feeling that she is a very attuned and rather excellent therapist. It may take a while to recognise that this is part of the gridlock dynamic in which she is not allowed to be other than perfectly attuned; in other words, she is not allowed to be separate. Once the therapist can get into a separate position, she can work with this dynamic. Enactments like this are not altogether a bad thing as although the work, while gridlocked, may not have progressed very much, the therapist, having got out of it, has quite a good understanding of what it is like to be in it, including its stuck and claustrophobic nature.

Alongside these more disturbed narcissistic dynamics in couples there are less extreme problems in allowing the other to be psychically separate and different. Also, there is a less disturbed form of narcissism in which either partner might become self-preoccupied and temporarily not interested in the other. But, as has been pointed out, we cannot be object relating all the time. Sometimes we need to not relate to others, but to relate just to ourselves. A functioning relationship can allow for these transient states, with space to be an individual and a couple, to be separate and together. For some individuals and couples, this oscillation between these states of mind feels extremely disturbing. With more ordinary narcissistic problems, the therapist, in the way she relates to the couple and the way she interprets, helps them develop more psychic space in their relationship. In a relationship, there needs to be room for love and hate, for interest and curiosity in the other and in one's self, for relating and non-relating, for misunderstanding as well as understanding. Clearly these aspects can be completely out of balance, and with too much hate or self-interest and misunderstanding, but sometimes it is the other way around. The couple feels it is catastrophic if there are misunderstandings or negative feelings towards each other, or if there is a wish for some existence separate from the other. Some couples have the phantasy that a creative relationship is perfect togetherness and harmony, and there are many popular images to support this view. A truly creative couple relationship actually looks rather different.

Chapter 8

The couple's psychic development, sex, gender and sexualities

In this chapter, I revisit the subject of the psychic development of a couple, which I described in my paper "On Being Able to Be a Couple: The Importance of a 'Creative Couple' in Psychic Life" (Morgan, 2005). Here I suggest that the capacity to become a couple is not only an important stage of psychic development, but that, within a couple relationship, further psychic development takes place; in particular, it furthers the coming together of an internal creative couple. A sexual relationship is a part of being an adult intimate couple and what sex means to the couple is part of any couple's therapy. Sometimes it is difficulties in the couple's sexual relationship which have made them seek help, sometimes sexual problems come to light in the course of the therapy. I will explore one area of sexual difficulty, one of the most commonly brought, the loss of desire. I also touch on some issues for same-sex couples. However, sex, gender and different sexualities are topics so vast that I cannot do them full justice here.

Psychic development from birth to being a couple and beyond

It goes without saying that what an intimate adult couple relationship is or what a couple aspires to for their relationship varies enormously. At the same time, I think there are developments and states of mind that might define an adult intimate couple relationship. One of these is a psychological sense of being a couple, an entity that has a boundary around it and, if the relationship is functioning well, the couple feels contained by. The boundary has flexibility, as the couple can include others, importantly children, but others too, and exclude others when appropriate. Within the psychic boundedness of their relationship, the couple allows for separateness as well as intimacy between them. The adult intimate relationship differs from others in that it is usually sexual and is potentially procreative.

Reading this, it will be immediately apparent how culturally based the couple relationship is and how much of what I have described is a culturally determined notion of what a couple relationship is. Not all couples choose to, or are able to put a boundary around their relationship. In some cultures, couples living in extended families or apart from their spouse are challenged in physically and psychologically creating a boundary around their relationship. For many, being a couple implies monogamy, but some couples have an open relationship, and some couples – for example, some gay male couples – report this as an issue in their relationship. Others feel a monogamous relationship is a heteronormative construct that is not part of their idea of being a couple. In some cultures, polygamy is part of married life, and also in western cultures there is interest in polyamorous relationships and a wish not to be constrained by societal norms of intimate relating. Normative and cultural differences also challenge us to think about psychoanalytic theories of development, since experiences of the 'primary object' or the 'Oedipal situation' will be different in some cultures and the kind of couple that develops might also be different.

In my earlier paper, I highlighted developments in the individual that seemed to me important precursors in the process of becoming a couple (Morgan, 2005). Psychic development, stimulated by physiological developments and the response of the environment, has for many a natural trajectory towards being an adult intimate and creative couple. Couple therapists encounter couples in whom these developments have been halted, resisted or rejected. The couple who present may be in a committed relationship, perhaps with children, but are more like two friends, two siblings or a mother–baby couple. While for some, this might be the relationship they choose to have, others feel that they can't become the sexual, adult, intimate couple they want to be. These may be the underlying reasons why the couple is seeking help. Or they may be coming for help because they are fearful of 'becoming a couple', because of what this means to them, unable to commit but equally unable to separate. Understanding the psychic developments and the accompanying anxieties that lead to becoming a couple is a helpful perspective here. Individuals and couples may need help in becoming aware of their own unconscious phantasies or beliefs about sex and an adult couple relationship and the way that these can distort their relationship or prevent them getting into a relationship.

Early development: the first couple

"The committed couple relationship, because of its intensity, intimacy and longevity, makes possible an interaction between two people at greater depth than any other, except for that of early infancy" (Ruszczynski, 1993a, p. 203).

From the beginning of life, there is a 'couple' as psychoanalysts among others have expressed. Winnicott, for example, writes, "There is no such thing as an infant, meaning of course that whenever one finds an infant one finds maternal care" (Winnicott, 1958/1975, p. xxxvii). Others have stressed that along with the biological drive to seek out an object, seen in other animals too, there is in the human infant the unconscious phantasy of there being an 'other' with whom the infant links or seeks attachment (Fairbairn, 1946/1952; Bion, 1962, 1963; Money-Kyrle, 1968, 1971; Bowlby, 1969). This can be thought of as something unconsciously 'known', waiting to be experienced so that it can be recognised. As Money-Kyrle puts it,

> [A]n innate preconception, then, if it exists, is something we use without being able to imagine it. I think of it as having some of the qualities of a forgotten word. Various words suggest themselves to us, which we have no hesitation in rejecting, till the right word occurs which we recognise immediately. I think this is what Bion means by an "empty thought". It is also something which, though it cannot be imagined, can be described as analogous, say, to a form waiting for a content.
>
> (Money-Kyrle, 1968, p. 692)

It does seem that the infant is born with an innate preconception of there being an object, and therefore of 'coupling' or 'linking'. Although the newborn infant might not be fully aware of the mother as a separate object, the idea of there being an object is important. It means that there is, in the infant's mind, the idea of an 'other' into which something can be evacuated or projected and from which something can be taken in, and through which he can link up. Through being in a relationship with another, the infant can process internal experiences and psychically grow. This is a template for the idea that it is through linking with another that one can better understand oneself and the world, a development which later forms part of being a 'creative couple'.

Following this, as Money-Kyrle has stated, it is also probable that the idea of a couple coming together sexually is derived from innate knowledge (Money-Kyrle, 1971). Just as at the beginning of life, the infant seeks the mother's breast, the nipple and the mouth forming a vital link, real and symbolic, so there is a development of this imperative later in life in the drive to create a sexual couple, symbolised and sometimes actualised by the link between penis and vagina. Thus, at the earliest stage of development, there is the beginning of a template for an adult sexual relationship. This is described evocatively by Clulow and Boerma:

> It is, of course, true that the early stages of a love relationship incorporate behaviour that is reminiscent of infant attachment. The importance of eye contact, of the special gaze between lovers, of exclusive physical contact and stimulation, echo relationship patterns between mothers and babies. The process of discovering and enjoying the other's body marks the specialness of the relationship, the privileged access that each partner accords to the other, and a symbolic as well as physical intimacy. The

wish to be in tune, to be responsive to every movement and gesture, to engage in baby talk and to find any separation intolerable suggests a wonderfully regressed state of mind, providing "uppers" and "downers" that most drugs would find hard to match (and, of course, there is an endomorphinal, pheromonal "buzz" to being in love). Indeed, the regions of the brain activated by maternal love are the same as those activated by romantic love, and use the same neurological pathways as those activated by addiction (Fonagy & Bateman, 2006). The state of being "in love" is a kind of intoxication, desire a variant of addiction, and in this heightened state interpersonal boundaries buckle under the pressure from lovers to melt into and merge with each other. Falling in love, if not the psychosis that Freud would have it to be, certainly approximates a borderline condition.

(Clulow & Boerma, 2009, pp. 81–82)

However, the mother–baby relationship, though a template for intimacy, allowing curiosity about mother's 'alpha function' to stimulate the beginning of thinking, differs from the adult couple relationship. There are several important ways in which it is different. One is that the infant is utterly dependent on the mother, dependent on the mother for his wellbeing and actually his survival, as Winnicott describes above. Another is that infantile sexuality is very different from adult sexuality; it is about the infant's uninhibited pleasure as the body is explored as an object because the emotional meaning of a penis inside a vagina, or any sexual variation of this, isn't yet there. Another is that the infant, at the beginning, does not feel fully separate from the mother, and this is only gradually achieved. Later in life, when forming a couple, difficulties stemming from this early stage of development can manifest, in particular states of mind, with an overdependence of one partner on the other, a struggle of "who is to be the baby" (Lyons & Mattinson, 1993, p. 108).

Some adult couples find it difficult to allow the other to be separate, sometimes even physically separate in allowing the other to come and go, but more often, psychically separate, accepting their different thoughts and feelings. If this early stage of development has gone awry, it can also give rise to tightly held unconscious beliefs about what a couple relationship is, as I described previously (Morgan, 2010). There may be a belief that the other should meet all one's needs, just like a tiny baby utterly dependent on the mother. If these aren't met, it is felt to be the other's failure. The unconscious recreation of the phantasised early mother–baby relationship may meet the needs of both partners, one directly and one vicariously as needs are projected into the 'baby'. Failure to maintain this unconscious arrangement is nearly always inevitable and there is disappointment, blame and conflict, one partner feeling they are completely justified in being angry with the other who has not been able, or chosen not to meet the needs of the former.

There are other versions of this 'mother–baby couple' that feel disturbing in a different way. The partners in the couple can feel that the reverse of containment is happening, they feel that the other is constantly projecting into them. Being part of a couple is then felt to be dangerous and defences may get set up to protect the self from intrusion. There are also mother–baby couples in which the other is experienced as impenetrable and unable to take in any of the other's communications (Fisher, 1993; Morgan, 2010). These kinds of beliefs have their roots in unconscious phantasies originating in the early relationship to the primary object. Rather than challenging these unconscious phantasies, later experiences have reinforced them.

A couple functioning as a version of a mother–baby couple is likely to have difficulties when there is an actual baby. The child's need may be felt to usurp the position of the 'adult baby' and be experienced as an attack on limited resources. If the couple had a comfortable mother–baby union, the baby may be felt as an intrusion into the couple's bond. The bond may then be disrupted as one partner, usually the mother, develops an exclusive relationship with the baby, while the question of who is the baby remains.

The Oedipal situation: another couple

The early Oedipal situation is a challenging part of psychic development as it requires the relinquishment of the exclusive relationship with the primary object, facing and being able to tolerate the special link between the parents. This is a crucial psychic development ushering in the depressive position. It is important to point out that here I am not referring to the sexual Oedipal situation, also an important part of development described by Freud. This occurs later, between the ages of three and five, in which for boys and girls, there is the wish to sexually possess the parent of desire in both the heterosexual and homosexual version of the Oedipus complex.

The trigger for the early Oedipal situation is the discovery of the absence of mother. At a certain point, after the baby has developed sufficient resources to be more aware of what is really happening, the original explanation for hunger, namely an attack from a 'bad breast', is discovered to be untrue. The baby sees that there is not a bad breast, but an absence. In this early stage, the baby's relationship is with the primary object and he fears that his rage with the bad breast has destroyed her. When the mother reappears, the baby is able to reassure himself that mother isn't destroyed, but he is left with the problem as to what caused the absence. His ideas of relationship as either good or bad, represented by the Kleinian images of good and bad breast (Klein, 1946), allow for only one possible explanation: mother must be having a good breast experience somewhere else. This means that, even if there is no actual father in the family, the baby now conceives of mother in relationship with somebody else.

However, with this painful loss of the phantasy of an exclusive twosome with the primary object, a different kind of space opens up with different possibilities, that which Britton (1989) has described as 'triangular space'.

> If the link between the parents perceived in love and hate can be tolerated in the child's mind, it provides him with the prototype for an object relationship of a third kind in which he is a witness and not a participant. A third position then comes into existence from which object relationships can be observed. Given this, we can also envisage being observed. This provides us with a capacity for seeing ourselves in interaction with others and for entertaining another point of view whilst retaining our own, for reflecting on ourselves whilst being ourselves.
> (Britton, 1989, p. 87)

It is at this point that the baby's sense of identity takes on the form that is often described as 'the Oedipal triangle'. The baby begins to experience himself as loved by a loving couple. With this development, the child can also experiment with being at different points in the triangle – in a relationship with either parent, observed by the other, or witnessing the parents' relationship as the excluded observer.

The capacity to take a third position is a crucial psychic development in being able to be ourselves and reflect on ourselves and it opens up psychic space, and develops thinking. It is also essentially part of being a creative couple and having the capacity for a 'couple state of mind', as I will discuss later. Although the child has been subjectively part of a couple with the mother, there is now, from the position of being outside a couple, the idea of a couple as an entity. This is important in being able to internalise a couple as an object which will be part of the basis for his own actual couple relationship.

With the awareness of the mother as part of a parental couple might come an awareness now that there has, in fact, been a couple all along. While this may or may not exist in external reality, the child might become more aware of an internal creative couple inside the mother. This, Birksted-Breen argues, is part of the mother's containing capacity that

> already combines both the maternal function of being with and the paternal function of observing and linking. In order to contain her infant, a mother (and an analyst) has to receive the projections empathically (the maternal function) and also take a perspective on this (paternal function).
> (Birksted-Breen, 1996, p. 652)

In this sense, containment involves a bisexual aspect: "the breast has to do with the function of being with, the penis with the function of giving structure" (Birksted-Breen, 1996, p. 653).

Birksted-Breen also shows how the 'penis-as-link' has an important structuring influence on the mind.

> Mental space and the capacity to think are created by the structure that allows for separateness and link between internal objects, and self and other, instead of fusion or fragmentation. The penis-as-link represents both that separateness and link of the parental relationship and forms the backbone of healthy mental functioning, which is a bisexual functioning.
>
> (Birksted-Breen, 1996, p. 655)

This capacity to be separate and linked to internal and external objects is fundamental to psychic health and to the capacity to form a creative couple relationship.

The couple relationship, once established, can provide the opportunity to continue reworking the early Oedipal situation, as the couple has to manage other 'thirds', which need to be included and excluded. If there has not been much working through of this Oedipal situation, then the couple will be quite challenged by managing children, parents and the other's separate interests and preoccupations such as work. If there are difficulties in this area, the parent may turn to the child and exclude the other parent, or anxieties may lead to the couple preserving their coupledom by overly excluding the children. At different stages in life there are challenges; for example, as Wrottesley points out, "The grandparental couple, like the child, must stand outside of the procreative young couple's relationship, and look upon what they cannot have" (Wrottesley, 2017, p. 193).

Adolescence:- separating from the parental couple

Physiological changes in the body and the brain and new hormones bring about puberty. For many adolescents, these changes are quite alarming; changes in the body can be rapid, and powerful sexual feelings can be very confusing and frightening because they are new. The triangular configuration of the Oedipal situation helps adolescents in their ambivalent state between wanting this independence but still feeling at times very dependent, taking ownership of their own body and mind, excluding themselves from the parental couple and developing their own identity (see Laufer, 1975). For a while, this sense of independence can be idealised and the parents rejected in order for the adolescent to separate. The adolescent task that Laufer describes is to take possession of the adult sexual body. The struggles of adolescence reach a point that could be described as 'young adult'. The urges that the adolescent has been struggling with can clearly give rise to the illusion, based upon the infant's view of adults, that the outcome of being adult is to become somebody who is autonomous and independent. The young adult might also think of himself as available for occasional intimacy. This is a stage that, although appearing to be the end of adolescence, is not really the state of a fully-grown adult. It seems very likely that the next part of development is triggered by something biological to do with forming stable parent relationships as well as something psychological triggered by an actual relationship with someone whom one finds oneself wanting to stay with.

But at the point of this new developmental imperative, biological and psychological, to form a couple, it is hopefully from a position of being an adult with a separate identity and mind, not from a position of wanting to return to a child/parent relationship. As Waddell has stated,

> One of the main undertakings of adolescence is that of establishing a mind of one's own, a mind which is rooted in, and yet also distinct from, the sources and models of identification that are visible within one's family, or in the wider school and community setting.
> (Waddell, 1998, p. 176)

The internal structuring which is achieved as an outcome of the early Oedipal situation helps the adolescent move between identifying with his internal objects and also feeling separate from them in the process of discovering who he is. In late adolescence, this experimentation can become very enjoyable, which is why some individuals resist taking the step of becoming part of a couple because of the fear of losing a sense of one's own separate identity and one's own mind, often represented by the new pleasures associated with the status of young adulthood.

Once one is part of a couple, it can be challenging to create enough psychic space in the relationship for each partner to be their separate individual selves and their couple self. "A predictable and inevitable dynamic in every couple relationship is that of the tension between, on the one hand, the needs and wishes of the individuals and, on the other hand, the requirements of the partnership they aspire to" (Ruszczynski, 1993a, p. 99). This is not only a tension, but also a capacity to be separate and linked with another.

Regression: stages of development and states of mind

Becoming a couple can stir up longings and anxieties from any of these earlier stages of development. Tracking the psychic development of a couple can have a deterministic feel as if we all pass through certain important stages and come out the other end as a fully formed couple. If an earlier stage has not been worked through, the adult couple relationship may be the arena in which unresolved aspects of earlier stages and the accompanying anxieties and states of mind, are brought and may be worked through. The truth is that none of us works through earlier stages of psychic development in a complete or perfect way, so inevitably, some of what is still unresolved will be brought into the adult couple relationship. And in fact, a healthy adult couple relationship can contain some regression and the couple can help each other work through unconsciously recognised shared areas of difficulty, or they may recreate earlier difficulties which they get stuck in and need help with.

Klein's paranoid schizoid and depressive positions are linked to stages of development, the paranoid schizoid in the first few months of life and the depressive position towards the middle of the first year of life (Klein, 1935, 1940, 1946). Ogden suggests an earlier stage, the 'autistic contiguous position', a stage of symbiosis preceding the paranoid schizoid position (Ogden, 1989). However, these 'positions' also represent constellations of types of defences, anxieties and states of mind that we move between, not just in early development, but throughout life.

Keogh and Enfield have explored how a couple coming for help might need to work through the developmental anxieties of all three stages, autistic contiguous, paranoid schizoid and depressive.

> First, a stage where the self and other are experienced in a sensory mode and the self tends to merge with its object; second, a stage where difficult-to-manage aspects of the self are split off and projected into the object of attachment; and third, a point in development where all aspects of the self are (initially painfully) integrated. This results in a relatively autonomous self where the other can be perceived as separate from oneself, enabling a true psychological marriage.
> (Keogh & Enfield, 2013, pp. 31–32)

While some couples move between these stages, towards 'true psychological marriage', other couples coming for help might be thought of as functioning with anxieties and defences predominantly at one stage, usually the autistic contiguous or paranoid schizoid, with moments of more depressive position relating.

How the therapist works with a couple might be influenced by the couple's developmental stage and accompanying states of mind. Keogh and Enfield (2013) argue that sometimes for fragile couples, those in the autistic contiguous position, more important than interpreting is the holding provided by the setting and the therapist's couple state of mind. For couples functioning in a paranoid schizoid mode, interpretation is focused on their splitting and projection; and in the depressive position, on the withdrawal of projections, guilt, disillusionment, but also the potential of a relationship in which the separateness of the other can be borne. In this state of mind, there are now two people in the relationship and potential for creating thirds, a development the therapist can support.

The movement between less integrated to more integrated states of mind is also captured by Fisher, though he focuses on the shifts in the capacity to relate to another as a separate other, the movement from narcissism to object relating.

> Marriage, in the sense of a capacity for what we in our psychoanalytic language term object relating, is not a once-and-for-all achievement. As with Bion's description of the oscillation between the paranoid-schizoid and depressive positions, which he images as Ps ↔ D, can we imagine a similar oscillation between narcissistic and object-relating states of mind?
> (Fisher, 1999, p. 8)

In fact, it is not possible to be in the depressive position or an object relating state of mind all the time, and some writers have described not only the inevitable movement between more primitive and more mature states of mind, but the necessity of this process in terms of development. Bion (1970), building on the work of Klein, has conceptualised that a change in one's way of thinking and relating involves the dismantling of previous views and theories, and that this dismantling can have the quality of a psychic catastrophe, a going to pieces (Grier, 2005b). This can be thought to be a move into the paranoid schizoid position (Klein, 1946). The reforming of a new set of views and theories is a synthesising move into the depressive position (Klein, 1935, 1940). Creative effort can therefore be viewed as a process, on a small scale, of movements to and from the paranoid schizoid and depressive positions. The tolerance of a degree of disintegration without resorting to omnipotent primitive defence mechanisms, or a turning back to a previously held position, is essential for creative thinking and living. At each point of development, fluctuations between the paranoid schizoid and depressive positions will occur. Britton describes the process of moving from the depressive position to what he calls a 'post-depressive position', in other words, a new one. This entails moving from a situation of integrated understanding into a new situation of uncertainty and incoherence, a new paranoid schizoid position, before moving on to a new and as yet unimaginable resolution incorporating the new facts, a new depressive position (Britton, 1998d). As these writers show, regressive behaviour and states of mind are not to be considered as simply psychopathological states, nor only as the products of disruptions caused by life transitions and environmental impingement or traumas. Such states are necessary as a result of the inevitability of psychic disruption towards the paranoid schizoid position likely to arise at points of new learning and growth. Once the new learning has been established, an internal reintegration takes place and there can then be a move forward towards a new depressive position.

The creative couple stage of psychic development

When we think about psychic development from infancy to adulthood, we can see that at each stage, there are, if things go well, important developments. From earliest infancy, we learn about and experience dependence on an object, intimacy, love, curiosity and how interacting with the mind of another is the fulcrum for our own development. With early Oedipal development, we learn about and have to come to terms with the link between the parents, including their sexual relationship, from which we are excluded. But this also provides us with triangular space and the awareness that the mother who contained us was a mother internally linked to a father. It helps us understand about linked separateness and provides us with an arena in which later we can experiment with being part of a couple and being separate within a couple. In adolescence, we struggle with powerful feelings of dependence and independence, identifying with important objects (including aspects of our parents), but also needing to be separate from them and have a mind of our own. We take ownership of our own separate and sexual body which no longer has anything to do with the parents (Laufer, 1981). And then, for most of us, at some point, we choose to make an adult sexual relationship of our own and become a couple, though as Waddell points out, "developing such a capacity may, for some, take many more years and possibly several different attempts" (Waddell, 1998, p. 176).

Psychic development doesn't cease on becoming a couple. The early clinicians of Tavistock Relationships understood the therapeutic potential of the couple relationship within which earlier and current conflicts and anxieties can be reworked and contained. The relationship itself is internalised by the partners in the couple as a symbolic third; it is something the couple turns to in their minds that functions as a container for them (Colman, 1993; Morgan, 2005).

But a couple relationship can be not only therapeutic and containing for the couple, but also creative for them. In this way, in the creative couple development, the Oedipal triangle is reconfigured so that the third point on the triangle is the couple's relationship, a symbolic third, to which the couple can turn to find a place in their minds from which each partner can observe themself in their relationship. Moving between our subjective experience of our self and our relationship to a more objective reflection on it, the couple can think together about what they are creating and also be creative in thinking together.

Over time, the couple experiences their relationship as an entity, as a resource, something they have created and continue to create together, the whole being greater than the sum of the parts. When there is something difficult to manage, identifying with their internal creative couple helps the two come together in their different ways to try and think about it. It supports the couple in letting go of previous certainties, being able to not

Psychic development, sex and sexualities   137

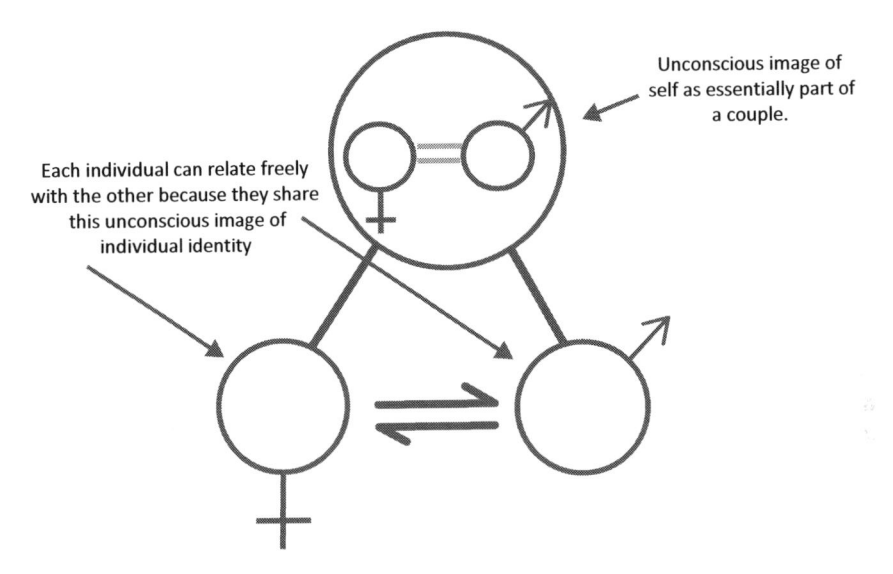

Figure 8.1 The creative couple developmental stage

know, and realising that while it may not be immediately apparent, an as yet unknown creative outcome to their difficulty might be possible.

The contribution of link theory (el vínculo) provides a discourse which puts the creation of something 'new' as an outcome of the couple's relating centre stage (Jaitin, 2016; Kaes, 2016; Kleiman, 2016; Nicolo, 2016; Scharff, 2016). The 'presence' of the other is an 'interference' for the subject, and on their previously held conceptions. This can lead to instabilities in a relationship, but also developments. This concept of interference is, as Berenstein states,

> about making room for the other as a different subject. It is about the couple members' ability to produce something new and different, instead of reproducing what each carry from childhood and what he or she has brought to the couple.
> (Berenstein, 2012, p. 576)

In this way, ideas from this perspective resonate with the creative relating of a couple. Link theorists are not thinking of this as a developmental achievement, but as something that continually occurs in the link between subjects in relationships of every kind. They are not suggesting that what is created by any particular link is necessarily positive. In the creative couple, I am describing a developmental achievement and the couple's capacity for creative outcomes, but it is, as also described by link theory, to do with what is created in the relationship 'between'.

> This production is not a mere externalisation of the internal contents of the linked subjects, but a new production. In this way, the link, any link, is not the result of the algebraic sum of the contents of the psychic apparatuses involved (including the conscious and the unconscious) or of the transfer of information from one participant to the other. What characterises the link is the development in the virtual spaces in-between participants surpluses and emergents that did not exist before the encounter.
> (Moreno, 2014, p. 4, cited in Kleiman, 2016, p. 177)

The creative couple is not to be seen as a stage of development in which, once achieved, the couple is always able to come together in a creative way. It is about tolerating not knowing, allowing previously held views to break down and be reconfigured in an intercourse with another. It rests on a belief that out of this disintegration, further integration will occur and lead to new, previously unknown, creative development.

This developmental perspective helps the therapist think about the kind of couple she has in the consulting room. It is another lens through which to view how the couple is relating and whether something in their development towards being a creative adult intimate couple has been halted. Sometimes development is feared. Becoming part of a couple may give rise to anxieties about a loss of independence or more primitive fears of being engulfed, losing one's sense of self or losing one's mind. There may be serious deficits in the couple's early experience which results in them putting pressure on the relationship to function in primitive ways, such as extreme dependence and lack of separateness. Although the couple might feel they have found just what they need in a relationship, and the opportunity to regress feels quite magical, it can rarely be sustained. The undeveloped regressive nature of the relationship kills it unless the couple finds the means to change and develop.

> Periods of transition are the ordinary stuff of life, shifts that mark life's inconspicuous continual growth. These periods draw upon a reservoir of creativity that enables us to take what we are up to at a certain point and reinvent ourselves. We retain this creative developmental potential to change how we live all of our lives (Scarf, 1987; Viorst, 1986).
> (Scharff, 2014, p. 215)

Some couples come into therapy with these kinds of developmental difficulties and they are often fearful of change and resistant to the therapist's efforts. But understanding these anxieties and defences and having a sense of when regression is not in the service of growth, but in the service of a kind of retreat from being a grown-up couple, are helpful.

The meaning of a couple's sexual relationship

> Human sexuality responds to and expresses the need for magic, for overstepping one's boundaries, and for endowing one's sensuality and profound corporeality with meaning, a meaning that is both clarifying and mystifying, that is both linked with the other, and is forever lacking and searching for 'the' object and (at the same time or intermittently) drawn into himself.
>
> (Stein, 1998, p. 266)

A sexual relationship is one of the defining aspects of an adult intimate couple relationship, but what sex means for each couple consciously and unconsciously is complex and changing within the development of their relationship. Sex is also a drive, part of human nature, and seeks expression and, in that sense, it is different to other issues that the couple experiences. It is not simply the case that the better a couple's relationship, the better their sexual relationship is. Sex in a transitory relationship, in one that is unsettled and uncommitted, or in which there is hatred and conflict, can be the most exciting. However, when sex takes place outside the marriage, as in an affair, it can feel that the foundations of the whole relationship have been breached. Having said this, for some couples with open relationships, sexual excitement outside the relationship, though challenging, might be felt to be what sustains the intimacy between the committed couple. For many, if sex goes wrong within the relationship, it can feel that the sense of being a couple is threatened. As well as that, there is something that remains unknowable or as Stein describes it, 'enigmatic'. Grier argues,

> None of us is ever quite sorted out in the area of sex, and it is perhaps both a torment and a comfort to realise that we shall never be, that an ultimate resolution is impossible, and that never fully solving this dilemma is part of what makes us human and alive rather than god-like and dead.
>
> (Grier, 2009, p. 46)

Loss of desire or different desire?

The loss of desire has been explored by a number of writers in relation to couple dynamics, linked to problems in separateness, the integration of love and hate and the influence of attachment patterns (Abse, 2009; Clulow & Boerma, 2009; Shmueli & Rix, 2009; Sehgal, 2012; Caruso, 2014). For the couple, loss of desire is often experienced as a sudden realisation, they notice they are not having much, or any, sex; that neither is initiating it and the urgency and excitement that went with sex before are gone. Very often this happens after the early years of child rearing when the couple at last feels there is a bit of time, space and energy for sex, and then discover that neither are that interested. This can be quite alarming, anxiety provoking and disturbing. As the wife in one couple said sadly, "I didn't think sex was going to come to an end in my mid 40s"; another partner said, 3 years after having twins, "Our sexual relationship used to be awesome, I want to get back to 'awesome', instead we are just irritated with each other"; and another couple reported, "We have sex, but just to convince ourselves that we are still ok". Later in life, couples often report a waning of their sexual relationship, or at least the excitement in their sexual relationship as sex becomes more infrequent and less exciting. But sometimes it is the incapacity to face inevitable change. Balfour, reflecting on older age and a poem by Thomas Hardy, says:

> It is, as Hardy puts it, the "part stolen/part abiding" that brings forth grief: the continued life of the body and the mind, the awareness of desires and, at the same time, of physical changes such as loss of youthful physical attractiveness and potency. A solution can be to wish away the desire, to "shrink the heart", in Hardy's words, to withdraw from bringing to life sexual desire or involvement and intimacy.
>
> (Balfour, 2009, p. 232)

Having an active sexual relationship often feels like a form of validation for each partner, in affirming their sense of being desirable, masculine, feminine, and as a hallmark confirming their relationship. There is an important relationship dynamic here too; it is very difficult to desire the other, to be in a state of 'wanting' when the other does not seem to want sex. The other closing down on desire can quickly lead to the partner following suit to avoid the unpleasant unsatisfied state of sexual excitation. But maintaining this disequilibrium can create a disturbing dynamic in the relationship, with one partner wanting and expecting sex and the other not wanting sex, and sometimes just making their body available because they feel it would be too conflictual or threatening to their relationship to refuse.

The loss of desire is an experience that all therapists, including sex therapists, find hard to treat, particularly if the relationship appears good in other ways and there are no physiological difficulties. Abse speaks of listening to couples describing

> sexual encounters that seem to leave both myself and the patient puzzled. Stories of sexual comings together that have failed, stories of the arousal of desire that has been lost, and stories that speak to the emptiness where arousal and desire would ordinarily be found.
>
> (Abse, 2009, p. 109)

It is important to say that loss of desire is a normal and ordinary experience. There will be exceptions to this, and it is interesting to think about why. It also doesn't mean that many couples do not continue to have sex which is enjoyable and satisfying, if not always as exciting as it once was. Here it is important to distinguish between sexual desire and having sex. One couple who noticed their loss of desire found that when they did "make themselves" have sex, it was really enjoyable. They said that to get to that place, "there was a wall to climb over, but it turned out to be quite a small wall".

A more current view of low sexual desire suggests that what couples consider to be low desire within their relationship is actually different desire between partners. Couples who struggle with difference tend to organise this by labelling difference with a dysfunction (hypo desire or hyper desire) which assumes that one partner has normal desire levels and the other does not. Low desire diagnosis that includes complete absence of masturbation and sexual fantasy for more than 6 months is actually quite rare (Blair, personal communication).

There are two particular aspects of sex and sexuality that I want to draw attention to in relation to the loss of desire – its enigmatic nature and the aggression and transgression that accompany sexual excitement.

The enigmatic nature of sexuality

Both Stein (2008) and Target (2007) have argued that because our sexuality as infants cannot be mirrored accurately by our mothers in the way other feelings can, there remains something unknowable and enigmatic in our sexuality and we discover it through another person later in life.

> Incongruent mirroring disrupts self-coherence, generating a sense of pressure and contradiction in relation to the psychosexual. The aroused baby interprets the mother's responses as a mirror of his own experience and identifies them as his own, but since they are not mirrored 'contingently' (in a manner faithful to his own affects and experiences), they are simultaneously experienced as not his own, as alien. This sense of incongruence within the self is then associated with sexual feelings, even when in other areas the self may feel well integrated. Sexual arousal can never truly be experienced as owned. There will always be a pressure to find someone to share it with, through projection and reintrojection. ... The enigmatic dimension of sexuality creates an invitation that calls out to be elaborated, normally by an other.
> (Target, 2007, p. 523)

Even if an invitation for elaboration is responded to by another, neither the discovery of our own sexuality nor the identification of what works will be necessarily straightforward. Working out what we like, could like and don't like sexually, and negotiating this with another, is often difficult and even when we manage this, things can go wrong. As Blair points out,

> Sex is very rarely perfect ... erections go at a time when they are most needed, ejaculation sometimes happens immediately and sometimes takes too long, people experience discomfort and pain in sex for a whole host of reasons, and this is normal.
>
> (Blair, 2018, p. 42)

For couples who can bear the trials and errors and imperfections of sex, many do achieve a sexually fulfilling relationship in which they elaborate this part of themselves within an intimate relationship. The problem, though, is what happens over time as we start to discover, know and own our sexuality? As Fonagy concludes,

> The experience of the partner is then partially reinternalised through a preconscious identification that gradually (over years) replaces enigma with familiarity. ... The upside of this is a better integrated, less troubled sense of self and the emergence of a powerful attachment relationship rooted in the experience of having been accurately reflected by one's partner. The downside ... well the downside is obvious. Over the normal course of an adult psychosexual life, as integration increases and the driven need for intense experience with a partner is reduced, libido is apparently reduced.
>
> (Fonagy, 2008, p. 25)

This theory about sexuality makes sense of our biological imperative to partner and have sex, and once we have procreated, for this need to diminish. Having said this, I do wonder whether our sexuality is ever completely mirrored by another and known by us. If we remain open to its unknowable and changing aspects, it continues to intrigue and tantalise. But this requires the couple to bear the transient nature of sexuality, what was "awesome" once may not be awesome now, and there is changing sexual desire and changing bodies. The sexual relationship has to be re-found and reconfigured over time, involving loss and change. Sexuality is such a fragile area for some that they deal with this by seeking sexual excitement and validation outside the relationship. Interestingly, following the discovery of an affair, sex between the couple sometimes becomes more exciting for a while, but something still has to be re-found that sustains excitement.

Sex, aggression and transgression

Sexual desire, and specifically sexual excitement, can be linked with aggression and transgression. Penetration in itself involves aggression, to enter another body not softly and gently, which could lead to a loss of erection, but with some force and for the woman to allow her body to be entered by another. A complex aspect of sexuality is that the aggression is more than an act of sex, it is also alive in our fantasies. Many sexual fantasies involve aggression (Freud, 1919; Kahr, 2007). Stoller argues,

> In the absence of special physiologic factors (such as a sudden androgen increase in either sex), and putting aside the obvious effects that result from direct stimulation of erotic body parts, it is hostility – the desire, overt or hidden, to harm another person – that generates and enhances sexual excitement. The absence of hostility leads to sexual indifference and boredom.
> (Stoller, 1979, p. 6)

This might seem an extraordinary statement, but it is one that speaks to the fact that sex is not just a physical act, but also a complex psychological one. In Stoller's view, the hostility that is part of sexual excitement is an attempt to undo traumas and frustrations from earlier in our lives, which threatened our masculinity and femininity. For Kernberg, while transgression is about a triumph over the Oedipal couple, in this stage of development of becoming a couple, one is a sexual couple, rather than the excluded third, and there is also pleasure in aggression towards the object of desire.

> Erotic desire includes a sense that the object is both offering and withholding itself, and sexual penetration or engulfing the object is a violation of the other's boundaries. In this sense, transgression involves aggression against the object as well, aggression that is exciting in its pleasurable gratification, reverberating with the capacity to experience pleasure in pain, and projecting that capacity onto the other. The aggression is also pleasurable because it is contained by a loving relationship.
> (Kernberg, 1995, p. 24)

When we think about aggression and sex, it is important to note that we are describing aggression in the context of love. Hewison, writing about the balance between love and aggression in couples, says,

> Where aggression is missing, erotic satisfaction is stunted or impossible. Where aggression is used in the service of love, to get through to someone, to connect by deliberately (and rapturously) breaching the boundaries of personal space and body surface in sex, relationship has the potential to be deepened through mutual satisfying erotic needs. Where aggression is paramount, eroticism is curtailed and becomes routine; connection between the couple is limited to acts and roles,

boundaries (emotional and physical) are turned into objects to be used, or used by, and love dies.

(Hewison, 2009, p. 166)

One of the clinical examples that often comes to my mind on this topic is that given by Grier. Drawing on Bion's conceptualisation of the emotional links between container and contained, the links of L (love), H (hate) & K (a desire to know the other) (Bion, 1967a), he describes work with a couple in which the knowledge about 'H' was a disowned and split-off part of their relationship. Interpretive work in this area with the couple was fruitful:

[T]o their intense surprise and relief, the result was not catastrophe, but a freeing of their capacity to love and get to know each other, which led spontaneously to their recovering sexual links in the marriage. Knowledge about H was engaged with, and this increased their desire for intellectual, emotional and sexual intercourse.

(Grier, 2009, p. 53)

Many writers have been drawn to Glasser's concept of the 'core complex' which describes the primitive claustro-agoraphobic nature of intimacy (Glasser, 1979). The infant's intense desire for the mother, and wish to merge with her, gives rise to anxiety about being engulfed and thereby annihilated. To preserve the self, the infant directs his aggression towards the mother, in order to effect his withdrawal. This then leads to anxieties about abandonment and the wish for closeness again. Although Glasser is talking about early development, it is clear that these anxieties remain in some form throughout life and are inevitably re-evoked in the adult couple relationship, the first exclusive relationship of such potential intimacy since the mother–infant relationship. We see these dynamics in a number of ways in couple relationships and the ways in which partners both seek and close down on intimate relating. Couples sometimes describe forms of intercourse in which they manage to have sex in a controlled way, that at the same time avoids intimacy, or we might say the trauma of intimacy, perhaps having its roots in a terrifying engulfing mother object. Those who have serial affairs, seeking affirmation by being desired, describe quickly bringing the affair to an end, often in a cruel way, as soon as there is a request for more intimacy or commitment.

These ideas point to the fact that within human development, intimacy is a complex and conflictual experience. We have a deep wish for, and deep anxieties about, intimacy. We see this struggle continue in the adult couple relationships, and in this sense, intimacy, like sex, is never resolved. We want it, passionately, aggressively, sometimes to be right inside the other, but in moments of achieving it, fear being lost inside or consumed by the engulfing object, just as the other who is entered into, unless there is also separateness, can feel taken over intrusively as described in Chapter Six. These are psychological and bodily aspects of being human and are expressed in a couple's sexual relationship, the excitement stemming, at least in part, from the risk-taking that sex involves through transgressing bodily and psychological boundaries.

The need for psychic separateness in both parties is fundamental in this, a prerequisite for good sex, and it seems that sexual excitement for most people comes into being on the cusp of being separate and being one. Kernberg, for example, states that the two crucial features of sexual love are, "the firm boundaries of the self and the constant awareness of the indissoluble separateness of individuals, on the one hand, and the sense of transcendence, of becoming one with the loved person, on the other" (1995, p. 43). Hertzmann, in looking at the experience of lesbian couples, highlights what can be an intense emotional and sexual experience in sexual union with another woman. A woman's sexual experience with another woman can be felt to be 'coming home', as the intensity of the "early regressed and embodied state with the internal Oedipal mother is made contact with again and finally symbolised" (2018, p. 33). She suggests that this can revive an unconscious belief that the Oedipal mother can be possessed. However, this revival of the original phantasy of possession, bringing with it unconscious repetition of loss is ordinarily understood to lead to an intensification of desire. Hertzmann states that, for some couples, this may not be the case, and instead can lead to an intensification of the loss rather than of desire, thereby resulting in loss of sexual desire. The mutual projective system of the couple's relationship, where both partners are dealing with this early and primal loss of the unconscious Oedipal mother, can, for some couples, make the emotional experience of separation following sex difficult (Hertzmann, 2018). Such feelings might be evoked in other kinds of couples too, who describe a sense of loss and sadness on separation after sex.

Specific sexual problems

While it is not possible within the constraints of this book to explore the range of sexual problems a couple might present with, knowledge about these different conditions is important for the couple therapist. The therapist has to think about the meaning the presented sexual problem has in terms of the couple's relationship: the way that sex represents something about each individual's psychology; a concrete enactment of the relationship difficulties; sexual ignorance or a block that requires its own focus; or even a medical problem that needs to be recognised as such. Common sexual disorders, as well as the loss of desire (or difference in desire in relationships) for both men and women, are, for men, erectile dysfunction, premature ejaculation, delayed ejaculation, painful sex or compulsive sexual behaviour. For women, there are sometimes problems in achieving an orgasm, vaginismus, dyspareunia (or sexual pain) and compulsive sexual behaviour. Trauma of any kind might affect the couple's sexual relationship, but particularly sexual abuse.

Sex therapists might approach these difficulties in a number of ways, but those working psychoanalytically would also think about the symptoms as elucidating the unconscious internal worlds of each partner and the couple. Sometimes the specific nature of the sexual relationship in a couple, problematic or not, can shed light on something important in the relationship. In this way, like a dream, it holds a condensed meaning. If it is problematic, understanding what is being expressed or disabled in the sexual relationship can help in understanding other non-sexual dynamics in the relationship. This understanding in turn can lead to a freeing up of the sexual relationship which had been constrained by the dynamics it was holding.

Blair gives the following examples:

> In premature ejaculation we might see shared issues around relationships being cut off too soon leaving the individuals with a sense that something is missing, spoiled, desecrated within their internal worlds; with vaginismus we could see the shared fear of penetrating and being penetrated linked to objects that seem to flick between over-intrusive relating and cut-off emotional states; in erectile dysfunction we could see shared fears of sadism linked to dominating cruel objects, the fear of which causes suppression of the libido. These sexual dysfunctions interlink, switch and shift in much the same way as couples' original presenting problems will develop, change, improve and worsen within couple psychotherapy. The interlinking of these dysfunctions (a woman with vaginismus might couple with a man with erectile dysfunction) and their development (erectile dysfunction turning to premature ejaculation) within treatment implies that there is a common thread running between all sexual problems.
>
> (Blair, 2018, pp. 37–38)

Talking with couples about sex

Sex is part of the territory of couples' therapy and it is useful for the therapist to introduce the topic, even if the couple doesn't, fairly early on in the therapy. Most couples are relieved that the therapist can talk about it in an ordinary way. It may be an area that the couple finds difficult to talk about between them. Their sexual relationship is part of the overall picture of who the couple is and may help us understand other aspects of their relationship.

Talking about sex can lead to certain transference and countertransference dynamics. The therapist can feel intrusive, stepping into a private arena of a couple's relationship, particularly if there is embarrassment – perhaps about particular kinds of sex the couple enjoy or areas that feel problematic and shameful; the female partner being non-orgasmic or a man being unable to sustain an erection; no sex or infrequent sex that makes the couple feel inadequate. Sometimes Oedipal dynamics get aroused in the therapist, either the sense of intrusiveness or the sense of being excluded by the couple as they keep the bedroom door shut on this aspect of their relationship. The couple might be affected by the gender of the therapist; for example, if an issue is the man's impotence and the therapist is female. It can also be hard for the couple to manage their own curiosity about the therapist's sexuality and sexual experience. If this curiosity is brought into the open, the couple's fantasies about the therapist might lead to further understanding about their sense of being seen and fully understood as a sexual (or non-sexual) couple.

Some couples have a different problem, a more 'perverse' one, in which they do want to talk about the details of their sexual relationship and recruit the therapist not only into understanding it, but also, in their minds, taking part in it, as they try and get the therapist excited. This dynamic can slowly dawn on the therapist and while helpfully revealing an aspect of the couple's relationship that needs understanding, it can be hard to analyse and requires the therapist finding a third position from which to interpret what is being enacted in the room.

Difference and different sexualities

How similar or different are same-sex relationships, or relationships when one or both partners are bisexual or transgender? Some couples describe themselves as mainly heterosexual, but within that have some leaning towards a same-sex orientation. Sexual identity and orientation can be quite fluid. In fact, being in touch with innate bisexuality, as described earlier, is part of being a creative couple – identifying with the male/female aspects in our relationship and in our own internal relating. There is an increasing questioning, especially among young people, about being confined to a binary sexual identity with regard to biological sex, gender or gender identity. Awareness of these possibilities can give them the opportunity to fully explore their sexuality before establishing their own sexual identity and orientation, but for some, it can also feel confusing and anxiety provoking.

The couple therapist seeks to explore with the couple the nature of their sexual relationship and any difficulties they are experiencing. This isn't a normative exploration, but it is perhaps too simplistic to say that whatever the couple does sexually is fine as long as they are not harming themselves or anyone else and they are happy with it. For example, as described earlier, aggression can be productive in a couple's sexual relationship (Kernberg, 1995), but it can also be overly expressed in the sexual relationship in a way that becomes damaging. Such split-off hatred was described by a deeply unhappy partner in one couple who felt that her husband "only wanted sex in ways that hurt her".

The couple therapist is also affected by his or her own gender and sexual orientation and, however much has been learnt about other genders and sexualities, this will be a limiting factor, as will cultural differences. How men and women construct their intimate relationship in one culture can be very different, and feel alien, to someone in another culture. Working with same-gender couples draws our attention to the many different kinds of couple relationships even, of course, within heterosexual relationships. We need to be mindful of not letting some version of a couple relationship in our minds have undue influence on us. It is different when two men make a relationship or two women or a man and a woman. Heteronormative assumptions can reduce same-sex relationships to meaningless stereotypes; for example, "the belief that lesbians, as a whole, are fused (unable to tolerate difference) and that gay men, as a whole, are polymorphously perverse (unable to tolerate intimacy" (McCann, 2014, p. 86). These assumptions not only are problematic in stereotyping, but also they can make it difficult to understand a couple relationship that is so different to one's own. As McCann again points out, "monogamous, long-term, emotionally intimate relationships, as opposed to polygamous relationships, or relationship structures that question the need for attraction and sexual passion always to be linked together" (2014, p. 86) is only one way of seeing relationships. In this process, we need to be aware that we do have our own "couple in the mind" (Ludlam, 2007), as I described at the beginning of this chapter. Awareness provides some protection against us unconsciously imposing our views on a couple, but might also help us allow these views to be challenged by encountering another view of a relationship.

Our own gender is also a limiting factor. A woman cannot really know what it is like to have a penis, just as a man cannot know what it is like to have a vagina, a womb or to be pregnant. We can't be all things. With couples, it is especially important for the therapist not to ally with what feels familiar and to actively explore the experience of being male or female for both partners. Does it matter to a couple what the gender of the therapist is? For example, might a lesbian couple feel more comfortable with a female therapist, or in heterosexual couples, does the gender of the therapist create an imbalance? There is often a gender imbalance or difference in the room that has to be kept alive as there may sometimes be the feeling that the partner who is the same gender as the therapist feels better understood, more aligned with, and the partner of the other gender feels ganged up on.

Inevitably, cultural norms and developmental experience affect how we feel about ourselves as a couple. Hertzmann and others (Downey &

Friedman, 1995; Frost & Meyer, 2009; Hertzmann, 2011) suggest that many gay and lesbian couples struggle with internalised homophobia, a sense inside them that they are not right or the norm, and this interferes with their capacity to be a functioning creative couple. "Internalized homophobia, functioning as an unconscious introject, acts as a host for aggressive acts of the superego potentially resulting in a very punitive attitude towards the homosexuality of the self and others" (Hertzmann, 2011, p. 350). This only reinforces the point that the couple therapist has to be aware of normative impulses inside her. But whatever the couple's sexuality, there is an issue of what is manageable and creative and what is not manageable – at least for one partner – and destructive for the couple.

Transsexual dynamics in a couple

Clinical example: David and Cheryl
David had started cross-dressing, first secretly and now in the presence of his wife, Cheryl. This felt important to David, and having discovered how it made him feel, he did not feel he could relinquish it. Cheryl said she had felt shocked and still found it challenging, but she loved David. They had been together a long time and come through other difficult times, including a termination they had regretted and later infertility problems. Cheryl felt she could be open to these changes in David, and for a while, his cross-dressing became part of their sexual relationship. She saw it as a feminine aspect of David that he wanted to express. But his cross-dressing, plucked eyebrows and hormonal bodily changes reached a point where she could no longer tolerate it. Together, we understood that the balance tipped when she felt that in sex she was required to be a woman sexually relating to another woman. She was losing her sense of being a woman relating to a man, albeit feminised. The dynamic changed between them from something more playful (though, I thought, containing aggressive aspects) to something more controlling of her, and she became resistant to being controlled by him, as she was required both to change her own sexuality and face the loss of her partner as male. This was painful for them. They both felt the loss of the relationship they once had, but could not return to.

Working with a couple's sexual relationship

There are many strands to working analytically with a couple's sexual relationship. One of the most basic is the understanding that a couple's sexual relationship, how they work it out and manage it, is unique to them. There may be aspects that are destructive, even abusive, which the couple needs help in thinking about and addressing. In order to facilitate this exploration, the therapist needs to be comfortable talking about sex, and able to reflect on, understand and manage some potentially difficult transference and countertransference dynamics.

I have come to think that one of the most important tasks a therapist has is that of helping a couple manage love and hate. There is a danger that as couple therapists, we tend more towards smoothing out a couple's relationship, seeking harmony rather than helping them with differences, and with managing hate as well as love; hate in the context of a relationship that is, though, fundamentally loving, or where one could say that the loving impulses have the upper hand. Being human means that we have a multitude of feelings under the heading of 'love', as well as those under the heading of 'hate'. If a couple can keep both these aspects alive and contained within a predominantly loving relationship, they will be able to be most alive, also sexually.

There may be specific sexual problems that the couple needs help with – either medically or with the intervention of a psychosexual therapist. If there has been sexual trauma such as childhood sexual abuse or rape, this needs special attention and working through; for example, in individual psychotherapy or analysis.

I think it helps a couple to know that loss of sexual desire is not unusual, but perfectly normal and not necessarily a catastrophe. When the couple is in touch with other good and alive aspects of their relationship, it is in fact possible to draw on these other live feelings to revitalise the sexual relationship.

Sometimes the sexual problem can elucidate an unconscious dynamic in the relationship which, if understood, can help the couple. Sometimes we approach it the other way around, thinking about dynamics in the relationship that throw light on the sex problem.

As well as 'L' and 'H' and the oscillation between them, 'K' is important in sex. A couple state of mind, providing the means to be both identified with oneself and be curious about and identified with the other, has been argued to facilitate good sex. Blair, I think, captures this well, and makes a link with the couple state of mind in the following comments: "Within sexual play an individual, quite subconsciously and automatically, inhabits three spaces simultaneously: that of herself, her partner and of an observer to their two bodies meeting. It is an identification from all three perspectives that allows for arousal" (2018, p. 41) and

> What is necessary within sex is an openness and curiosity about our partner's desires in order to understand them and we may need to experiment with our partner in order to understand what works and what doesn't. This ability to play requires flexibility within the couple fit that Morgan (2001) links to the couple state of mind; what we require sexually – in order to achieve genital identification – is curiosity in our partner and to be curious we need to be able to bear difference. Difference is relevant within both homo- and heterosexual relationships because no two people desire the same things whether they have 'matching' genitalia or not.
>
> (Blair, 2018, p. 40)

The therapist's attitude is one of enquiry into a couple's 'stated ambition' for their relationship, seeking out whether this ambition is a genuine expression of each partner's mature desire (as against blindly conforming to an external imposition) and then asking whether this ambition is a shared defence against relating, intimacy or difference and separateness, and finally, whether it is an expression of creativity.

Chapter 9

Interpretation[1]

The field of couple interpretation is complex but also potentially creative. I use the word 'field' to evoke the idea of a range of different but interrelating relationships and unconscious dynamics that can be understood and interpreted within the couple analytic setting. In this chapter, I first outline some framing comments about the nature of interpretation as I think of it. I'll then describe what I think of as specifically 'couple interpretation' before discussing a range of other kinds of interpretations used in analytic work with couples, as well as some other kinds of interventions. Interpretation is a far from perfect process and towards the end of this chapter, I'll suggest some of the things that can easily go wrong with interpretations.

The nature of interpretation

Interpretation is a specific form of communication to the couple, which shows them what the therapist might understand about the way they relate and what is happening in their relationship. The interpretations address various areas of the couple's relationship; for example, their projective system, transference relationship, shared phantasy, conflicts, anxieties, defences and beliefs. Particular attention is given to what the couple creates together as a consequence of their specific coupling.

Interpretation attempts to make conscious aspects of the couple relationship that are unconscious or partially so. They are not final statements, but part of the developing understanding between the couple and the therapist. The therapist, in different ways, puts into words aspects of, and dynamics in, the psychic life of the couple, so that there is the possibility that these can be thought about. This is a way for the couple to come to 'know' their relationship, aspects that they have been unaware of. With thinking comes the possibility of understanding, rather than enactment, working through and a different perspective.

Interpretations can only be made within the context of the analytic setting. The therapist takes care of the setting and provides the couple analytic space in which she can be attuned to, think about and analyse the couple's relationship. The setting also supports the therapist in having a state of mind receptive to the couple's unconscious, giving close attention to what they bring, the passing remarks, the affective tone of what is said, what is not being said or understood, the kind of unconscious pressure the partners exert on each other and the therapist. The couple analytic space, encompassing continuity and boundedness, also supports the couple in being able to be receptive to the therapist even though this might be difficult, and not always possible.

Giving an interpretation is part of a process. Interpretations, or what Poland has called an 'interpretive attitude', communicate to the couple that the therapist is trying to understand them, even though much of the time not making formal interpretations. Poland suggests, "*the analyst's attitude of analytic curiosity, ever aiming towards understanding and insight is the essential factor that shapes the psychoanalytic situation and makes possible the psychoanalytic value both of non-interpretive, noninsight-oriented activities, and of formal declarative interpretations*" (Poland, 2002, p. 817; emphasis in original).

Before an interpretation can be made, something has to come together in the therapist's mind, perhaps from several sources. This can be, for example, from countertransference, observation of the couple, a small enactment, or an image the couple brings that is saturated with symbolic meaning. Interpretation rests on a capacity for not knowing and allowing something to come together. As Bion observes,

> from the material the patient produces, there emerges, like the pattern from a kaleidoscope, a configuration which seems to belong not only to the situation unfolding, but to a number of others not previously seen to be connected and which it has not been designed to connect.
> (Bion, 1967b, p. 127)

Following Bion, Britton and Steiner describe this process as "the emergence of a *selected fact*", which they see "as a creative integration of disparate facts into a meaningful pattern" (1994, p. 1070; emphasis in original). In a couple interpretation, this process is complex and can be thought of as a "conjoint selected fact" as Pickering describes. "There is a selected fact which serves to sublate both selected facts, if not a series of selected facts. The word 'conjoint' refers to the *third thing* created by the combination of the two individual selected facts" (Pickering, 2011, pp. 59–60).

The emergence of a selected fact in the analyst's mind depends on her ability to maintain a state of what Freud (1912b) called 'evenly suspended attention' and Bion (1970) referred to as 'negative capability'. Without this negative capability and filled with collections of facts, thoughts, feelings and no sense of how they fit together, an alternative phenomenon can occur, which Britton and Steiner describe as an "overvalued idea", which, they suggest can "be used by the analyst to give a sense of integration to otherwise disparate and confusing experiences … [and] forced to fit a hypothesis or theory which the analyst needs for defensive purposes" (1994, p. 1070). This is part of the difficult work of analysis whether with a couple or an individual. For this reason, having made an interpretation, it's then important to see how it lands, how the couple responds, but also how the therapist feels having made it. This is an integral part of the process as it helps the therapist assess whether the interpretation was valid. This point is made clearly by Britton and Steiner:

> An essential part of the work of interpretation takes place after it is given. Then it becomes important to listen to the patient and take heed of his reaction to what has been said. Indeed, the evaluation of interpretations is so intimately connected with their formulation that we believe it cannot be separated from it, and an experienced analyst continuously monitors the effect his words have in the manner of a violinist who bends his ear towards his instrument to ensure that his intonation is correct.
> (Britton & Steiner, 1994, p. 1070)

But how do we do this? The therapist might consider the following kind of questions; for example, does the interpretation have an emotional impact, can it be understood and thought about, does it bring some relief, lead to further associations? Does it cause discomfort, which can be a good thing, but if too difficult to take in, may be rejected? If it is accepted and readily agreed with, it doesn't necessarily mean it is right, the couple could just be being compliant. Equally, sometimes the couple or one of the partners rejects the interpretation, but goes on to give evidence that it is correct. It could also be that the couple or one partner is not ready to take in the interpretation. These responses help the therapist understand more, which might be the basis of another interpretation later in the session or many weeks later, or it might help the therapist decide not to make this kind of interpretation for the time being, or that she has misunderstood something and needs to rethink.

We know that not all interpretations are correct, or perhaps sometimes only partially so, but even a wrong interpretation can help if the couple is in a reflective state of mind – the couple can say, no it's not like that, it's more like this. This can open more space for exploration, until eventually a more accurate interpretation can be made by the therapist or by the couple and therapist together. In this way, interpretations contribute to the ongoing relationship between therapist and couple. Interpretation, as Winnicott pointed out, shows the limits of the therapist's understanding, what the therapist does understand but also what she does not yet understand (Winnicott, 1969, p. 711).

Deciding where to interpret

In making an interpretation to a couple, the therapist is faced with what can feel like a bewildering range of choices about where to focus an interpretation, with the sessions feeling very 'busy'. This experience of a lot going on is probably more common in couple therapy than individual analysis. Thus, maintaining a state of mind in which to wait for a selected fact to emerge can be difficult and sometimes not possible as the couple recruits the therapist to intervene in various ways. With some couples, there is more of an empty or stuck feeling and the therapist finds it hard to think of anything to say. But even when it is not possible to interpret, the therapist is usually processing the material consciously and unconsciously. This can come together later, when the couple uses a particular word or expression, describe a particular event, avoid something or repeat a particular argument.

Sometimes it is thought, perhaps quite naturally, that couple therapists should only direct their interpretations to the couple about their relationship, usually referred to as 'couple interpretations'. I think the idea that this is what we 'only' do is a kind of myth about work with couples. If this were to be rigidly adhered to, it would make the work cumbersome and limited. The therapist can get into an unnecessarily uncreative place if she feels she has continually to link each partner's material to the other, or find a way of including both partners in each interpretation. If a 'couple state of mind' is secure, the therapist knows this is where she is heading, but there is quite a lot that needs to be understood by the therapist and quite a lot of psychic work in the couple that needs to take place before such interpretations are meaningful.

Having said this, in couple therapy, our interpretations are all leaning towards the couple's relationship and what they recreate from the past and newly create in the present. We try to elaborate the couple's living inner world. Until we reach this point we could say that the interpretation isn't finished. But there are other areas we think about and use as a basis for interpretation on the way to understanding the relationship itself; for example, the way either partner is relating separately or how they relate together to the therapist, the therapist's countertransference and the emotional atmosphere in the room, the inner worlds of each partner, and each partner's perception and experience of the other.

The therapist needs flexibility in this process, both in where she directs the interpretation, and also within herself, monitoring the emotional atmosphere, the countertransference, observing how the partners in the couple are relating to each other and to her, listening to the material as real and symbolic. Usually the therapist takes as her starting point what feels most alive; for example, a misunderstanding, a repetition, an absence, a presence, the countertransference, but she has as her organising frame of reference the relationship between the couple.

What is a couple interpretation?

Whilst one could say that in couple therapy all interpretations are 'couple interpretations', I think of a 'couple interpretation' as something specific. The interpretation is made from a 'third position' about the relationship and therefore offers a perspective that is not about who is doing what to whom, but what they are unconsciously creating together. If effective, it should, at least for a moment, bring an alternative state of mind from that of blame and accusation, and offer the couple a different way of seeing things. Couple interpretations aim to help the couple find a place, a third position, from which they can see what they are creating or recreating between themselves. Many such interpretations are made over the course of the therapy and if the couple can receive them, they develop an interest in their relationship and what they create positively and negatively together, rather than maintaining a focus on the other partner who is seen to be at fault. This is in contrast to the lived experience in their relationship in which they might feel blamed by the other or blaming of the other. They often expect that a version of this will take place with the therapist, who will support their view or their partner's. It can be met with relief when the therapist takes a third position, and provides a way of thinking about what is being created between them in their relationship.

A couple interpretation can come as a relief, but can also be difficult for the couple to receive. The requirement to make a shift in thinking from the belief that the partner is responsible for their difficulties to the idea that they are both responsible and actively part of creating something together might be strongly resisted, each might need to blame the other. If there is too much resistance, the therapist may decide not to make such interpretations for the time being. Equally, she might find that the interpretation is still worth making, as although not accepted in content, it introduces the different state of mind of the therapist, a different perspective and potentially more psychic space.

I am going to describe a range of different kinds of interpretations we might make to a couple in treatment, and for illustrative purposes will give fairly straightforward examples from several couples, rather than focus on more detailed clinical material and the interpretations that form part of a particular session.

A couple interpretation

Clinical example: Ann and Bill

The wife, Ann, is talking about sex and the way she feels her cues about wanting sex are not responded to by her husband, Bill. In his defence, he cites a few recent occasions when he has made quite a direct sexual advance to his wife and she has ignored it. The wife is dumbfounded and says she cannot remember any of these occasions. There is blame and recrimination, rejection and hurt. The therapist is addressing this and perhaps helping them think about how they might communicate their wish for sex more openly, more directly. However, the complaints are repeated in the next few sessions and the therapist becomes aware that she is being recruited to mediate. It feels rather fruitless. At some point, she is able to find a third position, her couple state of mind, in which she can think about what is happening in the 'relationship'. In this case, the couple is unconsciously creating a dynamic in which they can be certain that there will be no sex. This would be the basis of the couple interpretation and by now the therapist might also have some sense of what anxieties lie behind this 'no sex defence', which then might also be part of the interpretation, or be part of a later interpretation if the couple is able to connect with the idea that this is something they are creating together.

Couple interpretations are important because they introduce a different state of mind, both the therapist's, and as a possibility for the couple, and this creates more psychic space. They introduce a couple state of mind that over time can be introjected by the couple into their relationship. So, it is not just the content of the interpretation but also the offering of the couple state of mind in itself. Bion (1959, 1962), in his theory of containment, suggests that the mother processes 'beta elements' through her 'alpha function' and gradually transforms these unmetabolised elements into 'alpha elements' that can be thought about. Over time, the mother's capacity to do this, her 'alpha function', is also introjected. This helps the infant build up the capacity to process his own 'beta elements'. The introjection by the couple of the therapist's 'couple state of mind' is similar to this process in the couple, as it provides the couple with the capacity to think about the relationship, rather than deal with psychic pain or conflict by evacuation into, or acting out with, the partner.

Now I am going to describe some other kinds of interpretations in the field of couple analysis, showing the way they involve the therapist, either partner and the couple.

Interpretations involve all three

A fundamental difference between couple and individual therapy is that no interpretation is made to one partner alone, because it is made in the presence of the other partner. If the other partner is temporarily not present for a session, the therapist needs to be careful not to make an interpretation that she could not make again when both partners are present.

When making an interpretation that might temporarily focus on one partner or the other, the therapist is still thinking about this in relation to the couple, even though unable to formulate, or choosing not to make a couple interpretation at this point. If the couple has enough of an experience of the therapist doing this, they can build trust in the therapist's couple state of mind, and can tolerate the focus on one of them. If there is not enough of a sense of a couple state of mind, such interpretations can be experienced as a 'ganging up' on the partner who is in focus and the therapist needs to intervene to re-establish the couple focus. However, the fact that there are three in couple therapy, while having its challenges, is also something that makes the work creative in a different way to individual therapy or analysis. I shall say more about this later.

Working with transference in couple therapy

As described in Chapter 5, in couple therapy there are several transference relationships that can be thought about. There is a transference relationship between the two partners in the couple, as well as a transference relationship between the individual partners, both separately and as a couple, and the therapist. How does one interpret the transference between the individuals in the couple? And why is it also important to understand and interpret the transference to the therapist? Sometimes transference interpretations feel difficult to make and this can be even more difficult in couple therapy, when the couple can feel that the therapist bringing herself into the room is either irrelevant or intrusive. However, I think there are a number of reasons why the whole landscape of the transference has to be traversed in couple therapy too.

First of all, the transference between the partners and between the couple and the therapist are not separate things. In order to understand accurately the transference relationship between the couple and to help them move towards seeing each other in a less distorted way, the therapist's experience of the transference to her is very elucidating. The therapist can understand through her own experience and even enactment, something that might also occur in the couple. But in this position, she understands from inside herself, from her own emotional experience, rather than from the position of observing the couple, which is more outside, though often emotionally affected.

Second, by interpreting the transference between the couple and the therapist, a triangular space is created enabling more psychic space. The therapist becomes a third participant in the room. In analytic couple therapy, the therapist makes herself available for the couple to project into her and experience her in ways distorted by the projection. There is then the possibility that the couple can have these projections contained, rather than reacted to, by a mind capable of doing so. This is different to the partner who can feel persecuted by the projection and retaliates with counter projections. In addition, when something like this is happening between one partner and the therapist, the other partner can observe it in another relationship and it potentially opens up more thinking space.

The fact of there being three people in the room enables other possibilities – sometimes the therapist can make an interpretation of the transference to her and link it to the dynamics in the couple relationship. This triangular dynamic in which one of the partners is temporarily an observer of the partner/therapist couple increases psychic space, as that partner is able to take a third position on the dynamic in his or her own relationship. This is something that Balfour has described in relation to a couple he saw in which there was a lack of psychic space. The couple

> began to be able to see that it was no longer just the two of them enacting the dynamic in a linear way, but a three way affair, where within the "triangular configuration" in the room, each had witnessed the other playing out an aspect of this object relationship with me ... perhaps for a moment giving a perspective on something they were normally just "in" together.
>
> (Balfour, 2016, p. 69)

Some different uses of the transference in the triangular setting of couple therapy

i) An observing partner taking a third position on the relationship

Clinical example: Carly and James

James was a promising academic, but had very little sense of self. He had had a breakdown when an undergraduate, and had struggled in relationships, though he had succeeded academically. He was in a relationship with Carly who related to him very narcissistically. She told him what he thought and felt, and when he did attempt to express a different thought, she told him he was lying. In their twenties, the couple had only been together for a year and were unmarried. Despite an intense initial attraction when James timidly wooed Carly on an Under 30s Club holiday in Ibiza, the relationship had since become very abusive. The couple could only be calm together when they could get themselves into a place where there were no differences. Carly could not tolerate me having any alternate perspective to hers. It was only when James could witness her attempt to verbally obliterate me, including my interpretation of how anxious my possibly different view made Carly feel, that he could take any kind of third position on his own relationship. The couple only came to therapy for a few months and then they broke off. I did not feel I had been able to help them with their difficulties in being psychically more separate. However, a few weeks later, James came to see me on his own and told me that following an argument in which Carly had tried to bar him from leaving their flat, he had left her. He felt that it had only been by being in the couple therapy sessions that he could 'see' his relationship and realise how destructive it was for him. He was describing that with me in the room interacting with Carly, he could, from a third position, see himself in the relationship with Carly. Prior to this, he was simply 'in' the relationship with Carly, confused about what was him and what was her and unable to get hold of his own mind. Following this meeting, I felt very concerned about Carly and contacted her to see if she would like another appointment. She accepted, but then cancelled at the last moment and did not rearrange.

ii) Using the transference and countertransference between one partner and the therapist to understand the dynamic between the couple

Clinical example: Donna and Johnny

Six weeks into the therapy, Donna started the session expressing anger towards the therapist, who she felt had focused almost exclusively on Johnny in the previous session. She even thought that the therapist might be blaming her for Johnny's problems. The therapist responded defensively, saying she wasn't blaming Donna for Johnny's problems and acknowledged that there had been more of a focus on Johnny the previous week. However, as the session continued, the therapist noticed that each time she tried to make contact with Donna's distress, she was rebuffed. When Johnny came in again about something worrying him, Donna cut across him and changed the subject. The therapist had an experience of Donna feeling angry and let down by her but also an experience of being continuously rebuffed by Donna.

Observing the couple, she noticed that Donna couldn't bear the attention going to Johnny again, as if there would be a repeat of the experience of last week which was very painful for her. In this part of the session, the therapist was mainly focused on what was going on between her and Donna, the wish for her attention and the way it was rejected. She then started to think about this in relation to the couple. Did what was going on between her and Donna throw any light on a dynamic in the couple's relationship? The presenting problem was Donna's wish to leave the relationship because she could no longer bear to "mother" Johnny, but the therapist could see from her own experience the more nuanced aspects of this – Donna wanted to be cared for, but was fearful of it; did she not allow Johnny to provide this just as she didn't allow the therapist? Did she project her neediness into Johnny and mother that part of herself in him where it was safer, but then also resented him for getting his needs met – as in the previous session and feared at one point in this session? Does Johnny feel like the therapist, that his attempts to get close to Donna are rejected?

This was, of course, only part of the picture, mainly about Donna, and at this stage part of an hypothesis, but I am giving it as an example of how the therapist can work with other relationships in the room to help her understand the relationship (the couple's) that has come for help.

iii) An interpretation bringing together transferences to the therapist and transference between the couple

Clinical example: Will and Tamar
Will, one partner in a couple just starting therapy, seemed to be relating to me as if I were a judge presiding over him. He was unsure about making a long-term commitment and I felt he expected me to condemn his ambivalence and tell him to "get on with it". He also expressed irritation with what he called his girlfriend's "therapy-speak" (she was in a closely related profession and had been in individual therapy for some time). Tamar seemed more relaxed and expressed agreement with most of what I said. I had a strong countertransference response of being made into someone judgemental for Will and an even more uncomfortable one of being misperceived by both as if in an alliance with Tamar, as if we were two therapists analysing him. I therefore made an interpretation to Will that he felt I was judging him in his uncertainty about the relationship, but I included an interpretation to the couple – the idea that they both felt I was getting together with Tamar to judge him.

In this example, the transference of one partner to the therapist, to his partner, and from the couple to the therapist are all contained in the interpretation. It sounds complex, in some ways it is, but I think this is what happens in analytic couple therapy – we often navigate between and bring together the different experiences in the room.

A later interpretation explored Tamar's feeling that she needed to make an alliance with me. I explored why she felt she needed to do this and interpreted that this was her way of controlling me, as I was feared by her too as a potentially critical/judgemental figure. A few sessions later, these thoughts came together in a couple interpretation about a dynamic in the relationship, in which each feared judgement by the other, and the way in which they evoked the other to play a part in this judging/judged dynamic. Once the couple had some time to think further about this interpretation, which did make sense to them, they were, over time, able to bring this together with earlier experience and I was able to help them think about a very critical object that was part of their couple internal world.

These examples also illustrate the point that interpretations, wherever they are located initially, build up and gradually become more 'couple' and more complete. There is a note of caution here. In this approach, the therapist has quite a lot of scope to move around between the different relationships in the room, gradually building up an understanding of the couple. There are dangers in allowing oneself this flexibility, such as not being sufficiently even-handed, or the possibility and even likelihood that one will get 'caught up' with one partner or the other. If one is going to have the freedom to move between the different relationships and dynamics in the room, then one needs the anchor of a 'couple state of mind'. In other words, if the couple therapist has a 'couple state of mind' firmly inside her, then she does not need to concretely address everything, all the time, to the couple. Part of this analytic stance is knowing that, in fact, everything is indirectly addressed to the couple and the therapist's task is to take a third position in relation to all the relationships operating in the room, including her relationship to the couple.

Interpretations from the therapist's countertransference to the couple

Countertransference can be hard for the therapist to process and work through, as Brenman Pick has shown. For interpretations to have emotional depth, the analyst needs to make emotional contact with the experience the patient projects into her and this will be conveyed in the giving of the interpretation. "The contention that the analyst is not affected by these experiences is both false and would convey to the patient that his plight, pain and behaviour are emotionally ignored by the analyst" (Pick, 1985, p. 166). It takes time to process countertransference and to make use of it to understand unconscious aspects of the couple's relationship. It is helpful to think of Joseph's (1985) elaboration of transference as the total situation within which she includes the countertransference and the ongoing dynamics and subtle enactments between patient and analyst. Thought about in this way, the couple's dynamic can be expressed in any of the relationships in the room, and the countertransference, the therapist's conscious and unconscious response to the couple, is key in tuning in to this.

Clinical example: Tim and Rhoda
With one couple in therapy, the therapist had several weeks of struggling with her countertransference. The couple was often late or missed appointments, resulting in a frustrating experience. As soon as some understanding developed, it dropped away before the next session; nothing could be sustained. After a while, the therapist made a link in her mind with the couple's difficulty that she hadn't previously been aware of. It now struck her that although the couple outwardly stated that they wanted to be together, in fact, they were both very anxious about making a commitment. They were not talking about this in the room, quite the opposite, but they were telling her in this other way. She then became more aware of how this pattern of relating to her seemed to be about an anxiety in making contact, and a fear of the outcome of relating. When she interpreted this to the couple, it made sense to them and helped them think about their anxieties, not just about making a commitment but about connecting up properly with another, which the problem in the couple therapy symbolised.

Clinical example: Lois and Walt
The wife in another couple made several phone calls to the therapist before coming for a consultation. She wanted to establish that he was the right therapist, having

had several failed attempts at couple therapy. After an initial brief phase of idealisation, the therapist felt under constant attack from Lois. In different ways, Lois told him he was wrong, did not understand them and was making things worse. Walt was in the background of most sessions, was difficult to make contact with and gauge. The therapist often wished that he, Walt, could provide a third position on what was going on between him and Lois, but he sat back. At this stage, it was very difficult to understand much about the couple. The therapist dreaded seeing them, but despite threats from Lois to find a new therapist, they continued. After a lot of processing and consultation, the therapist realised that he had to be kept as the 'wrong therapist'. This could be understood as, in Racker's terms, a complementary identification and the dread that he felt before seeing this couple was Lois's dread, and possibly more hidden, Walt's, a concordant identification (Racker, 1968). The dread that he felt before seeing this couple was Lois's dread and possibly more hidden, Walt's. Lois was clearly desperate for containment, but had no belief in a benign containing object, so that the therapist's attempt to contain felt dangerous for fear that he would escalate her anxiety or project into her. With this couple, this issue of the right or wrong therapist was what had to be understood first, as this powerful dynamic threatened the possibility of even the next session. A lot of thought had to go into how to work with this fragile couple. It was only when the wife felt a measure of trust in the therapist that Walt could get more into the picture. He had to be kept by Lois as a neutral, ineffective and unthreatening object, which for his own complex reasons, he was prepared to be. It will probably be of no surprise to know that Lois had a psychotic mother and Walt a physically and emotionally abusive father from whom he tried to keep hidden.*

Interpreting the couple's transference on beginning therapy

As described in Chapter Three, starting couple therapy inevitably stirs up anxieties and the nature of these anxieties will be influenced by earlier experiences with helpful and persecuting objects. In the early stages of therapy, the transference to the therapist is often intense and primitive. There are often anxieties about what couple therapy is and what the figure of the couple therapist represents. The couple may experience the therapist as a parental or superego figure who is going to tell them they have failed or reprimand them. In fact, one of the hopes may be that she will reprimand the partner and bring him or her into line. The therapist may be experienced as someone exerting power and influence, someone who could keep the couple together or break them apart. There are often anxieties that the therapist will take sides and not be able to hold a couple state of mind. The therapist may be experienced as a very idealised figure, perhaps having extraordinary or magical insights into couple relationships or holding the 'knowledge' of what being a couple is. There can be anxieties about overwhelming the therapist and feeling that she will be unable to contain them. The transference to the therapist, the kind of figure she is and what she represents, needs to be interpreted to the couple at this early stage and is part of helping them engage in treatment.

There may be a particular atmosphere in the session in which one of the partners has more of a voice, tries to take charge in describing the problem, presents the couple problem as the other one's fault, sometimes overtly, sometimes in rather hidden ways, that suggests the couple (in their different positions) is seeing the therapist as likely to be one-sided or not evenly balanced in relation to them both. This may have been reflected in the referral, with one of the partners making the initial contact, or the couple being referred by one partner's analyst. Being able to make these transference interpretations is dependent on what the therapist is observing and experiencing in the countertransference. So, for example, does the therapist feel a pressure from one or both of them to fit in with a particular view with little room for thinking about it? Does the therapist feel there is no space in the room to speak, or in her mind to think? Is there an atmosphere of blame? It is quite useful to make these transference interpretations during this process of engagement when there are usually a lot of feelings and anxieties about the therapist; as well as being containing to the couple, it establishes early on in the therapy the idea of this being part of the dialogue between the therapist and couple.

So far, I have talked mainly about transference and countertransference between the couple and the therapist. Here is an example of the transference in the couple's relationship

The transference in the couple's relationship

Clinical example: Jimmy and Dale

Jimmy met Dale when he was an intern and Dale was his department head. They both complained that whenever they tried to think about and discuss something important together, their communication quickly broke down. Jimmy was considering a radical career change and resigning from his current job. In one session, just before communication broke down again, Dale said he thought that every time he spoke to Jimmy, Jimmy responded to him as if he, Dale, was trying to stop him making this career change. I said I felt this was accurate, Jimmy related to Dale as if he was an authority figure or parent against whom he had to rebel to establish a sense of his own identity. Jimmy agreed with this interpretation, but protested that this was because Dale was an authority figure. It was true that Dale could behave in an angry and somewhat authoritative way, and perhaps had done so to a greater degree earlier in their relationship, but it would be hard for anyone else not to notice how powerless, insecure and totally lacking in influence over Jimmy he now felt. I then took the interpretation a stage further and said to the couple that although it could look like Dale had the authority in the relationship, certainly from Jimmy's perspective, in fact it seemed they shared an experience of powerlessness and each easily perceived the other as in control. This time Jimmy was temporarily able to step outside the transference and consider this new thought.

Interpreting the projective system

When one partner is expressing something strongly, the therapist thinks about the ways in which what one partner is talking about links with the other, but these links are not usually obvious or straightforward. It may be that one partner is expressing something on behalf of the couple. The way the partners in the couple use the relationship to project unwanted aspects of the self into the other leaves the other carrying a 'double dose' of this aspect. Again, this may be for defensive or developmental reasons, but it can lead to the couple feeling very polarised; for example, one partner carrying all the dependent feelings, the other all the need for autonomy and separateness. Although one might imagine that the partner with the double dose may be burdened by the projection, they may also be reluctant to return it, as unconsciously it serves a protective function for the relationship, the conscious container, being unconsciously contained.

Clinical example: Harry and Bella
Harry wants to go away without their young children. Bella is reluctant and anxious about leaving them behind for any length of time. The therapist put it to them that this was a conflict in each of them, both were very attached to the children, and were reluctant to leave them while so young, but both also longed for adult time, with the children out of mind, and in particular to resume their previously good/exciting sexual relationship. They dealt with this by each representing one side of the conflict so the internal conflict was now one between them. Following this interpretation, the couple reluctantly acknowledged their shared ambivalence about the trip and thought together about making it more manageable – they decided not to go away for so many days.

In the example of Harry and Bella, helping them see how they were managing an internal conflict, in each of them, by projecting one part of the conflict into the other, was helpful. What they were projecting into each other was not so far from consciousness and they were fairly easily able to reintroject the unwanted aspect of their feelings. But often the projective system is more forceful, more disowned and less available to being made conscious.

Clinical example: Kath and Christine
Kath and Christine had been in therapy for about a year. Although the therapist was aware of a powerful projective system, it was very difficult to shift it. Kath felt very let down by Christine, whom she experienced as very chaotic when it came to making arrangements, keeping appointments they had and keeping the house in

order. After 5 years of being unsure of their commitment, they had recently moved in together to see if they could make a go of it. Although these difficulties had been there before Christine moved in, Kath felt if they lived in the same place, she could feel more in control of Christine's chaos, and that with her influence, Christine would settle into a more ordered life. Instead she felt Christine was set on driving her mad. This belief ranged from mild irritation to moments of feeling she would really lose her mind.

The therapist was aware of something rather disorganised, even chaotic, in Christine, but she had also become aware of something quite disturbed in Kath. She could see in the to and fro of the sessions the way in which Kath projected this frightening part of herself into Christine and Christine all too readily accepted the projection. She tried to appease Kath, by acknowledging her faults, and while she did also protest a bit, she usually ended up promising to do better. It was as if she was aware of this disturbed part of Kath and unconsciously, for the sake of the relationship, she was prepared to take the projection, an example of the 'conscious container' (Kath) being the 'unconsciously contained'.

In this situation, trying to help Kath see that she was projecting a very frightening chaotic part of herself into Christine would not only be refuted, she would feel misunderstood and perceive the therapist as trying to force something disturbing into her. When working with and interpreting the projective system, it is important to remember the defensive aspect of this process; we split off and project parts of the self that cause us conflict, but also parts we cannot manage, that threaten to overwhelm us, even to destroy us. Therefore, showing the couple what they are projecting into each other is rarely enough to enable them to take this part back. I think it happens in a different way.

If we recognise that what we are witnessing in a couple is a manifestation of their projective system, a double dose of some psychic contents in one partner, we first of all have to work with it there, in that part of the relationship. We know that couples coming for help are often bringing a split-off part of themselves located in the other. In a sense, this is why they have to come for couple therapy. By working with this disowned and often frightening part of the self where it is located in the relationship, hopefully it becomes less frightening. The projecting partner can see that the therapist is not so frightened by it, is not judging it and is interested in understanding it. This is one of the ways in which the triangular nature of couple therapy can be very effective. Over the course of the therapy, it is sometimes possible for the projecting partner to become less frightened by this part of the self. It took a while, but Kath did start to be able to talk about her own internal chaos and there was an increased sense of something chaotic and fragmented that they both shared. However, at times of stress, the relationship went back to its default position of Christine carrying the disturbance, but again over time, the couple became aware of the dynamic, even though they could not always prevent it occurring.

Interpreting fantasy, unconscious phantasy and beliefs

Couples have many ideas about what a relationship is or should be. This is an important area in couple therapy because these assumptions, fantasies and unconscious beliefs are driving the relationship in some way. Unless they can be brought properly into consciousness and thought about, they can lead to a sense of never-ending conflict which, in the mind of the subject is justified, but in the partner, feels irrational or unfair. These ideas range from open assumptions to deeply unconscious beliefs. Conscious assumptions often need to be brought more into the open and thought about. It may be that each partner thinks these are shared views and discovers they are not. Here I would include such things as: the couple's idea that they should always be able to understand each other (Vorchheimer, 2015), like everything about each other, always find each other sexually attractive, never hate each other, never have an argument, be a united front. Although the couple may deny, if thought about rationally, that they have such fantasies, in fact, they are often in the grip of them more than they are aware. Sometimes there are phantasies more like Freud's use of the term as day dreams that are kept from reality testing and later become repressed (1911). Couples often have phantasies that the partner is, or should be, a particular way – in appearance, characteristics, behaviour, or that they should relate in an expected way to oneself, be happy, social, nurturing, undemanding and so on, and there is disappointment or even a grievance if the other is not.

Some of these assumptions may take the form of deep unconscious beliefs, such as the idea that relationships are essentially threatening or destructive or are about merging and so on. An unconscious belief exerts a powerful background influence on the relationship, usually accessed by the therapist in a difficult to process countertransference, or enactment. But these beliefs pose particular problems for interpretation. As Britton describes,

> [W]hen belief is attached to a phantasy or idea, initially it is treated as a fact. The realisation that it is a belief is a secondary process which depends on viewing the belief from outside the system of the belief itself.
>
> (Britton, 1998c, p. 9)

This means that when a couple is in the grip of an unconscious belief, there is an atmosphere of certainty which is difficult to challenge. They are not able to take a third position in relation to the belief and may be resistant to the third position of the therapist. The therapist may interpret, "You are talking together as if there is a belief that you should meet each other's needs all the time", and the couple might respond rather indignantly (as if the therapist is mad), "Isn't that what a couple relationship is?!" In this situation, the therapist offering a different view, instead of being experienced as increasing psychic space, is experienced as challenging, or threatening what in their minds is a fact. It can feel very difficult for the therapist to think and to find any useful way of formulating an interpretation. The countertransference is difficult to manage and there may be a pressure towards enactment. The therapist may herself respond with insistence or certainty, as in an 'overvalued idea'. In a way, as long as the therapist becomes aware of it, this is also useful as it is an indication to the therapist of the terrain she is in. It might help her monitor her interpretations to check that she is not responding to one overvalued idea with another.

Interpretation of symbols and dreams

Analytic listening is different to ordinary listening. As Zinner has noted, couple therapists can "get swept away by the manifest content, find ourselves, despite our efforts taking sides, tuning out, despairing, all the time searching for some intervention that will serve a constructive purpose". He suggests that "the manifest content of the argument be assessed for its metaphoric meaning. Further, that the argument be viewed as a stereotyped and patterned reaction to some underlying, often unconscious emotional strain in one or both partners" (1988, p. 1). Thus, one of the ways we listen to material is by trying to hear the unconscious symbolic meaning. If we can understand that the thing the couple is fighting about is not only the thing, but also what it represents, we sometimes have the means of bringing some light into a repetitive exchange of misunderstanding. The couple finds the apparent thing they were fighting about is not quite the thing they thought it was.

Clinical example: Sadie and Paul

An issue common to many couples faced with the demands of young children is that of feeling not looked after by the other. Sadie and Paul had three young children, and Sadie in one session was expressing her extreme disappointment that Paul rarely brought her a cup of tea in bed at the weekend. He did get up before her, got the children up and started getting breakfast underway, and she heard him in the kitchen, heard the kettle and the chink of china, but when he reappeared in the bedroom, there was no tea! She said this and showed with a collapse in her body what a huge disappointment this was. Paul was listening and indicating that he thought her expectations were unreasonable. After all, he was getting on with things and he was giving her a lie in! For a while I could go along with Paul, wasn't Sadie being a bit unreasonable? But then I started to listen differently, with a 'third ear' and saw that it wasn't just the longed-for tea, it was what it represented to Sadie. It became clear that the tea represented the consistent and reliable maternal care which she herself had never had, felt more acutely now that she was required to provide this most of the time for the children. Furthermore, hearing Paul in the kitchen was tantalising, generating hope, which was dashed, again and again. Although her affect seemed extreme in relation to this event, I realised this was the quality of care she experienced with her emotionally unavailable mother; there was the tantalising promise of care, which was only too frequently dashed.

Clinical example: Charlie and Erica
This couple came to see me in an urgent state as they had recently argued and Charlie had pushed Erica. They hadn't been together long, but had both felt this was the relationship they wanted to commit to. Erica said that despite what had happened, she thought she loved Charlie. In the first few sessions we tried to process how their fighting had escalated to physical violence. Then in one session, they told me they had argued because Charlie had not dealt with a faulty smoke alarm as he'd agreed to, and it went off in the middle of the night waking them. Charlie's not attending to the smoke alarm spoke to a tension between them that we were starting to become aware of, about who was looking after whom and, in particular, a wish in Erica to feel more taken care of by Charlie than he was able to manage. But the image of the smoke alarm was most helpfully thought about in terms of its symbolic meaning – the alarm going off inside both of them and the relationship. Working with the material in this way brought them both into contact with a panic and terror they felt about the relationship and had not been fully aware of, as they realised there was not really a relationship of any substance between them.

A dream brought to couple sessions is also symbolic material for the couple. Although one partner has the dream, we can think of it as a version of 'social dreaming', the dream having its source and meaning beyond the dreamer. Furthermore, the decision to bring the dream into the couple analytic space suggests that the dreamer is already associating to his or her relationship.

A female patient brings the following dream:

> She was at a dance. The setting was hazy, but she was able to see the gray suit worn by a man who asked her to dance. They danced around the room, and suddenly her partner steered her to a corner and pressed himself against her. She could feel his erect penis.
>
> (Giovacchini, 1982, cited by Roth, 2001, p. 533; emphasis added)

This is in fact an excerpt of a dream used by Priscilla Roth in her paper "Mapping the Landscape", as an example through which she describes different levels of transference interpretations (Roth, 2001, p. 533). It is interesting to think how this might be taken up in a couple session if one of the partners were to bring it. First, I think the couple might both associate to the dream. It could be that this kind of object relationship between someone pressurising and another who feels pressurised is an object relationship both partners know about internally or externally in their families of origin (perhaps either or both had oppressive, pushy or sexually inappropriate mothers/fathers, for example).

It could also be an aspect of the way they experience each other, a relationship between a pressuring and a pressurised object that might be part of the unconscious belief the couple has about the nature of relationships. It might also be a communication about their sexual relationship, an eagerness for sex, or a fear of sex.

Thought about in relation to the therapist, it could be that the couple experiences the therapist like the man in the dream or possibly like the woman in the dream, under pressure from them as they join forces and pressurise her. It could also be what is being felt by one or both parties towards the other now in the session, rather like what Hobson (2016) calls a 'self-representing event' in that what is being talked about, out there in the dream, is at the same time happening right now in the session. In other words, the dream might have come to mind at that point in the session because of an unarticulated dynamic going on in the room.

As well as actual dreams, we can also approach the couple's stories as dreams, as Fisher describes, not as simply factual accounts, but as shared unconscious phantasy and "as attempts to communicate emotional experiences" (1999, p. 152). Working with couples, the most alive moment in the session can be anywhere in the room, and the therapist has to make a judgement about where this is at any particular moment. These kinds of stories, whether in dreams, or something reported from everyday life, thought about symbolically, lend a deeper meaning to something about the relationship, and possibly something happening at this moment in the relationship.

Other kinds of interventions

Making links with history

Many links to the couple's history – both individually and the history of their relationship – will be made in the course of the therapy. Usually some history is gathered in the assessment interviews. Links to history can provide the couple with a sense of continuity and help in the process of integrating their present experience. Sometimes the therapist feels she needs to know a bit more of the history in order to understand something better.

Having said this, my own view is that, as long as there is knowledge of significant aspects of history, it is important, in most cases, not to spend a lot of time elaborating a detailed history at the beginning of treatment, unless this is led by the couple. As described in Chapters Two and Three, couples often present in a crisis and need help to understand what is happening to them now. They can feel unheard and uncontained if the therapist asks them too many questions about their background. Sometimes therapists do this because of anxiety about not knowing and having to wait. It can also lead to premature linking of their current difficulties with the past.

Integration of the past with the present often occurs at a more meaningful level when the couple makes links themselves. For example, when Kath (of Kath and Christine above), eventually felt safe enough to acknowledge her own internal chaos, she herself linked it to her early experience with her "nut case of a mother". At that point, it really helped to elaborate her lived experience of this, both for her and for Christine. I knew a little about her mother, but if I had asked her to talk about this before, I think she would have felt persecuted or accused by me. As well as that, by the time Kath did talk about her mother, I had already lived out in the room with them this experience of madness and chaos. From the transference and countertransference, I had a good idea of what this experience was like for her, which I could not have had in the same way from her recounting events in her childhood earlier on in the therapy. This illustrates the point that the value of recounting historical events without the emotional experience of them in the present is limited. In Chapter Five, I talked about a living inner world, a world which is created both by experience of the environment, past and present, but also crucially our response to it. What a "nut case of a mother" means to one patient will not be the same as what it means to another patient. So, without this live experience with the couple, we can only guess what it means or worse, bring our own associations.

'Translating'

One of the things the couple therapist can find herself doing a lot is what I would describe as 'translating' what each partner is saying, feeling, experiencing to the other. Most couples that come for help have problems in communication and helping the partners understand each other better, more accurately, is a valid activity. However, it is important not to get so caught up in this that one loses sight of what the couple is creating together. It may be that the partners in the couple mishear each other, don't want to hear each other – or at least, don't want to hear some particular thing that is difficult to hear – or there is something hinted at, but that can't quite be spoken about. It is important that the therapist can notice the pressure to take up this role of translator so that she can think about the meaning for the couple of getting her to do this. Then she will have re-established something more of a third position, a couple state of mind. From this position, instead of translating, the therapist might interpret; for example, that there is something particular they can't talk about, or that there seems to be a deliberate wish to misunderstand or distort what the other is saying if it doesn't fit with the listening partner's view, or simply that there is a problem in listening to each other.

Fisher likens listening to the meaning of the emotional experience behind the couple's different versions of events to listening to music. He cautions that

> sometimes we are too keen as therapists to translate what we hear from our patients into a language more familiar to us, more under our control without giving ourselves time to listen to the music of what we are hearing.
>
> (Fisher, 1999, p. 153)

Analytic listening and reflecting back

Meltzer, in discussing analytic listening, says, "to listen is not like listening to a recording machine. It is really listening to the language, listening to the music, listening for special uses of words that strike one as having symbolic references" (Meltzer, 1995, p. 133). As described earlier, analytic listening requires us to try to hear the latent content of the couple's discourse. We try to do this, but couples put enormous pressure on us to work with the manifest content. Sometimes they try to recruit us to confirm the words one or the other actually said, asking, "Did I say that?" I am suggesting a kind of listening which asks the question, "What unconscious narrative is going on in each partner as they speak?" While we might often think that the way the partners in the couple are talking to each other is slightly 'mad', perhaps with the concept of unconscious belief, we can think, "It is mad because they are relating to each other as if relationships are like this".

In couple analytic therapy, listening is also key because the partners often find it hard to listen to each other and, when they are listening, they often don't hear each other accurately. Attention is given by the therapist to what is said, and the way it is said, what is not said and the silences. With a couple, the therapist is interested in what the other partner hears and what cannot be heard. In fact, it is not always easy to understand another person, or to take in what they are actually saying, especially if it is painful to the self, or threatens one's own view or beliefs about the relationship. Yet, as described earlier in Chapter Seven, many couples have an expectation that they should understand the partner and be understood by them (Vorchheimer, 2015).

Questioning and reflecting back

Sometimes the therapist wants to ask the couple something in an attempt to understand more of the emotional quality of what is being discussed, not to gather more facts or details, unless something blatant is missing. To do otherwise risks gathering up material that the couple themselves have not brought into the room rather than staying with what they have brought. The therapist might also want to check how the partner heard something the other was talking about, but usually this kind of question comes with an observation the therapist is making; for example, "I noticed when 'X' was speaking, you 'Y' seemed to switch off?".

Observation of the couple

Couple analytic therapy, unlike much individual work, is conducted with the couple sitting up. The couple's appearance and body language, who sits where and if they turn to each other or away from each other, what they do with their hands, eyes – tearful perhaps, but in a hidden way, and whether the other partner notices or not – are all sources of information for the couple therapist. Infant observation, which is part of many psychoanalytic training programmes, as well as providing the opportunity to observe an infant's very early development and relating, also provides a training in maintaining an analytic attitude of quiet reflection (Rustin, 1991) and in being able to closely observe. Sometimes the couple is interacting and the therapist is in the position of observer, sometimes one of them is engaging the therapist and the other is silent. The couple therapist is just as interested in the silent one. Alperovitz gives an example of this in couple psychotherapy, when she observes the familiar crying of Peggy, the partner of Jack, and begins to wonder about it.

> What I saw was this: I noted that when Peggy began to cry she balled up both fists and placed the knuckle of each index finger deeply into her eyes at the bridge of her nose and then twisted them roughly. At the same time, her speech became whiny and cranky as though she was an infant who could not make the transition from sleep to waking or from waking to sleep – and who was not being helped. As she became more agitated, she took a tissue from the box and folded it – first in half and then in half again. She lifted the tissue and placed it just under the lower edge of her left eye – and then she moved the folded Kleenex to the lower edge of her right eye – as though to blot the tears before they could spill from her eyes.
>
> (Alperovitz, 2005, pp. 11–12)

Alperovitz takes what she has observed as a communication to her and to Jack. She comments on the way Peggy tries to stop the tears before they fall on her cheek. Both Jack and Peggy immediately have associations to this and it leads to insights into their individual and shared internal worlds, in particular an "unspoken common bond and similar dilemma with each other – a deep longing for intimacy and for dependency and an equally intense fear of allowing that to happen" (Alperovitz, 2005, p. 13).

Some things that can go wrong with interpretations

Interpretations and unprocessed countertransference

Sometimes the therapist makes interpretations out of anxiety, often something has been projected into the therapist that makes her uncomfortable and she wants to do something with it. The interpretation can then be more like an evacuation, as it hasn't yet been understood or brought into connection with other elements by the therapist. It is sometimes possible to recognise a pressurised feeling when the therapist is saying more than she needs to, or too quickly, or maybe putting something in a complicated way that is hard for the couple to understand. Not knowing or understanding and feeling helpless can be difficult to manage and result in the therapist interpreting, based on previous knowledge or experience, which might not be close enough to this couple's experience, or as Britton and Steiner (1994), have described it, an overvalued idea.

Compliance

Some couples set the therapist up in their minds as an expert who has the last word on what a relationship is, on reality, on who in their relationship is right or wrong and so on. With this kind of transference, yet to be worked through, it might be hard for them to receive an incorrect or imperfect interpretation, which there will always be. Hopefully the therapist picks up their compliant response, perhaps in the way the couple too readily agrees with it, but can't make any associations to it. This situation between the couple and therapist then leads to another interpretation about the compliance and the need to keep the therapist as this 'expert', all-knowing figure.

An incorrect couple interpretation

Therapists, particularly those less experienced and with a less developed 'couple state of mind' sometimes feel they have to see everything in terms of the couple's projective system and they over-interpret this dynamic in the couple. For example, one of the partners is feeling abandoned or angry, or jealous or depressed, the other apparently not, and it may be that this partner's feeling is part of the couple projective system; that is, that it exists in each of them and there is an unconscious agreement that one of them carries this difficult experience, a 'double dose of it'. But this is not always the case. This might be an example of an 'overvalued idea' that gets in the way of recognising the true clinical picture. If this is the case, it can make the couple, or one of them, feel very misunderstood, and if repeated too often, can make the couple feel that something rather mad is going on.

Timing of interpretations

Well-timed couple interpretations usually bring some relief and enable a shift from a blaming dynamic to more reflectiveness on what the couple is creating together – a temporary couple state of mind. However, sometimes the couple cannot move into this state of mind, they want to blame and hold onto the idea of the other at fault. A couple interpretation makes them feel misunderstood. Similarly, interpreting the projective system feels unhelpful, as there is a need to evacuate an unwanted or frightening part of the self. The couple isn't ready to reintroject something that is so split off that it feels alien and is probably part of the defensive structure of the relationship. When we think about the timing of an interpretation, we think about all the preparative work that goes before. In the case of projection, part of this is understanding the anxiety that leads to the projection. The projection needs to be understood by the therapist, felt by the therapist and worked through in the countertransference, mainly unconsciously. This takes time for the couple and the therapist. A question that sometimes is raised in clinical discussions is – what if the interpretation is right for one partner and not the other? Earlier on, I was talking about interpretation as a process and this is very relevant here. If we discover that an interpretation is helpful to one and not the other, this fact becomes part of the next interpretation: "I think 'X', you found this other perspective I offered quite helpful, but 'Y', I think it left you feeling unheard or misunderstood"; or if the interpretation is more shared, "I think you are both interested in the possibility of thinking about what is going on between you in this different way, but it's hard to stay with this as the pull towards your more familiar way of seeing the other as at fault is strong".

Interpretation is an imperfect and complex process. We all struggle to understand our patients and to communicate this understanding to them in a way that they can take in. Sometimes, for a long time, they can't take it in and we have to find different ways of keeping in contact with them. Sometimes we get interpretations right and sometimes we don't; in many therapies this is tolerated, in others it is not. There is a process, but not just a developing relationship between two people, as in individual therapy; rather, it is a triangular dynamic that lends itself to understanding through the many 'couples' in the room being at different times participant and observer, which helps the couple to develop a couple state of mind.

Note

1 A version of this chapter has previously been published as Morgan, M. (2018) Complex and creative: the field of couple interpretation. *fort da*, 24 (1), 6–21

Chapter 10

Endings and the aim of couple therapy

> The couple hopefully have come to a point at which they are able in the dynamics of their relationship to allow the other the kind of emotional freedom that either makes the continued loving presence of the other a gift, or allows the other to leave to form a new relationship. It is sometimes as clear as that – sometimes, but not often.
>
> (Fisher, 1999, p. 283)

Ending is a special issue in couple therapy. As with other forms of therapy, there is the question of the aim of the therapy and the ending of the therapy. In couple therapy, there is also very often the question in the minds of the couple from the beginning about whether the relationship can endure, whether the couple can, should or wish to stay together. This might make either member of the couple anxious that they will be left by their partner. The fear that couple therapy might result in the relationship ending can complicate the process of engaging in therapy. And, of course, although many couples stay together, sometimes ending the relationship *is* the outcome of couple therapy. There is also, as described above by Fisher, sometimes an emotional 'letting go' of the other – releasing the other from whom we need them to be, what we have imbued them with, and constrained them by, which might lead to separation, but equally might lead to a more psychic space and a more creative relationship. In this chapter, I will explore both the ending of therapy and the ending of the couple relationship.

Engagement, beginnings and premature endings – why some end before they've begun

At the point of the initial consultation and beginning of therapy, the future of the relationship and the idea of ongoing therapy are often intertwined in a complex way. Many couples come because they want to find a way to make the relationship work, to be understood better by each other, to re-find some lost and now longed-for part of the relationship, or to find their way through a crisis. Often there is the question in the couple's mind about whether or not the relationship should end. But even when there is a wish to end, this is rarely an easy decision; otherwise one imagines it would have already happened without the thought of seeking couple therapy. There is a lot at stake in ending a committed couple relationship. Perhaps there are children, or perhaps the relationship has endured for many years. Even in a relatively new relationship, a lot of hope for the future can have been invested. Deciding to go into couple therapy can be perceived by the members of the couple as a symbolic act. It is an acknowledgement that there are difficulties, but an investment in and a commitment to the relationship. For others, it might feel the beginning of the end, a process that will sooner or later result in the relationship ending. One partner may feel manipulated into coming and highly suspicious of the whole thing. These anxieties manifest in ambivalent states of mind in each partner, though within their projective system, each may carry one polarised set of feelings.

As described in Chapter Five, the transference to the therapist can be quite saturated at this point and this can be difficult for the therapist to navigate and contain. On the one hand, the therapist can be perceived as an unrealistic and idealised figure, an 'expert' to whom the couple can hand their relationship over, to hold together at a time when it seems to be falling apart. On the other hand, there are fears and anxieties about letting the therapist in at all, because of anxieties about being exposed and about loss of control. There are often hidden hostile feelings because the therapist is not wanted in the relationship, but is needed. The therapist as an idealised figure can quickly disappoint and the dawning reality of what therapy involves emotionally and practically, including the fact that it will take some time, may lead the couple to prematurely drop out. Although this may follow from a recognition that couple therapy is not right for them or not right for them now, at other times, it is because they are full of these kinds of anxieties and have not been held in this initial stage, which is in fact not always easy for the therapist to do.

When one or both partners say they want to end the relationship

Quite frequently, in the course of couple therapy, one or both of the partners say they want to end the relationship. Often this is said in the heat of the moment, expressing a sense of frustration or despair, or it is an attempt to have an impact on the other, a threat or coercion. In fact, many couples come into therapy in this way; as one husband put it, "I've come with a gun to my head". So, when it comes up in this way during the course of therapy, it is important that the therapist doesn't jump to the conclusion that the couple actually wants to end their relationship, but instead helps the couple think about what is being expressed. It may be a heightened expression of other emotions. "I feel so angry with you I can't bear to be in the same room with you", or "I feel so hopeless about our relationship it would be better if we just called it a day". In both of these exclamations, the wish to end the relationship is more about unmanageable anger or despair and this is what the couple wants understood.

The wish to separate might also be a need for more psychic separation, a need to create more psychic space within the relationship so that the couple can be both with and without each other. This might be what is being expressed when one partner says they want to end, but the other doesn't. In their projective system, one of them is holding onto the need for more separateness and the other to the need for more togetherness and intimacy, but actually, the balance between the two is what they are both struggling with. It might also be a transference communication to the therapist. In fact, when a couple expresses the wish to end the relationship, the therapist is often for a moment unclear about whether they mean the therapeutic relationship or the couple relationship.

Although it is important not to take the couple's expression of the wish to separate as a statement of fact, equally we have to be careful not to collude with couples in avoiding looking at one or both partners' wish actually to end their relationship. Sometimes one partner has decided to leave and can't bear the guilt or anxiety of doing so, so they want to leave their partner with the therapist. In this situation, there may be an ongoing affair, openly acknowledged or hidden. The affair, which may be the 'real' relationship for the partner who is having it, has a continuously undermining effect on the couple in the room. Even if there isn't another actual relationship, there is the fantasy of an 'other', whether this be a different partner, a different life or way of being, including being on one's own. The partner who has taken "emotional leave of absence" (Britton, 2003a, p. 175) may consciously or unconsciously unpick any progress made in the direction of healing the relationship. The other partner, who wishes to hold onto the relationship, exerts a different kind of pressure on the relationship and on the therapist. Any hint of the relationship being over is experienced as blasphemy. The therapist may feel under pressure to support the partner who does not want to be left or the one who is saying they want to leave. Some therapists, as discussed in Chapter Five, for their own unresolved reasons feel they should hold the couple together, they feel that the couple separating is a failure of the therapy. This is a complex issue in couple therapy, both in terms of understanding what kind of separation is needed, and also in terms of not being drawn into enacting something for the couple or for one of the partners.

In a previous paper (Morgan, 2016), I described this dilemma in relation to a particular couple.

The wife in one couple stated very clearly early in the therapy that she was leaving the relationship and wanting to set up home with the man with whom she was having an affair. But she was very anxious about leaving and felt paralysed. Her husband was completely unable to accept that the relationship was over, and she became unable to raise this possibility in any way that he would acknowledge. They kept coming week in and week out and not talking about this, and as the therapist I felt in a difficult position. If I brought up her stated wish to leave that now could not be spoken about, was I supporting her attempt to end the marriage? If I did not, was I supporting his attempt to maintain the status quo? Also I had to consider whether the difficulty in talking about ending was also the expression of an unconscious wish in both of them to continue the relationship.

(Morgan, 2016, p. 46; emphasis added)

When one partner leaves

With many couples, ending the relationship isn't a joint decision. In couple therapy, if one partner decides to leave, it either brings about the end of the couple's therapy or the focus changes radically from the understanding of the couple's intimate relationship to help in managing a separation. But the partner who has decided to leave the relationship may do so quite quickly as it feels too difficult continuing the sessions with the other, who perhaps cannot accept the decision. The needs of each partner might no longer be met in the intimate context of the couple therapy.

Clinical example: Bill and Janet

Bill and Janet had come into therapy because Bill had been having an affair with a younger work colleague, Cara. He said the affair was over, but Janet remained very distressed. She wanted Bill to get rid of the colleague and, if he couldn't, to leave his job. The therapy was difficult because Janet wanted to know every detail of the affair and Bill wanted to move on and not talk about it anymore. He felt they had already discussed it excessively. The therapist felt that giving up the affair had not been easy for Bill and he was privately mourning the loss. But he couldn't express this openly with Janet and became more and more withdrawn. This too increased Janet's distress as she felt anxious about where Bill was. After a few months, Bill announced he was still in love with Cara and he wanted to end the relationship with Janet. He couldn't bear to continue the sessions. He said, "I can't be what Janet wants me to be, nor can I be myself". Bill did continue for a few more sessions before leaving. Janet could not accept his decision and had unresolved feelings towards the therapist, whom she felt should have kept them together.

When this happens, it can be difficult for the therapist and the remaining partner who are both left, an 'abandoned couple', but now it is not clear how to carry on. In individual therapy, the loss of a significant relationship is a point at which the therapist is most needed. There are different views about how to proceed at this stage in the context of couple therapy. Most usually, a limited number of sessions are agreed on between the therapist and that partner to work towards the ending of the couple therapy. Part of this work may be consideration of and a referral for individual therapy. Sometimes the partner who has been left with the couple therapist wants to continue in individual therapy with the couple therapist. They make the case that the couple therapist knows them well, *they* haven't chosen to end their therapy and still feel in a therapeutic process with that therapist, and they have no wish to start again with someone else. And, as in the case above, Janet was left with a lot to work through with her therapist.

This is a complex issue that needs thought. Some couple therapists may work with individuals as well as couples and feel they could change the frame and proceed to individual work. I don't think this ever really becomes individual work, since the frame has been established as couple therapy and the therapist has worked with the patient's partner too. That partner will have a presence in the mind of the therapist, and her experience with and knowledge of that partner will have an impact on what she thinks, understands and interprets. Therefore, in most cases, the remaining partner is worked with towards an ending of the couple therapy and, if helpful, a referral for individual therapy. There may be situations in which there is a thought-through decision to continue with one partner, but in this case, I think that two facts remain. One is that this therapy remains a form of couple therapy, that is its history and how it was set up and will always be part of it. Second, if there is the decision to continue in this way, any future couple therapy – should the couple resume their relationship or indeed one of the partners start a new relationship that he or she wants help with – would not be possible. While I think in couple therapy that it is possible to manage the absence of one of the partners occasionally, it is not possible once this has occurred for an extended period of time. In such a situation, were the couple therapy to resume, the therapist's couple state of mind would be impossible to maintain.

Does the therapist ever tell the couple to separate?

Contrary to the beliefs of some couples, the couple therapist is not there to make a judgement about whether a relationship is viable or not. Sometimes couples put pressure on the therapist to give a view on this, which the therapist is unlikely to be drawn on. However, one of the difficult aspects of couple therapy can be witnessing the couple's destructive behaviour and the effect this has on them both, the relationship and family life, especially young children. Destructiveness takes many forms, and sometimes there is a turning point for the therapist in which she may feel she has been supporting a relationship which is too destructive – even inadvertently enabling it to continue only because of the glue the therapy provides. An important part of the work is addressing the couple's destructiveness when present, so that they can be more aware of it and the damage it causes. The couple may have lost all perspective on it or be very reluctant to face it, but with awareness and understanding of the dynamics behind it, they may be able to bring about changes. Clearly, if there are concerns about the safety – physical, emotional or sexual – of members of the couple or their children or other family members, this has to be addressed, even though it may mean the therapy ends.

When the relationship is already over

Some couples come for help when the relationship is already over, and there is no desire to give more life to it. The couple may feel they should attempt couple therapy because they want to tell themselves or others they have tried, but they don't actually want to stay together. They may not be able to face the fact that the relationship is over and need help in letting it go. When this is very much unacknowledged in the couple, the therapist can have a countertransference experience of feeling stuck, useless and not getting anywhere. This kind of countertransference is very often to do with resistance in the couple, and therefore has to be borne and understood. But it can also be to do with the fact that there is no conscious or unconscious cooperation in the couple. When the therapist starts to understand that this is what she is up against, or to put it another way, that this is the issue the couple is bringing, it is difficult to know what to do with it. The couple has communicated this to her unconsciously. They are coming to the therapy as if they are a couple wanting help with their relationship. Interpreting to the couple that this may not be the case may feel like a kind of assault on the couple, though if the interpretation is well timed, it may provide enormous relief, even if one or both partners are still holding onto the relationship. They are helped to relinquish the painful experience of continually trying to hold onto a present absence.

For others, the relationship being over is openly acknowledged and they want help to end the relationship in the best way possible. This can take some time, as the couple wants to understand what has happened and make sense of it. They want help in mourning the relationship they once had, which may have worked well for them at an earlier stage. Often, there were many good things about the relationship, but the relationship did not evolve with the changing needs of the partners. Some couples have a traumatic event to deal with, and this opens up a fault line that has always been present in the relationship and now cannot be ignored. If the couple can manage it, important work can be done at this stage in understanding and coming to terms with the ending of their relationship.

Unwanted endings

Sometimes the ending has to happen without anyone wanting it. The therapist has to stop work (for health, or age and retirement reasons), or because she is moving too far away, or the couple is no longer able to come for a variety of reasons. And, of course, sometimes the therapy has broken down and has to be brought to an end. Usually, if the therapist has to stop, there is some time to work with this, including the possibility of referring the couple to a colleague. This is also a point at which the therapist has to consider what to say to the couple in terms of what is happening in her life, balancing their need for some information with a wish not to burden them with too much information about the therapist's personal circumstances. Clearly, if the therapist is suffering ill health, this may already have been picked up by the couple and is being worked with. The most difficult situation is when the therapy has broken down. At Tavistock Relationships and in other clinical services, the couple who are allocated to a therapist may decide they want to see a different therapist. They may feel something has gone wrong in the therapy, or they don't like the therapist and are unable or unwilling to think about what this might mean. I remember once in co-therapy, the wife said she did not like the way my co-therapist looked at her. We tried to work with this, but it was such a paranoid anxiety and seemed impossible to contain in the room with four of us. We decided temporarily to meet in parallel single sessions, my co-therapist with the husband and me with the wife. Eventually, we were able to come back together. This is one of the advantages of co-therapy, but not possible with a single therapist. In a clinical service setting, if this situation feels impossible to manage, then it might be possible for the therapist who undertook the original assessment or another colleague to see the couple to try and understand the difficulty.

When is the right time to end? The aim of couple therapy

The aim of couple therapy is not prescriptive. The aim is not to help them stay together or achieve being a particular kind of couple. The couple may have an aim for themselves; for example, an increase in intimacy or better sex, the renewal of trust, better communication and increased understanding or less destructive arguments. Some writers have formulated criteria that help assess the couple's readiness to end. Fisher, for example, states:

> Ideally, we might think that when a couple come to a point when they can think together about their emotional experiences instead of trying to control the other through intrusive projections or emotional abandonment, they are also ready to be free of the therapy.
>
> (Fisher, 1999, p. 283)

Cachia and Savege Scharff (2014, p. 324) give a more extensive outline of criteria which I have summarised as:

- a capacity for concern for the other;
- an ability to recover from setbacks;
- some internal working through of 'unconscious blocks';
- a reduction in narcissism;
- a capacity to deal with separation;
- the withdrawal of projections and reintegration inside the self;
- better regulation of affect and sensitivity to partner's moods and feelings;
- increased containment of the self and containment in the relationship;
- more creative couple functioning;
- an establishment of a more creative internal couple – perhaps drawing on other internal couples as well as the internalised relationship to the therapist;
- a capacity to bear and mourn losses.

However, these authors conclude, "we feel most assured that the time for ending has come when we see that the analysing function of therapy has become installed" (Cachia & Savege Scharff, 2014, p. 325).

Colman takes it as inevitable that the partners in a relationship will project into each other and that "internal worlds are in continual interplay with the internal worlds of others via external relationships with those others" (1993a, p. 96). He considers that a functioning relationship is one in which

> there is sufficient alpha function to allow projections to be processed and made available for introjection. It is not one partner or the other who is doing this but both partners together as a function of the relationship that exists between them.
> (Colman, 1993a, p. 96)

Therefore, the aim of couple therapy "is to promote the capacity of marriage to function as a psychological container" (Colman, 1993a, p. 70). These ideas, though not identical, all highlight a development in a couple's state of mind as an aim of couple therapy. For Fisher, the aim is the couple being able to "think about their emotional experience" instead of managing it in other ways such as projection or withdrawal. For Cachia and Savege Scharff, the aim is that the "analysing function of therapy has [to] become installed" in the couple; and for Colman, the relationship needs to function better as a "psychological container" within which mutual projections can be processed. All these writers are in touch with how important this change in a *state of mind* within the couple is, and that whatever other developments the couple is able to make, this is what is crucial.

The introjection of a couple state of mind as the aim of couple therapy

I would put the aim of couple therapy in the following way. The couple state of mind, missing in the couple when they come for help, is provided by the couple therapist as a function of the therapist and gradually internalised by the couple over the course of the therapy. The couple state of mind becomes the third position in the couple relationship which for most couples coming for help was missing, either temporarily, or because it has not been sufficiently, or at all, developed. The couple unconsciously seeks this in the figure of a therapist who can take a third position in relation to them as a couple. That is what the couple therapist does, she speaks to the couple from a third position about their relationship. The couple relationship itself symbolically stands for the couple state of mind for the two members of the couple. In other words, when they turn to the relationship in their minds, they can move from the subjective position of their own thoughts and feelings in relation to the partner, to a more objective position in which they can observe the relationship and what they are creating together. The couple will inevitably still have difficulties, disappointments and challenges, but with a couple state of mind, they can see these in the context of their relationship. For some couples, as described in Chapter Eight, a further development takes place which I have described as a creative couple state of mind, in which the couple not only achieves a perspective on their relationship, as in the couple state of mind, but increases the capacity to think together, in a way that they could not do, each on their own. This capacity in the couple is also an individual development, as the experience of being a creative couple in the *relationship* becomes an internal capacity, an 'internal creative couple' in the *individual*.

In couple therapy that is going well, an alive sense of the ending of the therapy is present somewhere in the minds of the couple and the therapist. The couple often thinks about it around the time of breaks, pausing before the long summer break to think about where they are in the therapy. The therapist may do the same thing, but also does something else. The therapist notices the development of a couple state of mind. Are the partners in the couple able to think about what is going on between them and how they both contribute to that? Instead of coming to the session and reporting an argument, and maybe continuing or recreating the argument in the session, expecting the therapist to be able to think about it and help them understand it, the couple has already done it. They report the argument but also their reflection on it. In other words, the couple develops a capacity to think about what is happening to them, what they may be creating together, and moving away from the idea that one of them is to blame.

The therapist notices these developments in the couple and when this capacity is in evidence, it is important to acknowledge it. Eventually this capacity feels more or less secure. I say 'more or less', because in reality, the capacity to use a couple state of mind comes and goes, but it is nonetheless installed in the psyche of the couple. Once it is internalised, the therapist may feel that the couple does not need her in the same way, and that she can start to imagine an exit from their relationship. This capacity to use a couple state of mind is an indication of development in the couple and is an indication that the couple is progressing towards ending. It may not be for a while, it could be in a year or more, but as long as the couple sustains this, an ending is in sight. The mourning of the loss of the analyst, as Steiner (1996) has pointed out, is an important part of the internalisation of what the analyst has held for the patient. This capacity is the equivalent of what in individual work is a self-analytic function that continues after an analysis has ended; it is the couple analytic function.

Problems in the introjection of a couple state of mind

In a previous paper (Morgan, 2016), I contrasted two couples. For one, the ending of therapy arose in a natural way and there was a thoughtful ending process. For the other, the ending of the therapy was never brought up by the couple and rarely by the therapist, for whom the experience with the couple felt never ending. These contrasting clinical situations illustrate both a psychic development in the couple which enables a successful ending and what might be the impediment to a couple and their therapist, in feeling they can end.

The couple that felt 'never ending', a couple I called Ralph and Suzy, I described in the following way:

> As long as the therapy went on, I could be attuned to each of them, but neither had to be attuned to the other. Thus, the only way there could be a third position in the relationship, a couple state of mind, was if I occupied that position.
>
> (Morgan, 2016, p. 56)

I enjoyed working with this couple and the work went on for several years. Perhaps this was a lot to do with the fact that they were able to use my couple state of mind; thus, I could help them, they felt understood by me and sometimes, with my help, they could understand what was happening between them. However, it did not feel that they were *internalising* a couple state of mind themselves. And without being able to do that, it was hard to see how the therapy would end. The therapy did eventually end, though not in a satisfactory way. The husband was required by his employer at quite short notice to relocate to a different country. There was unfortunately a shortened period of time to end, and I was left wondering how much of our work together had been internalised, particularly how much of a couple state of mind.

This also raised questions in my mind about whether the fact of not really being able to talk about ending with this couple was largely driven by countertransference and hindered the internalisation of a couple state of mind. As I said, in that paper,

> When ending never gets thought about, or only in the sense of feeling one will never be able to end, then one has to wonder whether the couple and therapist are stuck together in an enactment of a phantasy in which therapy can go on forever.
>
> (Morgan, 2016, p. 57)

But what is this and why? The therapist as a more concrete entity has become part of the couple's relationship. In the sessions with the therapist present, there *is* a couple state of mind, but it does not continue outside this context. It is experienced by the couple *in the therapist*, but there is no development of this capacity *in the couple*.

I have found two ideas that I think address this in some way. The first is in the work of Steiner (1996) who underscores the mourning required in the process of reintrojection; and the other is from the work of Bleger, translated by Bleger and Churcher (1967/2013), helpfully elaborated by Churcher (2005) and Churcher and Bleger (1967/2013), which throws light on the deep meaning of the setting, what is contained there and what can stay lodged there.

The re-acquisition of projected parts of the self (Steiner, 1996)

Steiner suggests that there are two stages involved in "the re-acquisition of projected parts of the self" (1996, p. 1076):

> In the first stage the patient internalises an object containing parts of the self still inextricably bound to it, and the loss of the object during actual separations is denied by a phantasy of omnipotent possession of it. The relief from anxiety comes from a sense of being understood by the analyst and relies on the analyst's authority. Understanding as opposed to being understood has to arise from within and depends on a capacity to think and judge for oneself, so that it involves a relinquishment of a dependence on the views and judgements of authority figures, including the analyst.
>
> (Steiner, 1996, p. 1076)

In the second phase, "the reality of dependence on the object has to be acknowledged and then the reality of the loss of the object has to be faced in order for mourning to be worked through, and both are often vehemently resisted" (Steiner, 1996, p. 1077).

For part of any couple therapy, the couple state of mind and the therapist are felt as one and the same thing. While the process of introjection takes time for any couple, for some couples, it seems that the psychic shift required for introjecting the couple state of mind into the relationship is too difficult. Steiner suggests that the process of reintrojecting parts of the self that have been contained by the analyst is difficult because it involves separating from and therefore mourning the loss of the analyst. This is an important idea in thinking about the problem of reintrojecton within the projective system of the couple – the difficulty in giving the other their freedom from the projections we have needed them to carry, as described by Fisher earlier in this chapter. Here I am drawing on this idea to think about the problem in being able to separate from the therapist, and through that process, reintroject an aspect of the couple, a couple state of mind.

However, reintrojecting a couple state of mind might only be an accurate description for those couples who have temporarily lost it and then re-found it in the therapist. As I have been describing in this book, many couples have never developed this capacity and it appears initially in the therapist and develops within the couple in the process of therapy. For some couples, this newly developed capacity, which could be introjected into their relationship, is resisted. I think this might link each of them to the painfulness of making this psychic development, which involves the loss of the previous, more infantile, states as well as the loss of the therapist. Sometimes, therapists with couples who cannot end describe a comfortable kind of countertransference in which no one wants to end. In the light of the ideas above, we might think of this as a therapeutic collusion in which the therapist joins the couple in avoiding the loss and supports the couple's resistance against making this psychic development.

What Steiner is pointing out is that containment is not enough; the containing object has to be relinquished. In this process, as Freud (1917) showed so beautifully in his paper "Mourning and Melancholia", the lost object, or in my terms here, the therapist representing 'the couple state of mind', becomes set up inside the self. This has also been described eloquently by Meltzer, and cited by Fisher in *The Uninvited Guest* (1999, p. 278): "When an object can be given its freedom to come and go as it will, the moment of experience of relationship with that object can be introjected" (Meltzer, 1978, p. 468).

Symbiosis and the setting (Bleger)

We know the setting, as discussed in Chapter Three, to be important, but perhaps we have not been able to articulate to ourselves quite why it is so important at a deeper level, even though we feel it, and know it, in our analytic selves. Churcher (2005) points to the fact that there is a surprising paucity of literature on the psychoanalytic setting, though it is an area that has been interestingly elaborated by the Argentinian analyst José Bleger. Bleger suggests that it is in the setting that the symbiosis (that exists in all of us) or, what Bion (1967c) described as the psychotic part of the personality, can take refuge. Churcher describes Bleger's symbiotic position as follows:

> [P]rior to the paranoid-schizoid position as described by Melanie Klein, there is a position which he called the 'glischro-caric' (from the Greek words *glischros*, meaning 'sticky', or 'viscous', and *karion*, meaning 'nut' or 'nucleus'). The characteristic anxiety of this position is confusional rather than persecutory, and the object relation is one of symbiosis with a primitive 'agglutinated nucleus'.
>
> (Churcher, 2005, p. 4)

This is similar to Ogden's 'autistic-contiguous' position (1989), put forward by him many years later and taken up by Keogh and Enfield in relation to couples, "where the self and other are experienced in a sensory mode and the self tends to merge with its object" (2013, p. 31). The couple they discuss, who are at this earlier developmental stage, are described in the following way:

> Our couple had a regression point that involved primitive states of mind, wherein the sense of a bounded self with a psychic skin, was not developed. When their tenuous psychic equilibrium was disturbed, they collapsed into a state of primitive anxieties: the autistic-contiguous mode of functioning.
>
> (Keogh & Enfield, 2013, p. 44)

Bleger argues that "the patient's setting is his most primitive fusion with the mother's body and that the psychoanalyst's setting must serve to re-establish the original symbiosis but *only* in order to change it" (1967/2013, p. 240). The working through of this symbiotic part of the self is often missed because it is contained in the setting.

> The normal, silent, continuous, background presence of the setting thus furnishes the patient with an opportunity for repeating the original symbiosis of the infant with the mother. The psychotic part of the patient's personality, the undifferentiated and unresolved part of the primitive symbiotic relationship, is deposited in the setting, where it silently persists as a 'phantom world', undetected but nonetheless psychically real.
>
> (Churcher & Bleger, 1967/2013, pp. xxix–xxx)

Bleger differentiates the setting (non-process) from the analytic work (process), but says that at some point, what is going on in the non-process needs analysing too. However, it may be missed as it is hidden in the setting or it can function as a kind of psychic retreat (Steiner, 1993b) in which this part of the self remains.

Bleger also discusses the symbiosis operating in external relationships where "we observe a crossed projective identification in which each depository acts according to complementary roles of the other, and vice versa" (Churcher & Bleger, 1967/2013, p. 32). It is both heartening and interesting to see that this understanding, of what at Tavistock Relationships we would call the 'couple's projective system', has arisen completely independently in another scientific community. His use of the term 'symbiotic' is perhaps particularly close to the idea of projective gridlock in which the projective system leads to symbiotic relating and confusional states. As I described previously, such couples

> have great anxieties about either allowing the other a separate psychic existence and/or in being able to feel psychically separate in the relationship. They often describe a feeling of there only being one person in the relationship or a feeling of confusion between them about who thinks and feels what.
>
> (Morgan, 1995, p. 34)

One of the things those working with couples discover, sooner or later, is how much disturbance and regression can be ignited in an intimate adult couple relationship. The confusion, emotional dysregulation and primitive behaviour that can form part of a couple therapy session, sometimes week in and week out, can come as quite a shock. Particularly as the couple reports that in their lives outside the sessions it is not so bad. Having said this, sometimes it is as bad, but there are couples who seem to function reasonably well in their ordinary outside life – sometimes as extremely competent and responsible professionals – and yet the inside of the relationship which is brought to the therapy is something quite different. Having experienced this many times, I have come to think that, although it is true that the intimate adult couple relationship provides for regression with the opportunity for development and working through, for some, the regression becomes lodged unhelpfully in the couple relationship. This is brought to the therapy, sometimes in the tangible way expressed above. But I think what Bleger helps us see is that this is not always so obvious and may be missed. Thus, while Steiner (1996) is addressing the problem of the re-acquisition of parts of the self that have been contained by the analyst because it involves separating from the analyst, Bleger's contribution helps us consider that the couple may not be able to end because they are not psychically separate either from each other or from the therapist. In the couple's mind, the therapist may feel installed in their relationship, part of the relationship, as described earlier with Ralph and Suzy. The degree of symbiosis in any particular couple will vary, perhaps quite considerably, but I think always needs to be considered when there is a difficulty in feeling that the couple therapy could end, because it might be that the symbiosis, unworked through, is lodged in the therapeutic relationship.

How to think about a planned ending of therapy?

In a planned ending, the decision to end the therapy will take place over several weeks or months. It is really important to take time to get this right. There can easily be some enactment in the decision to end. It might be led by the couple who after several 'good' sessions take a flight into health. The therapist who is finding the work difficult with a couple might jump at the couple's suggestion of ending, when really the issue coming up is more to do with a sense of despair and stuckness which first needs understanding. It might lead to a decision to end if it feels no further work is possible, but it might also lead to further understanding of what feels so stuck and a sense that further work is possible.

Once the decision to end has been thought through, including when the ending will be, some time needs to be given to the ending phase. It can also help to make the decision following a break, which can help the couple connect to the experience of the therapist no longer being there. Ending at the time of a break can also work well, with an uninterrupted period leading up to the final break.

What happens in the final phase

During the ending phase, there is the chance to review what has happened in the therapy, what has changed, what has not changed and thoughts about going forward. Sometimes new things spontaneously arise as there is some added freedom in the thought of ending. This can be good, though there will need to be the recognition that limited time can be spent on what is new – it will be taken forward by the couple themselves. It is also important to talk about the actual ending and what it means to the couple. It may evoke other unresolved endings, anxiety, disappointment and positive feelings. The couple does have some experiences of ending – through the end of each session and the holiday breaks.

Often there is a regression in the couple during this phase, but it is usually temporary, although, in the therapist and couple, it can cause anxiety that it is a mistake to end. The couple sometimes avoids talking about ending and, surprisingly, therapists also report that this can get lost in the ending phase. This may be unconsciously avoided by both the therapist and the couple. But as I described earlier, the process of separation, mourning, introjection and giving up the unconscious symbiosis with the therapist is essential to the work.

The final session

The final session can be an emotional experience for the couple and the therapist. And it can be difficult working within the frame of the final session, to make it meaningful without opening up something that cannot be dealt with within the session. It can be hard to keep in mind that this *is* the final session and to properly acknowledge this. Some couples do so by bringing a gift for the therapist; it is sometimes important to the couple to find a tangible way of expressing their appreciation and marking the ending. Sometimes the couple wants to leave something of themselves behind, some kind of object left in the therapist's consulting room, a permanent reminder of them. This usually cannot be fully analysed in the constraints of the last session and it could be argued that it should not be and just needs to be acknowledged. Sometimes the ending is avoided by the couple and the session feels like any other session. The therapist is then left to keep the ending in mind and frame her interpretations within this context. During the final phase of the work or in the last session, the couple may ask if they can come back if they need to in the future. Unless the therapist is retiring or moving a long way away, the couple probably already knows that if a crisis arose and they needed further help, the therapist would respond if she could.

Some endings are more unsatisfactory. Perhaps one partner has already exited, or wants to end the therapy while the other does not. It might be that the couple's development has not gone at the same rate, one ready to end and the other not. It might mean that one or both partners will be continuing or beginning individual therapy with other therapists. Perhaps the work has not gone well, or the outcome of the therapy has been difficult, the couple deciding to separate or stay together facing disappointments in their relationship. The therapist may have brought the therapy to an end, due to personal circumstances that make it impossible to continue, occasionally because she feels she can't work with the couple, or that the therapy is doing more harm than good. In these circumstances, the final session can be very challenging. The couple may be angry or blaming of the therapist and there may not have been time to work through much of this in previous sessions so that a lot of feelings erupt in the final session. With the time constraints, perhaps the main thing that can be done is that the couple feels heard and the therapist doesn't become too defensive or caught up with the couple in something that cannot be resolved.

Those therapists new to the work sometimes get anxious about the final moments, how to say goodbye. There are no rules about this, but the therapist usually develops as part of her normal practice some procedure that feels appropriate to her; for example, shaking each partner's hand and wishing them well. This would be different as the therapist would not expect to have physical contact during the therapy or be wishing the couple well, and in this way, it marks a difference captured in this moment.

References

Abse, S. (2009). Sexual dread and the therapist's desire. In: C. Clulow (Ed.), *Sex, Attachment and Couple Psychotherapy: Psychoanalytic Perspectives* (pp. 103–118). London: Karnac.

Alperovitz, S. (2005). Learning to call the game: Some lessons from infant observation for the couple therapist. In: *Psychoanalytic Perspectives on Couple Work, 2005*: 9–18.

Aznar-Martínez, B., Pérez-Testor, C., Davins, M. & Aramburu, I. (2016). Couple psychoanalytic psychotherapy as the treatment of choice: Indications, challenges and benefits. *Psychoanalytic Psychology, 33* (1): 1–20.

Balfour, A. (2009). Intimacy and sexuality in later life. In: C. Clulow (Ed.), *Sex, Attachment and Couple Psychotherapy: Psychoanalytic Perspectives* (pp. 217–236). London: Karnac.

Balfour, A. (2016). Transference and enactment in the "Oedipal setting" of couple psychotherapy. In: A. Novakovic (Ed.), *Couple Dynamics: Psychoanalytic Perspectives in Work with the Individual, the Couple, and the Group* (pp. 59–84). London: Karnac.

Balint. E. (1993). Unconscious communication between husbands and wives. In: S. Ruszczynski (Ed.), *Psychotherapy with Couples: Theory and Practice at the Tavistock Institute of Marital Studies* (pp. 30–43). London: Karnac.

Bannister, K. & Pincus, L. (1965). *Shared Phantasy in Marital Problems: Therapy in a Four-person Relationship*. London: Institute of Marital Studies.

Baranger, M. & Baranger, W. (2008). The analytic situation as a dynamic field. *International Journal of Psycho-Analysis, 89*(4): 795–826.

Berenstein, I. (2012). Vínculo as a relationship between others. *Psychoanalytic Quarterly, 81* (3): 565–577.

Bianchini, B. & Dallanegra, L. (2011). Reflections on the Container–Contained Model in couple psychoanalytic psychotherapy. *Couple and Family Psychoanalysis, 1* (1): 69–80.

Bion, W. R. (1959). Attacks on linking. *International Journal of Psycho-Analysis, 40*: 308–315.

Bion, W. R. (1961). *Experiences in Groups and Other Papers*. London: Karnac.

Bion, W. R. (1962). *Learning from Experience*. London: Karnac.

Bion, W. R. (1963). *Elements of Psycho-Analysis*. London: Heinemann.

Bion, W. R. (1966/2014). Catastrophic change. Published (1966) in *The Bulletin of the British Psychoanalytical Society*, 5; reprinted (2014) in: C. Mawson (Ed.), *The Complete Works of W. R. Bion*, Vol. VI. London: Karnac Books.

Bion, W. R. (1967a). A theory of thinking. In: W. R. Bion, *Second Thoughts* (Chapter 9; pp. 110–119). London: Karnac.

Bion, W. R. (1967b). Commentary: A theory of thinking. In: W. R. Bion, *Second Thoughts* (Chapter 10; pp. 120–166). London: Karnac.

Bion, W. R. (1967c). The differentiation of the psychotic from the non-psychotic personalities. In: W. R. Bion, *Second Thoughts* (Chapter 5). London: Karnac.

Bion, W. R. (1970). *Attention and Interpretation: A Scientific Approach to Insight in Psycho-Analysis and Groups*. London: Tavistock.

Birksted-Breen, D. (1996). Phallus, penis and mental space. *International Journal of Psycho-Analysis*, 77: 649–657.

Blair, L. (2018). Intimate sex and sexual dysfunction: The role of the third space and a couple state of mind. *Journal des Psychologies, March*. At: www.jdpsychologues.fr/article/relations-sexuelles-intimes-et-dysfonctionnement-le-role-de-l-space-tiers-et-du-couple

Bleger, J. (1967/2013). *Symbiosis and Ambiguity. A Psychoanalytic Study*. Edited by J. Churcher & L. Bleger. London & New York: Routledge.

Bollas, C. (1987). *The Shadow of the Object: Psychoanalysis of the Unthought Known*. London: Free Association Books.

Bolognini, S. (2008). *Passaggi segreti. Teoria e technica della relazione interpsichica*. Turin: Bollati Boringheieri.

Bott Spillius, E., Milton, J., Garvey, P., Couve, C. & Steiner, D. (2011). *The New Dictionary of Kleinian Thought*. London & New York: Routledge.

Bowlby, J. (1969). *Attachment and Loss: Volume I: Attachment*. The International Psycho-Analytical Library, Vol. 79 (pp. 1–401). London: Hogarth Press and the Institute of Psycho-Analysis.

Britton, R. (1989). The missing link: Parental sexuality in the Oedipus Complex. In: J. Steiner (Ed.), *The Oedipus Complex Today: Clinical Implications* (pp. 83–101). London: Karnac.

Britton, R. (1998a). Belief and psychic reality. In: R. Britton, *Belief and Imagination: Explorations in Psychoanalysis* (pp. 8–18). London: Routledge.

Britton, R. (1998b). Subjectivity, objectivity and triangular space. In: R. Britton, *Belief and Imagination: Explorations in Psychoanalysis* (pp. 41–58). London: Routledge.

Britton, R. (1998c). *Belief and Imagination. Explorations in Psychoanalysis*. London: Routledge.

Britton, R. (1998d). Before and after the depressive position Ps (n) → D (n) → Ps (n +1). In: R. Britton, *Belief and Imagination. Explorations in Psychoanalysis* (pp. 69–81). London: Routledge.

Britton, R. (2003a). Narcissistic problems in sharing space. In: R. Britton, *Sex, Death, and the Superego: Experiences in Psychoanalysis* (pp. 165–178). London: Karnac.

Britton, R. (2003b). *Sex, Death and the Superego: Experiences in Psychoanalysis*. London: Karnac.

Britton, R. & Steiner, J. (1994). Interpretation: Selected fact or overvalued idea? *International Journal of PsychoAnalysis*, 75(5–6): 1069–1078.

Brookes, S. (1991). Bion's concept of containment in marital work. *Journal of Social Work Practice*, 5(2): 133–141.

Buss-Twachtmann, C. & Brookes, S. (1998). Marital typology. *Society for Couple Psychoanalytic Psychotherapy Bulletin*, 5 (May): 4–9.

Cachia, P. & Savege Scharff, J. (2014). The ending of couple therapy with a couple who recovered joy. In: D. E. Scharff & J. Savege Scharff (Eds.), *Psychoanalytic Couple Therapy: Foundations of Theory and Practice* (pp. 323–334). London: Karnac.

Caruso, N. J. (2014). Sexual desire disorder: A case study from a dynamic perspective. *Couple and Family Psychoanalysis*, 4(2): 166–185.

Churcher, J. (2005). Keeping the psychoanalytic setting in mind. Paper given to the Annual Conference of Lancaster Psychotherapy Clinic in collaboration with the Tavistock Clinic, at St Martin's College, Lancaster, 9 September 2005. An earlier version was given to the Fourteenth Annual General Meeting of the Hallam Institute for Psychotherapy, Sheffield, 8 May 2004. Available at: www.academia.edu/4527520/

Churcher, C. & Bleger, L. (Eds.) (1967/2013). Editorial introduction. In: J. Bleger, *Symbiosis and Ambiguity. A Psychoanalytic Study* (pp. xvii–xlv). London & New York: Routledge.

Cleavely, E. (1993). Relationships: Interaction, defences, and transformation. In: S. Ruszczynski (Ed.), *Psychotherapy with Couples: Theory and Practice at the Tavistock Institute of Marital Studies* (pp. 55–69). London: Karnac.

Clulow, C. & Boerma, M. (2009). Dynamics and disorders of sexual desire. In: C. Clulow (Ed.), *Sex, Attachment and Couple Psychotherapy: Psychoanalytic Perspectives* (pp. 75–101). London: Karnac.

Clulow, C., Dearnley, B. & Balfour, F. (1986). Shared phantasy and therapeutic structure in a brief marital psychotherapy. *The British Journal of Psychotherapy*, 3 (2): 124–132.

Cohen, L. (1992). Anthem, *The Future*. New York: Columbia Records.

Colman, W. (1993a). Marriage as a psychological container. In: S. Ruszczynski (Ed.), *Psychotherapy with Couples: Theory and Practice at the Tavistock Institute of Marital Studies* (pp. 70–96). London: Karnac.

Colman, W. (1993b). The individual and the couple. In: S. Ruszczynski, (Ed.), *Psychotherapy with Couples: Theory and Practice at the Tavistock Institute of Marital Studies* (pp. 126–141). London: Karnac.

Colman, W. (2005/2014). The intolerable other: The difficulty in becoming a couple. *Couple and Family Psychoanalysis*, 4 (1): 22–41. (Previously published [2005] without the author's "Afterword" in *Psychoanalytic Perspectives on Couple Work*, 1: 56–71.)

Cowan, C. P., Cowan, P. A., & Heming, G. (2005). Two variations of a preventive intervention for couples: Effects on parents and children curing the transition to school. In: P. A. Cowan, C. P. Cowan, J. C. Ablow, V. K. Johnson & J R. Measelle (Eds.), *The Family Context of Parenting in Children's Adaptation to Elementary School* (pp. 277–312). Monographs in Parenting series. Mahwah, NJ: Lawrence Erlbaum Associates Publishers.

Cudmore, L. & Judd, D. (2001). Thoughts about the couple relationship following the death of a child. In: F. Grier (Ed.), *Brief Encounters with Couples: Some Analytical Perspectives* (pp. 33–53). London: Karnac.

Dearnley, B. (1990). Changing marriage. In: C. Clulow, *Marriage: Disillusion and Hope. Papers Celebrating Forty Years of the Tavistock Institute of Marital Studies*. London: Karnac.

de Botton, A. (2016). Why you will marry the wrong person. (Online) *The New York Times*, May 28 2016. At: www.nytimes.com/2016/05/29/opinion/sunday/why-you-will-marry-the-wrong-person.html?mcubz=3

Dicks, H. V. (1967). *Marital Tensions. Clinical Studies towards a Psychological Theory of Interaction*. London: Karnac. (Reprinted 1993.)

Downey, J. I. & Friedman, R. C. (1995). Internalised homophobia in lesbian relationships. *Journal of the American Academy of Psychoanalysis*, 23 (3): 435–447.

Evans, C., Mellor-Clark, J., Margison, F., Barkham, M., Audin, K., Connell, J. & McGrath, G. (2000). CORE: Clinical Outcomes in Routine Evaluation. *Journal of Mental Health*, 9(3): 247–255.

Ezriel, H. (1972). Experimentation within the psychoanalytic session. *Contemporary Psychoanalysis*, 8 (2): 229–245.

Fairbairn, W. D. (1952). Object-relationships and dynamic structure. In: *Psychoanalytic Studies of the Personality* (Chapter V; pp. 1–297). London: Tavistock Publications Limited. (Chapter originally published 1946.)

Feldman, T. (2014). From container to claustrum: Projective identification in couples. *Couple and Family Psychoanalysis*, 4 (2): 136–154.

Fisher, J. (1993). The impenetrable other: Ambivalence and the Oedipal conflict in work with couples. In: S. Ruszczynski (Ed.), *Psychotherapy with Couples: Theory and Practice at the Tavistock Institute of Marital Studies* (pp. 142–166). London: Karnac.

Fisher, J. (1999). *The Uninvited Guest. Emerging from Narcissism towards Marriage.* London: Karnac.

Fisher, J. (2006). The emotional experience of K. *International Journal of PsychoAnalysis*, 87: 1221–1237.

Fisher, J. V. (2009). Macbeth in the consulting room: Proleptic imagination and the couple. *fort da*, 15 (2): 33–55. Reprinted (2017) as "The Macbeths in the consulting room" in: S. Nathans & M. Schaefer (Eds.), *Couples on the Couch. Psychoanalytic Couple Therapy and the Tavistock Model* (pp. 90–112). Abingdon & New York: Routledge.

Fonagy, P. (2008). A genuinely developmental theory of sexual enjoyment and its implications for psychoanalytic technique. *Journal of the American Psychoanalytic Association*, 56(1): 11–36.

Fonagy, P. & Bateman, A. (2006). Mechanisms of change in mentalization-based treatment of BPD. *Journal of Clinical Psychology*, 62 (4): 411–430.

Freud, S. (1911). Formulations on the two principles of mental functioning. In: *The Standard Edition of the Complete Psychological Works of Sigmund Freud, Volume XII (1911–1913): The Case of Schreber, Papers on Technique and Other Works* (pp. 213–226). London: Hogarth Press.

Freud, S. (1912a). The dynamics of transference. In: *The Standard Edition of the Complete Psychological Works of Sigmund Freud, Volume XII (1911–1913): The Case of Schreber, Papers on Technique and Other Works* (pp. 97–108). London: Hogarth Press.

Freud, S. (1912b). Recommendations to physicians practising psycho-analysis. In: *The Standard Edition of the Complete Psychological Works of Sigmund Freud, Volume XII (1911–1913): The Case of Schreber, Papers on Technique and Other Works* (pp. 109–120). London: Hogarth Press.

Freud, S. (1913). On beginning the treatment (further recommendations on the technique of psycho-analysis I). In: *The Standard Edition of the Complete Psychological Works of Sigmund Freud, Volume XII (1911–1913): The Case of Schreber, Papers on Technique and Other Works* (pp. 121–144). London: Hogarth Press.

Freud, S. (1914). Remembering, repeating and working-through (further recommendations on the technique of psycho-analysis II). In: *The Standard Edition of the Complete Psychological Works of Sigmund Freud, Volume XII (1911–1913): The Case of Schreber, Papers on Technique and Other Works* (pp. 145–156). London: Hogarth Press.

Freud, S. (1916–1917). The paths to the formation of symptoms. Lecture 23. In: *The Standard Edition of the Complete Psychological Works of Sigmund Freud, Volume XVI (1916–1917: Introductory Lectures on Psycho-Analysis (Part III)* (pp. 358–372). London: Hogarth Press.

Freud, S. (1917). Mourning and melancholia. In: *The Standard Edition of the Complete Psychological Works of Sigmund Freud, Volume XIV (1914–1916): On the History of the Psycho-Analytic Movement, Papers on Metapsychology and Other Works* (pp. 237–258). London: Hogarth Press.

Freud, S. (1919). "A child is being beaten": A contribution to the study of the origin of sexual perversions. In: *The Standard Edition of the Complete Psychological Works of Sigmund Freud, Volume XVII (1917–1919): An Infantile Neurosis and Other Works* (pp. 175–204). London: Hogarth Press.

Freud, S. (1920). Beyond the pleasure principle. In: *The Standard Edition of the Complete Psychological Works of Sigmund Freud, Volume XVIII (1920–1922): Beyond the Pleasure Principle, Group Psychology and Other Works* (pp. 1–64). London: Hogarth Press.

Freud, S. (1923). The ego and the id. *The Standard Edition of the Complete Psychological Works of Sigmund Freud, Volume XIX (1923–1925): The Ego and the Id and Other Works* (pp. 1–66). London: Hogarth Press.

Friend, J. (2013). Love as a creative illusion and its place in psychoanalytic couple psychotherapy. *Couple and Family Psychoanalysis, 3* (1): 3–14.

Frost, D. M. & Meyer, I. H. (2009). Internalised homophobia and relationship quality among lesbians, gay men, and bisexuals. *Journal of Counseling Psychology, 56* (1): 97–109.

Garelick, A. (1994). Psychotherapy assessment, theory and practice. *Psychoanalytic Psychotherapy, 8*(2): 101–106.

Gill, H. & Temperley, J. (1974). Time-limited marital treatment in a foursome. *British Journal of Medical Psychology, 47* (2): 153–161.

Glasser, M. (1979). Some aspects of the role of aggression in the perversions. In: I. Rosen (Ed.), *Sexual Deviations* (pp. 278–305). Oxford: Oxford University Press.

Grier, R. (Ed.) (2001). *Brief Encounters with Couples. Some Analytical Perspectives*. London: Karnac.

Grier, F. (Ed.) (2005a). *Oedipus and the Couple*. London: Karnac.

Grier, F. (2005b). No sex couples, catastrophic change, and the primal scene. In: F. Grier (Ed.), *Oedipus and the Couple* (pp. 201–219). London: Karnac.

Grier, F. (2009). Lively and deathly intercourse. In C. Clulow (Ed.), *Sex, Attachment and Couple Psychotherapy: Psychoanalytic Perspectives* (pp. 45–61). London: Karnac.

Harold, G. T. & Leve, L. D. (2012). Parents as partners: How the parental relationship affects children's psychological development. In: A. Balfour, M. Morgan & C. Vincent (Eds.), *How Couple Relationships Shape our World: Clinical Practice, Research and Policy Perspectives*. London: Karnac.

Heimann, P. (1950). On counter-transference. *International Journal of Psycho-Analysis, 31*: 81–84.

Hertzmann, L. (2011). Lesbian and gay couple relationships: When internalised homophobia gets in the way of couple creativity. *Psychoanalytic Psychotherapy, 25* (4): 346–360.

Hertzmann, L. (2018). Losing the internal Oedipal mother and loss of sexual desire. *Journal of Psychotherapy, 34*(1): 25–45. doi: 10.1111/bjp.12343

Hewison, D. (2009). Power vs. love in sadomasochistic relationships. In: C. Clulow (Ed.), *Sex, Attachment and Couple Psychotherapy: Psychoanalytic Perspectives* (pp. 165–184). London: Karnac.

Hewison, D. (2014a). Projection, introjection, intrusive identification, adhesive identification. In: D. E. Scharff & J. Savege Scharff (Eds.), *Psychoanalytic Couple Therapy: Foundations of Theory and Practice* (pp. 158–169). London: Karnac.

Hewison, D. (2014b). Shared unconscious phantasy in couples. In: D. E. Scharff & J. Savege Scharff (Eds.), *Psychoanalytic Couple Therapy: Foundations of Theory and Practice* (pp. 25–34). London: Karnac.

Hewison, D., Casey, P. & Mwamba, N. (2016). The effectiveness of couple therapy: Clinical outcomes in a naturalistic United Kingdom setting. *Psychotherapy, 53*(4): 377–387.

Hewison, D., Clulow, C. & Drake, H. (2014). *Couple Therapy for Depression. A Clinician's Guide to Integrative Practice*. Oxford: Oxford University Press.

Hobson, R. P. (2016). Self-representing events in the transference. Paper presented at the Scientific Meeting of the San Francisco Center for Psychoanalysis, June.

Humphries, J. (2015). Working in the presence of unconscious couple beliefs. *Couple and Family Psychoanalysis, 5* (1): 25–40.

Humphries, J. & McCann, D. (2015). Couple psychoanalytic psychotherapy with violent couples: Understanding and working with domestic violence. *Couple and Family Psychoanalysis*, 5 (2): 149–167.

Ibsen, H. (1996). *A Doll's House*. London: Faber & Faber.

Isaacs, S. (1948). The nature and function of phantasy. *International Journal of Psycho-Analysis*, 29: 73–97.

Jaitin, R. (2016). Ways and voices in the psychoanalysis of links according to Enrique Pichon-Riviere. *Couple and Family Psychoanalysis*, 6 (2): 159–172.

Joseph, B. (1985). Transference: The total situation. *International Journal of Psycho-Analysis*, 66(4): 477–454.

Joseph, B. (1989a). Psychic equilibrium and psychic change. In: M. Feldman & E. Bott Spillius (Eds.), *Psychic Equilibrium & Psychic Change: Selected Papers of Betty Joseph* (pp. 168–180). London & New York: Tavistock/Routledge.

Joseph, B. (1989b). Projective identification: Some clinical aspects. In: M. Feldman & E. Bott Spillius (Eds.), *Psychic Equilibrium & Psychic Change: Selected Papers of Betty Joseph* (pp. 181–193). London & New York: Tavistock/Routledge.

Kaes, R. (2016). Links and transference within three interfering psychic spaces. *Couple and Family Psychoanalysis*, 6 (2): 181–193.

Kahr, B. (2007). The traumatic roots of sexual fantasy. In: B. Kahr, *Sex and the Psyche* (pp. 280–310). London: Allan LaneFile.

Kelly, J. B. & Johnson, M. P. (2008). Differentiation among types of intimate partner violence: Research update and implications for interventions. *Family Court Review*, 46 (3): 476–499.

Keogh, T. & Enfield, S. (2013). From regression to recovery: Tracking developmental anxieties in couple therapy. *Couple and Family Psychoanalysis*, 3(1): 28–46.

Kernberg, O. F. (1995). *Love Relations: Normality and Pathology*. New Haven, CT: Yale University Press.

Kleiman, S. (2016). The links: What is produced in the space between others. *Couple and Family Psychoanalysis*, 6 (2): 173–180.

Klein, M. (1935). A contribution to the psychogenesis of manic-depressive states. *International Journal of Psycho-Analysis*, 16: 145–174.

Klein, M. (1940). Mourning and its relation to manic-depressive states. *International Journal of Psycho-Analysis*, 21: 125–153.

Klein, M. (1946). Notes on some schizoid mechanisms. *International Journal of Psycho-Analysis*, 27: 99–110.

Klein, M. (1952). Notes on some schizoid mechanisms. In: M. Klein, P. Heimann, S. Isaacs & J. Riviere (Eds.), *Developments in Psycho-Analysis* (pp. 292–320). London: Hogarth Press.

Klein, M. (1958). On the development of mental functioning. *International Journal of Psycho-Analysis*, 39: 84–90.

Lanman, M. (2003). Assessment for couple psychoanalytic psychotherapy. *British Journal of Psychotherapy*, 19(3): 309–323.

Laufer, M. (1981). The psychoanalyst and the adolescent's sexual development. *The Psychoanalytic Study of the Child*, 36: 181–191.

Links, P. S. & Stockwell, M. (2002). The role of couple therapy in the treatment of narcissistic personality disorder. *American Journal of Psychotherapy*, 56: 522–538.

Losso, R., De Setton, L. & Scharff, D. E. (2018). *The Linked Self in Psychoanalysis: The Pioneering Work of Enrique Pichon Riviere*. London: Routledge.

Ludlam, M. (2007). Our attachment to "the couple in the mind". In: M. Ludlam & V. Nyberg, *Couple Attachments* (pp. 3–22). London: Karnac.

Ludlam, M. (2014). Failure in couple relationships – and in couple psychotherapy. In: B. Willock, R. Coleman Curtis & L. C. Bohm (Eds.), *Understanding and Coping with Failure. Psychoanalytic Perspectives* (pp. 65–71). London & New York: Routledge.

Lyons, A. (1993a). Husbands and wives: The mysterious choice. In: S. Ruszczynski (Ed.), *Psychotherapy with Couples: Theory and Practice at the Tavistock Institute of Marital Studies* (pp. 44–54). London: Karnac.

Lyons. A. (1993b). Therapeutic intervention in relation to the institution of marriage. In: S. Ruszczynski (Ed.), *Psychotherapy with Couples: Theory and Practice at the Tavistock Institute of Marital Studies* (pp. 184–196). London: Karnac.

Lyons, A. & Mattinson, J. (1993). Individuation in marriage. In: S. Ruszczynski (Ed.), *Psychotherapy with Couples: Theory and Practice at the Tavistock Institute of Marital Studies* (pp.104– 125). London: Karnac.

Mattinson, J. (1975). *The Reflection Process in Casework Supervision.* London: Institute of Marital Studies. (Republished 1992.)

Mattinson, J. & Sinclair, I. (1979). *Mate and Stalemate. Working with Marital Problems in a Social Services Department.* Oxford: Blackwell.

McCann, D. (2014). Responding to the needs of same sex-couples. In D. E. Scharff & J. Savege Scharff (Eds.), *Psychoanalytic Couple Therapy: Foundations of Theory and Practice* (pp. 81–90). London: Karnac.

Meltzer, D. (1967). *The Psychoanalytical Process.* Perthshire, Scotland: Clunie Press.

Meltzer, D. (1978). A note on introjective processes. In: A. Hahn (Ed.), *Sincerity and Other Works: Collected Papers of Donald Meltzer* (pp. 458–468). London: Karnac.

Meltzer, D. (1986). *Studies in Extended Metapsychology: Clinical Applications of Bion's Ideas.* London: Karnac.

Meltzer, D. (1992). *The Claustrum: An Investigation of Claustrophobic Phenomena.* Perthshire, Scotland: Clunie Press.

Meltzer, D. (1995). Donald Meltzer in discussion with James Fisher. In: S. Ruszczynski & J. V. Fisher (Eds.), *Intrusiveness and Intimacy in the Couple* (Chapter 6; pp. 107–144). London: Karnac.

Milton, J. (1997). Why assess? Psychoanalytic assessment in the NHS. *Psychoanalytic Psychotherapy, 11* (1): 45–58.

Money-Kyrle, R. (1968). Cognitive development. *International Journal of Psycho-Analysis, 49*: 691–698.

Money-Kyrle, R. (1971). The aim of psychoanalysis. *International Journal of Psycho-Analysis, 49*: 691–698.

Morgan, M. (1994). Some aspects of assessment for couple psychotherapy within the setting of the Tavistock Marital Studies Institute. *Society of Psychoanalytical Marital Psychotherapy Bulletin, May*: 27–29.

Morgan, M. (1995). The projective gridlock: A form of projective identification in couple relationships. In: S. Ruszczynski & J. V. Fisher (Eds.), *Intrusiveness and Intimacy in the Couple* (pp. 33–48). London: Karnac.

Morgan, M. (2001). First contacts: The therapist's "couple state of mind" as a factor in the containment of couples seen for initial consultations. In: F. Grier (Ed.), *Brief Encounters with Couples* (pp. 17–32). London: Karnac.

Morgan, M. (2005). On being able to be a couple: The importance of a "creative couple" in psychic life. In: F. Grier (Ed.), *Oedipus and the Couple* (pp. 9–30). London: Karnac.

Morgan, M. (2010). Unconscious beliefs about being a couple. *fort da*, 16 (1): 36–55. Reprinted (2017) in S. Nathans & M. Schaefer (Eds.), *Couples on the Couch. Psychoanalytic Couple Therapy and the Tavistock Model* (pp. 62–81). Abingdon & New York: Routledge.

Morgan, M. (2016). What does ending mean in couple psychotherapy? *Couple and Family Psychoanalysis*, 6 (1): 44–58.

Morgan, M. & Ruszczynski, S. (1998). The creative couple. *Unpublished paper presented at the Tavistock Marital Studies Institute's 50th Anniversary Conference*.

Morgan, M. & Stokoe. P. (2014). Curiosity. *Couple and Family Psychoanalysis*, 4 (1): 42–55.

Nathans, S. (2009). Discussion of "Macbeth in the consulting room: Proleptic imagination and the couple", *fort da*, 15(2): 33–55. Reprinted (2017) as "The Macbeths in the consulting room" in S. Nathans & M. Schaefer (Eds.), *Couples on the Couch. Psychoanalytic Couple Therapy and the Tavistock Model* (90–112). Abingdon & New York: Routledge.

Nicolo, A. M. (2016). Thinking in terms of links. *Couple and Family Psychoanalysis*, 6 (2): 206–214.

Novakovic, A. (2016). The quarrelling couple In: A. Novakovic (Ed.), *Couple Dynamics. Psychoanalytic Perspectives in Work with the Individual, the Couple and the Group*, (pp. 85–105). London: Karnac.

Novakovic, A. & Reid, M. (Eds.) (2018). *Couple Stories: Applications of Psychoanalytic Ideas in Thinking about Couple Interaction*. London: Routledge.

Nyberg, V. (2007). An exploration of the unconscious couple fit between the "detached" narcissist and the "adherent" narcissist: One couple's shared fear of madness. In: M. Ludlam & V. Nyberg (Eds.), *Couple Attachments. Theoretical and Clinical Studies* (145–156). London: Karnac.

Ogden, T. (1979). On projective identification. *International Journal of Psycho-Analysis*, 60: 357–373.

Ogden, T. (1994a). *Subjects of Analysis*. Northvale, NJ: Jason Aronson.

Ogden, T. H. (1989). On the concept of the autistic-contiguous position. *International Journal of Psycho-Analysis*, 70(1): 127–141.

Ogden, T. H. (1992). Comments on the transference and countertransference in the initial analytic meeting. *Psychoanalytic Inquiry*, 12(2): 225–247.

Ogden, T. H. (1994b). The analytic third: Working with the intersubjective clinical facts. *International Journal of Psycho-Analysis*, 75: 3–19.

Pick, I. B. (1985). Working through in the countertransference. *International Journal of Psycho-Analysis*, 66(2): 157–166.

Pickering, J. (2006). The marriage of alterity and intimacy. *Psychoanalytic Perspectives on Couple Work*, 2: 19–39.

Pickering, J. (2011). Bion and the couple. *Couple and Family Psychoanalysis*, 1 (1): 49–68.

Pincus, L. (1960). Relationships and the growth of personality. In: L. Pincus (Ed.), *Marriage: Studies in Emotional Conflict and Growth* (pp. 13–34). London: Institute of Marital Studies.

Pincus, L. (1962). The nature of marital interaction. In: The Institute of Marital Studies, *The Marital Relationship as a Focus for Casework* (pp. 13–25). London: Institute of Marital Studies.

Poland, W. S. (2002). The interpretive attitude. *Journal of the American Psychoanalytic Association*, 50 (3): 807–826.

Racker, H. (1968). *Transference and Counter-transference*. London: Hogarth Press.

Rey, J. H. (1988). That which patients bring to analysis. *International Journal of Psycho-Analysis*, 69: 457–470.
Riviere, J. (1936). A contribution to the analysis of the negative therapeutic reaction. *International Journal of Psycho-Analysis*, 17: 304–320.
Rosenfeld, H. R. (1983). Primitive object relations and mechanisms. *International Journal of Psycho-Analysis*, 64: 261–267.
Roth, P. (2001). Mapping the landscape: Levels of transference interpretation. *International Journal of Psycho-Analysis*, 82 (3): 533–543.
Rustin, M. (1991). Encountering primitive anxieties. In: L. Miller, M. Rustin, M. Rustin & J. Shuttleworth (Eds.), *Closely Observed Infants* (pp. 7–21). London: Duckworth.
Ruszczynski, S. (Ed.) (1993a). *Psychotherapy with Couples: Theory and Practice at the Tavistock Institute of Marital Studies*. London: Karnac.
Ruszczynski, S. (1993b). The theory and practice of the Tavistock Institute of Marital Studies. In: S. Ruszczynski (Ed.), *Psychotherapy with Couples: Theory and Practice at the Tavistock Institute of Marital Studies* (pp. 3–26). London: Karnac.
Ruszczynski, S. (1994). Enactment as countertransference. *Journal of the British Association of Psychotherapists*, 27 (Summer): pp. 41–60.
Ruszczynski, S. (1995). Narcissistic object relating. In: S. Ruszczynski & J. Fisher (Eds.), *Intrusiveness and Intimacy in the Couple* (pp. 13–32). London: Karnac Books.
Ruszczynski, S. (1998). The "marital triangle": Towards "triangular space" in the intimate couple relationship. *Journal of the British Association of Psychotherapists*, 34 (31): 33–47.
Ruszczynski, S. & Fisher, J. V. (Eds.) (1995). *Intrusiveness and Intimacy in the Couple*. London: Karnac.
Sandler J. (1976). Countertransference and role-responsiveness. *International Review of Psycho-Analysis*, 3: 43–47.
Scarf, M. (1987). *Intimate Partners: Patterns in Love and Marriage*. New York: Random House.
Schaefer, M. (2010). Discussion of "Unconscious beliefs about being a couple". Beliefs about a couple and beliefs about the other. *fort da*, 16 (1): 56–63. Reprinted (2017) in S. Nathans & M. Schaefer (Eds.), *Couples on the Couch. Psychoanalytic Couple Therapy and the Tavistock Model*. Abingdon & New York: Routledge.
Scharff, D. E. (2014). How development structures sexual relationships. In: D. E. Scharff & J. Savege Scharff (Eds.), *Psychoanalytic Couple Therapy: Foundations of Theory and Practice* (pp. 215–227). London: Karnac.
Scharff, D. E. (2016). The contribution of Enrique Pichon-Riviere: Comparisons with his European contemporaries and with modern theory. *Couple and Family Psychoanalysis*, 6 (2): 153–158.
Scharff, D. E. & Palacios, E. (Eds.) (2017). *Family and Couple Psychoanalysis*. London: Karnac.
Scharff, D. E. & Savege Scharff, J. (2011). *The Interpersonal Unconscious*. Northvale, NJ: Jason Aronson.
Scharff, D. E. & Savege Scharff, J. (2014). *Psychoanalytic Couple Therapy: Foundations of Theory and Practice*. London: Karnac.
Scharff, D. E. & Vorchheimer, M. (Eds.) (2017). *Clinical Dialogues on Psychoanalysis with Families and Couples*. London: Karnac.
Scharff, J. (1992). Projective and introjective identification, love and the internal couple. In: J. Scharff, *Projective and Introjective Identification and the Use of the Therapist's Self* (Chapter 6; pp. 133–157). New Jersey & London: Jason Aronson.

Searles, H. (1955/1965). The informational value of the supervisor's emotional experience. In: H. F. Searles (1965), *Collected Papers on Schizophrenia and Related Subjects* (pp. 157–176). London: Hogarth Press. (Reprinted: London: Karnac Books, 1986.)

Segal, H. (1983). Some clinical implications of Melanie Klein's work: Emergence from narcissism. *International Journal of Psycho-Analysis*, 64: 269–276.

Sehgal, A. (2012). Viewing the absence of sex from couple relationships through the "core complex" lens. *Couple and Family Psychoanalysis*, 2(2): 149–164.

Shmueli, A. & Rix, S. (2009). Loss of desire and therapist dread. In: C. Clulow (Ed.), *Sex, Attachment and Couple Psychotherapy: Psychoanalytic Perspectives* (119–140). London: Karnac.

Spillius, E. B. (2001). Freud and Klein on the concept of phantasy. *International Journal of Psycho-Analysis*, 82 (2): 361–373.

Spillius, E. B., Milton, J., Garvey, P., Couve, C. & Steiner, D. (Eds.) (2011). *The New Dictionary of Kleinian Thought*. London & New York: Routledge.

Stein, R. (1998). The poignant, the excessive and the enigmatic in sexuality. *International Journal of Psycho-Analysis*, 79(2): 253–268.

Stein, R. (2008). The otherness of sexuality: Excess. *Journal of the American Psychoanalytic Association*, 56 (1): 43–71.

Steiner, J. (1987). The interplay between pathological organisations and the paranoid-schizoid and depressive position. *International Journal of PsychoAnalysis*, 68: 69–80.

Steiner, J. (1992). The equilibrium between the paranoid-schizoid and the depressive positions. In: R. Anderson (Ed.), *Clinical Lectures in Klein and Bion* (pp. 46–58). London: Routledge.

Steiner, J. (1993a). Problems in psychoanalytic technique: Patient-centred and analyst-centred interpretations. In J. Steiner, *Psychic Retreats: Pathological Organisations in Psychotic*, Neurotic and Borderline Patients (pp. 131–146). London: Routledge.

Steiner, J. (1993b). *Psychic Retreats: Pathological Organisations in Psychotic, Neurotic and Borderline Patients*. London: Routledge.

Steiner, J. (1996). The aim of psychoanalysis in theory and in practice. *International Journal of Psycho-Analysis*, 77(6): 1073–1083.

Stoller, R. J. (1979). *Sexual Excitement: Dynamics of Erotic Life*. London: Karnac.

Storr, A. (1960). *The Integrity of the Personality*. London: Heinemann.

Strachey, J. (1934). The nature of the therapeutic action of psycho-analysis. *International Journal of Psycho-Analysis*, 15: 127–159.

Symington, N. (1985). Phantasy effects that which it represents. *International Journal of Psycho-Analysis*, 66: 349–357.

Target, M. (2007). Is our sexuality our own? A developmental model of sexuality based on early affect mirroring. *British Journal of Psychotherapy*, 23 (4): 517–530.

Tarsh, H. & Bollinghaus, E. (1999). Shared unconscious phantasy: Reality or illusion? *Sexual and Marital Therapy*, 14 (2): 123–136.

Teruel, G. (1966). Recent trends in the diagnosis and treatment of marital conflict. *Psyche*, 20(8).

Turquet, P. (1985). Leadership, the individual and the group. In: D. Colman & M. H. Geller (Eds.), *Group Relations Reader 2* (pp. 71–87). Florida: A. K. Rice Institute.

Vincent, C. (1995a). Consulting to divorcing couples. *Family Law*, December: 678–681.

Vincent, C. (1995b). Love in the countertransference. *Society of Psychoanalytical Marital Psychotherapists Bulletin*, 2 (May): 4–10.

Vincent, C. (2004). Touching the void: The impact of psychiatric illness on the couple. In: M. Ludlam & V. Nyberg (Eds.), *Couple Attachments. Theoretical and Clinical Studies* (pp. 133–144). London: Karnac.

Viorst, J. (1986). *Necessary Losses*. New York: Simon & Schuster.

Vorchheimer, M. (2015). Understanding the loss of understanding. Paper presented at the IPA Congress, Boston.

Waddell, M. (1998). *Inside Lives: Psychoanalysis and the Growth of the Personality*. London: Karnac. (Revised edition published in 2002 by H. Karnac [Books] Ltd.)

Wanless, J. (2014). But my partner "is" the problem: Addressing addiction, mood disorders, and psychiatric illness in psychoanalytic couple treatment. In: D. E. Scharff & J. Savege Scharff (Eds.), *Psychoanalytic Couple Therapy: Foundations of Theory and Practice* (pp. 310–322). London: Karnac.

Willi, J. (1984). The concept of collusion: A combined systemic-psychodynamic approach to marital therapy. *Family Process*, 23(2): 177–185.

Winnicott, D. W. (1958/1975). *Through Paediatrics to Psychoanalysis: Collected Papers*. The Institute of Psychoanalysis. London: Karnac.

Winnicott, D. W. (1969). The use of an object. *International Journal of Psycho-Analysis*, 50(4): 711–716.

Woodhouse, D. (1990). The Tavistock Institute of Marital Studies: Evolution of a marital agency. In: C. Clulow (Ed.), *Marriage: Disillusion and Hope* (pp. 69–119). London: Karnac.

Wrottesley, C. (2017). Does Oedipus never die? The grandparental couple grapple with "Oedipus". *Couple and Family Psychoanalysis*, 7(2): 188–207.

Zinner, J. (1988). Projective identification is a key to resolving marital conflict. *Unpublished paper*.

Index

abandonment:
　emotional 182
　vs. separateness 60
Abse, S. 139, 140
acquisitive identification 91, 92
acquisitive projective identification 91–93
acting out, dangerous 28
addiction 28, 30, 33, 129
adherent narcissism 115
adolescence 4, 136
　separating from parental couple 132–133
Adopting Together 27
affair(s) 18, 33, 36, 43, 82–85, 139, 142, 144, 159, 178, 179
agglutinated nucleus, primitive 188
aggression and sex 143
aggressive object relation 89
alcoholism 30, 31, 33, 36
Alperovitz, S. 173
alpha elements 90, 157
alpha function 90, 129, 157, 183
alterity 6
analyst, loss of, mourning of 185
analytic couple, relating in 9
analytic couple therapy 7, 9, 31, 158, 161
analytic curiosity 153
analytic listening 168
　and reflecting back 172
analytic setting, couple xix, 73, 87
　establishment of 34–53
analytic space, couple 15, 17, 19, 34, 51–53, 152, 153, 169
analytic third, intersubjective 75
analytic work, couple xviii, xix, xx
androgen 143
anger and aggression, dysregulated, difficulty in managing 28
annihilation, psychic 115

anorexia 32
anti-depressant medication 30
anxiety(ies):
　and phantasies about couple psychotherapy 34–35
　paranoid 182
　primitive 188
　　about survival of self 64
　　in autistic-contiguous stage 23
　shared 21, 60
archetypes 63
art 104
assessment(s):
　couple 14–33
　　psychoanalytic xix, 14
　couple therapy:
　　importance of providing containment in 15
　　key elements of 19–27
　extended 16
　formulating couple problem in 19
　as initial consultation 16
　initial interpretation in 18
　as part of ongoing process 33
　psychoanalytic, complex nature of 14
　risk: *see* risk assessment
　setting of 15–16
　structure of 17–19
　of suitability for psychoanalytic couple therapy 19
　see also initial consultation
assumptions, in couple relationships 68–69
attachment xviii, 22, 45, 58, 120, 134
　infant 128
attachment-based couple therapy xviii
attachment patterns 139
attachment relationship 142
attachment theory xviii

attributive identification 91
attributive projective identification 91–93
autistic-contiguous position 23, 134, 188
autistic-contiguous stage, primitive anxieties in 23
autonomy, adolescent sense of 4
Aznar-Martínez, B. 27

babes in the wood marriage 23
baby–mother dyad 70
bad breast 130
Balfour, A. ii, 7, 52, 82, 140, 159
Balint, E. 2, 3, 6, 13
Bannister, K. xxi, 3, 13, 57–59, 65, 95, 103
Baranger, M. 62
Baranger, W. 62
basic assumption dependence 86
basic assumption fight-flight 86
basic assumption modes 86
basic assumption pairing 86
Bateman, A. 129
Berenstein, I. 7, 8, 9, 62, 137
beta elements 157
Bianchini, B. 46
Bion, W. R.
    alpha elements/function 90, 129, 157, 183
    analyst's pre-conception 22
    basic assumption modes 86
    container–contained, theory of xii, 89–91, 144, 157
    empty thought 128
    group unconscious phantasy 87
    innate preconceptions 54
    negative capability 153
    paranoid-schizoid and depressive positions, oscillation between 135
    projective identification 93
    psychotic part of personality 188
    valencies 49
Birksted-Breen, D. 131, 132
bisexuality 131, 132
    innate 147
Blair, L. 141, 142, 146, 150
Bleger, J. 41, 42, 62, 186, 187, 188, 189
Boerma, M. 128, 129, 139
Bollas, C. 92
Bollinghaus, E. 64, 66
Bolognini, S. 46
borderline condition, falling in love as 129
Bott Spillius, E. 91
Bowlby, J. 128
BPAS: *see* British Psychoanalytical Society

British Psychoanalytical Society (BPAS) xv
Britton, R. xxi, 24, 112
    emotional leave of absence 178
    identification, acquisitive and attributive 91
    narcissism xxi, 86
    narcissism, detached and adherent 115
    Oedipus Complex xxi
    overvalued idea 22, 154, 168, 174
    post-depressive position 135
    psychic leave of absence 116, 119
    psychic space, sharing 6, 115–118
    selected fact, emergence of 153
    third position xxii
    triangular space xxi, 6, 52, 131, 136, 158
    unconscious beliefs xxi, 3, 5, 64, 65, 167
Brookes, S. 24, 46
Buss-Twachtmann, C. 24

Cachia, P. 183
Caruso, N. J. 139
castration 54
cat and dog marriage 23
Charles, Prince 113
child(ren):
    and inter-parental conflict 31–32
    loss of 99
Churcher, J. 41, 42, 186, 188, 189
claustrum, and intrusive identification 93–95
Cleavely, E. 3, 93
clinical examples:
    container, absence of (Matt and Abe) 101–102
    couple interpretation (Ann and Bill) 156–157
    disillusionment in relationships (Danek and Milena) 70
    early countertransference (Julia and Rob) 37–38
    extractive introjection (A and B) 92–93
    fantasy, assumptions, illusions (Jake and Simone) 68–69
    initial consultation (Leroy and Roxanne) 21–22, 23, 24
    interpretation, of symbols and dreams
        (Sadie and Paul) 168–169
        (Charlie and Erica) 169
    love and hate, struggle with (David and Kay) 10
    never-ending couple therapy (Ralph and Suzy) 185
    observing partner taking third position

(Carly and James) 159–160
projective gridlock (Stan and Frank) 120
projective identification (Dilan and Radhika) 105
projective system:
    functioning as container (Olivia and Jack) 107
    interpretation of (Harry and Bella, Kath and Christine) 165–166
    more creative functioning in (Rick and Sonia) 106
    with intrusive projective identification (Mario and Lula) 94
sado-masochistic dynamics (Johann and Anna) 122–123
separation, managing (Bill and Janet) 179
shared defensive behaviour (Mr and Mrs Avon) 60
shared phantasy:
    (Mr and Mrs Frazer) 63
    (Mr and Mrs Smith) 59
sharing psychic space:
    (Antonio and Camila) 116–119
    developmental problems in (Adam and Andrea) 119
therapist as observer (Peggy and Jack) 173
transference:
    gathering (Eva and John) 79–81
    in relationship (Jimmy and Dale) 164–165
transference and countertransference, use of (Donna and Johnny) 160
transsexual dynamics in couple (David and Cheryl) 149
Clinical Outcomes in Routine Evaluation (CORE) 31
Clulow, C. ii, xviii, 63, 64, 128, 129, 139
coercive controlling violence 29, 30
COFAP: *see* Couple and Family Psychoanalysis
cognitive behavioural therapy 27
Cohen, L. 112
collusion, therapeutic 187
Colman, W. xxi, 3, 24, 63, 93, 99, 110, 111, 114, 119, 121, 136, 183
communication:
    transference 178
    unconscious, couple's 19
complementariness, unconscious 97
complementary identification 163
compliance 174

concordant identification 163
conflicts and anxieties, early, unresolved, effect of 1
confusional states 189
conscious container, unconsciously contained 100–101
conscious fantasy(ies) 25, 34, 50, 54, 68
consultation, initial, assessment as 16
container:
    absence of, Matt and Abe (clinical example) 101–102
    /contained xii, 124, 144
        concept of 89–91
    marital 24
containment:
    flexible 98–99
    importance of, in couple therapy assessment 15
    as key element of couple psychotherapy assessment 19–20
    limited 90
    in marriage relationship 3
    maintaining a couple analytic space 19–20
    maternal 90
    in relationship 98, 183
    of self 183
    theory of 157
CORE: *see* Clinical Outcomes in Routine Evaluation
core complex 144
co-therapist 47, 48, 49, 50, 76, 182
co-therapy xix, 42, 49, 50, 51, 76, 182
    as way of working 47–48
co-therapy relationship, and reflection process 48–50
countertransference:
    in couple therapy 75–76
    concept of 74–75
    couple, therapeutic xix
    disturbing, elusive 5
    early 37–39
    enactment of 77
    erotic 87
    Freud's understanding of 74
    manic 23
    real 79
    therapist's 26, 86, 155, 162
        use of 78–79
    and transference xix, 19, 26, 34, 146, 149, 164
        and living inner world of couple 73–87
        living inner world of couple 73–87

Index

unprocessed 80, 174
use of, in formulating couple's problem 22
working creatively with 87
countertransference enactment 84
couple(s):
   analytic work with xv, xx, 9, 152
   creative 8, 9, 108, 125, 127, 128, 132, 137, 138, 147, 149
      internal xxiv, 126, 131, 136, 184
   living inner world of, and transference and countertransference 73–87
   need of two therapists 50–51
   projective system of xix, 8, 10, 25, 26, 59, 88, 94, 95, 97, 99, 174, 189
   psychic development of 126–151
   sexual relationship of xx, 126, 139, 145, 146, 147, 149
couple analytic function 185
couple analytic setting xix, 73, 87
   establishment of 34–53
couple analytic space 15, 17, 34, 51–53, 152, 153, 169
   maintenance of, in assessment 19
couple analytic work xviii, xix, xx
Couple and Family Psychoanalysis (COFAP) ii, ix, xvi, xvii, xx, 7
couple countertransference, therapeutic xix
couple dynamics 23–24, 139
   babes in the wood 23
   cat and dog 23
   defensive 23
   doll's house 23
   net and sword 23
   projective gridlock 23
couple fit xix, 2, 6, 7, 25, 65, 73, 88, 95
   flexibility within 150
   and shared phantasy and unconscious choice 61
   and unconscious partner choice 96–97
couple interpretation(s) xx, xxiv, 40, 46, 52, 65, 152–175
   Ann and Bill (clinical example) 156–157
   incorrect 174
   specific nature of 156
couple object relations 62
couple observation 173
couple problem 19, 164
   formulating 20–27
   understanding 20
couple projective system vii, 7, 174
   and projective identification 88–109

Couple Psychoanalytic Psychotherapy xvi, xx
couple psychotherapy, anxieties and phantasies about 34–35
couple relationship:
   adult intimate xviii, 3, 126, 139
   couple state of mind as third position in 184
   influence of past on 1–3
   intimate xviii, 3, 6, 76, 114, 126, 139
   as potentially therapeutic 3
   potential for development of 8–13
   psychoanalytic understanding of 1–13
   as symbolic third 136
   transference dimension of 25
   transference in 25, 164
couple state of mind (*passim*):
   capacity to use 185
   development of 184
   existence of, in couple 26
   introjecting 187
   introjection of 184
      problems in 185–190
   reintrojecting 187
   as third position in couple relationship 184
   therapist's use of 39–40
couple state of mind (passim) 1
couple therapy (*passim*)
   aim of 176–192
      introjection of couple state of mind as 184–185
   analytic 7, 9, 31, 158, 161
   anxieties about 163
   for depression xviii
   ending of 176–192
   indications and contraindications for 27
   mentalisation-based 28
   never-ending, Ralph and Suzy (clinical example) 185
   psychoanalytic, assessment of suitability for 19
   triangular nature of 82, 166
   triangular setting of 159
   triangular situation in 7
   working with transference in 158–165
couple transference relationship xix
Cowan, C. P. 31
Cowan, P. A. 31
creative couple xxi, xxiv, 8, 9, 108, 125–132, 136–138, 147, 149
   internal xxiv, 126, 131, 136, 184
creative couple developmental stage 136–139
creative couple functioning 183

creative couple state of mind 184
creative internal couple, establishment of 183
creativity 105, 138, 151
Cudmore, L. 99
curiosity 38, 40, 67, 113, 125, 129, 136, 150
    analytic 153
    and narcissism 114–115
    non-intrusive 114

Dallanegra, L. 46
day dreams 167
Dearnley, B. 13
de Botton, A. 69, 70
defence(s):
    manic 21
    primitive 5, 98
    shared 3, 54–72, 151
        and shared phantasy 60–61
defence mechanisms, omnipotent
    primitive 135
defensive relationship 60
delusion 66
    emotional strength of 65
dependency:
    basic assumption 86
    couples' 84
    couple's unconscious struggle with 4
    longing for and fear of 173
depression, acute or chronic 30
depressive position 98, 130, 134, 135
    anxieties in 24
desire, loss of or change in 139–141
destructive behaviour, couple's 180
detachment, narcissistic 115
development, psychoanalytic theories of 127
developmental relationship 60
developmental stage, couple's 134
Dicks, H. V. xxi, 7, 13, 97
discourse:
    latent content of 172
    symbolic references in 172
disillusionment 134
    in relationships 69
        Danek and Milena (clinical
            example) 70
disintegration, fear of 120
divorce and separation consultation service 27
divorcing couples 85
Doll's House marriage 23, 32
Downey, J. I. 148
dream(s) 167
    interpretation of 168–170
        Charlie and Erica (clinical example) 169
        as shared unconscious phantasy 170
        and symbols, interpretation of, Sadie and
            Paul (clinical example) 168–169
drug addiction 33
dynamics, couple: *see* couple dynamics
dyspareunia 146

early countertransference, Julia and Rob
    (clinical example) 37–38
early development, mother–infant couple
    127–130
ejaculation:
    delayed 145
    premature 145, 146
el vínculo (link) 7, 8, 137
emotional abandonment 182
emotional leave of absence 178
empathy 98, 114, 115
empty thought 128
enactment(s) 5, 47, 49, 190
    concrete, of relationship difficulties 145
    countertransference 84
    effect of unconscious belief on 167
    of phantasy of never-ending therapy 186
    pressure for 19, 26, 75, 168
    in therapy 37, 76
    therapist's vulnerability to 68, 78,
        82, 158
    subtle, between patient and analyst 162
    of transference 83
ending, as special issue in couple therapy
    176–192
ending phase 190
endings:
    premature 176–177
    unwanted 182
Enfield, S. 23, 134, 188
engulfment 120
erectile dysfunction 145, 146
erotic countertransference 87
erotic desire 143
erotic satisfaction 143
erotic transference 82, 83, 87
Evans, C. 31
evenly suspended attention 153
extractive introjection, A and B (clinical
    example) 92–93
Ezriel, H. 60

Fairbairn, W. D. 128
Family Discussion Bureau ix, xx, 1

fantasy vii, xix, 35, 54, 60, 70, 91, 141, 178
  and assumptions and illusions, Jake and Simone (clinical example) 68–69
  in couple relationships 68–69
  interpretation of 167–168
  vs phantasy 68
father:
  abusive 163
  intrusive 56
Feldman, T. 93
fight-flight basic assumption 86
Fisher, J. xxi, xxii, 38, 39, 56, 94, 102, 104, 110, 111, 130, 176, 182, 183
  couple's stories as dreams 170
  couple's versions of events as music 172
  interlocking adhesive and intrusive narcissistic dynamics 93
  movement from narcissism to object relating 135
  narcissism and the psychological state of marriage 6
  narcissistic relating and psychological state of marriage, move between 24
  narcissistic relating to a psychological state of marriage 97
  non-intrusive curiosity 114
  proleptic imagination 67, 77
  shared phantasy in couple therapy 63
  uninvited guest 36
  Uninvited Guest, The ix, xiv, 6, 103, 187
flexible containment 98–99
flight into health 190
Fonagy, P. 129, 142
frame:
  continuity of 43–45
  Tavistock Relationships 42–43
Freud, S. 45, 46, 78, 84, 129, 143
  Beyond the Pleasure Principle 2, 77
  countertransference 74
  day dreams 167
  Ego and the Id, The 74
  evenly suspended attention 153
  Mourning and Melancholia 187
  repetition compulsion 2, 73
  sexual Oedipal situation 130
  unconscious phantasy 54
Friedman, R. C. 149
Friend, J. 69
Frost, D. M. 149
fused relationship 26, 120

Garelick, A. 27
gay couples 149
gender, and sex and sexualities 126–151
Gill, H. 13
Glasser, M. 144
glischro-caric position 188
good breast 130
Grier, F. xxi, 20, 135, 139, 144

Hardy, T. 140
Harold, G. T. 31
hate, and love, managing 150
  difficulty, David and Kay (case example) 10–13
hatred, split-off 148
Heimann, P. 74
Heming, G. 31
Hertzmann, L. 145, 148, 149
Hewison, D. x, 23, 30, 32, 57, 59, 62, 119, 143, 144
history, making links with 170–171
Hobson, R. P. 79, 170
homophobia, internalised 149
Humphries, J. 3, 29, 30, 67
hyper desire 141
hypo desire 141
hypothesis 65, 154, 160
  vs. belief 66

IAPT: *see* Improving Access to Psychological Therapies
Ibsen, H. 23
idealisation 64, 69, 82, 84–86, 163
idealised figure, therapist as 177
idealising transference 84–85
identification
  intrusive 93, 102, 103, 104
  preconscious 142
illusion(s) 58, 65, 116, 119, 132
  in couple relationships 68–69
  and disillusion 69
illusory intimacy 119–120
imagination 96, 104, 115
  proleptic 67, 77
Improving Access to Psychological Therapies (IAPT) xviii
incongruence within self, sense of 141
individual therapy 27, 28, 34, 36, 42, 157, 158, 161, 175, 179, 191
  referral for 180
individuation 63
inertia, sense of 21

infant, primitive states of terror of 90
infant observation 173
initial consultation 15, 16, 17, 24, 27, 39, 43, 176
　Leroy and Roxanne (clinical example) 21; see also assessment(s)
innate phantasies 54
innate preconceptions 54
inner world of couple, living 76–77
Institute of Marital Studies xiv, xx
interference, concept of 137
internal object relations 1
International Association of Couple and Family Psychoanalysis xvii, xx, 7
International Psychoanalytical Association (IPA) xvi, xx, 7
International Psychotherapy Institute (IPI) xvi, xvii
inter-parental conflict, and children 31–32
interpretation(s):
　couple 40, 46, 52, 65
　　Ann and Bill (clinical example) 156–157
　　field of 152–175
　　incorrect 174
　　specific nature of 156
　decisions about 155
　of dreams 168–170
　of fantasy 167–168
　from therapist's countertransference 162
　initial, in assessment 18
　nature of 152–154
　of symbols and dreams, Charlie and Erica (clinical example) 169
　as process 175
　process, triangular dynamic of 159, 175
　of symbols 168–170
　timing of 175
　transference : see transference interpretation(s)
　and unprocessed countertransference 174
　of unconscious beliefs 167–168
　of unconscious phantasy 167–168
interpretive attitude 153
intersubjective analytic third 75
intimacy 26, 36, 70, 96, 99, 104, 115, 122, 126–129, 133, 136, 139, 140, 151, 178, 182
　couple's unconscious struggle with 4
　emotional 119
　illusory 119–120
　lack of 3

longing for and fear of 173
physical 128
primitive claustro-agoraphobic nature of 144
symbolic 128
as vehicle of change 6
intimate partner violence 29
intrapsychic tension xviii
introjection 95, 103, 157, 183, 184, 185, 187, 191
　extractive 92
intrusion 94, 104, 111, 130
intrusive identification 102, 103, 104
　and claustrum 93–95
intrusiveness 113, 114, 147
intrusive projections 102, 104, 124, 182
intrusive projective identification 99, 103, 105, 121
　projective system with, Mario and Lula (clinical example) 94
invasion 111
IPA: see International Psychoanalytical Association
IPI: see International Psychotherapy Institute
Isaacs, S. 54, 55

Jaitin, R. 137
Johnson, M. P. 29
joint personality
　marital 7
　marriage relationship as 3, 97
Joseph, B. 74, 75, 98, 162
Judd, D. 99
Jung, C. G., archetypes 63

Kaes, R. 137
Kahr, B. 143
Kelly, J. B. 29
Keogh, T. 23, 134, 188
Kernberg, O. F. 143, 145, 147
Kleiman, S. 137, 138
Klein, M. 11, 54, 65, 89, 94, 95, 135, 188
　good and bad breast 130
　paranoid schizoid and depressive positions 134
　projective identification 74, 88, 93, 96, 123
　splitting 74
　unconscious phantasy 55

language and meaning 112–113
Lanman, M. 15, 20, 21

Laufer, M. 132, 136
lesbian couple(s) 50, 145, 148, 149
lesbians 148
Leve, L. D. 31
life instinct 111
link (el vínculo) 7, 8, 137
Links, P. S. 27, 170
link theory (*el vínculo*) xvii, 137, 138
listening:
　analytic 168, 172
　well 113
loss:
　early, unresolved 24
　of self 120
Losso, R. 62
love:
　and hate
　　difficulty in managing, David and Kay (case example) 10–13
　　integration of 139
　　managing 150
　maternal 129
　romantic 129
Ludlam, M. 36, 37, 148
Lyons, A. 13, 101, 129

manic defence(s) 21
manualised therapies x, xi
marital container 24
marital fit 62, 96
marital personality, joint 7
marital triangle 7, 10
marriage:
　as psychological container 183
　psychological, true 134
　psychological state of 6, 24, 97
marriage relationship:
　containment in 3
　as joint personality 3, 97
masochism 86, 94, 123
maternal care 127, 168
maternal function, of being with 131
maternal introject 56
maternal love 129
Mattinson, J. 13, 23, 48, 101, 129
McCann, D. 29, 30, 148
Meltzer, D. 40, 41, 93, 103, 104, 172, 187
mental health 10, 28, 30
mentalisation-based couple therapy/treatment xviii, 28
mentalisation therapy, time-limited 27

Meyer, I. H. 149
Milton, J. iv, 27
Money-Kyrle, R. 54, 128
mood disorder 30
Morgan, M. xxi, xxii, xxiv, 3, 4, 5, 7, 23, 28, 38, 52, 67, 86, 88, 103, 105, 110, 115, 120, 126, 127, 129, 130, 136, 150, 178, 179, 185, 186, 189
mother:
　Oedipal, unconscious early and primal loss of 145
　psychotic 163
mother–baby couple(s) 119, 127, 130
mother–baby relationship 129, 144
mourning, of loss of analyst 185

nameless dread 90
narcissism xix, xxi, 6, 25, 135
　adherent 115
　and curiosity 114–115
　destructive 110
　detached 115
　entrenched 110
　ordinary 110
　and relating to an 'other' 110–115
　and sharing psychic space 110–125
narcissistic adherence, and sharing psychic space 115–118
narcissistic couple 101
narcissistic detachment, and sharing psychic space 115–118
narcissistic patients 86
narcissistic personality disorder 27
narcissistic relating 5–7, 24, 91, 97, 121
　adherent 6
　detached 6
Nathans, S. 67, 68, 77
National Institute for Health and Care Excellence (NICE) x
negative capability 153
negative transference 36, 82
net and sword marriage 23
NICE: *see* National Institute for Health and Care Excellence
Nicolo, A. M. 137
Novakovic, A. ix, 62, 63, 97
Nyberg, V. 6, 115

object-cathexis 74
object relating 110, 125, 135
object relations xvii
　aggressive 89

couple 62
internal 1
object relationship:
    conflictual 78
    traumatic 78
object relations theory 7, 62
object seeking 5
observation, of couple 173
Oedipal conflicts 78
Oedipal couple 143
Oedipal development, early 136
Oedipal dynamics 147
Oedipal mother 145
    internal 145
    unconscious, early and primal loss of 145
Oedipal situation 4, 6, 127, 130, 132, 133
    another couple 130–132
    sexual 130
    triangular configuration of 132
Oedipal triangle 131, 136
Oedipus complex xxi, 130
Ogden, T. 6, 52, 75, 91, 100, 134, 188
oneness 87, 110
    basic assumption 86
orgasm, problems in achieving 146
other:
    being with, impact on partner of 5
    foreign aspect of 9
    otherness of 6, 17
overvalued idea 154, 168, 174
    vs. selected fact 22

pairing, basic assumption 86
Palacios, E. 7
paranoid anxiety 182
paranoid-schizoid position 86, 89, 134, 188
    anxieties in 24
    and depressive position, oscillation between 135
paranoid-schizoid state of mind 86
parental relationship 132
    feelings of exclusion from 78
    inappropriate inclusion in 78
Parents as Partners 27
partner:
    transference to 26
    unconscious choice of xix, 2, 7, 25, 61, 88, 95, 96, 104
parts of self, splitting off and projecting 166
past, repetition of 73, 78; *see also* repetition compulsion
paternal function, of observing and linking 131

PCPG: *see* Psychoanalytic Couple Psychotherapy Group
penis-as-link 132
personality, psychotic part of 188
phantasy(ies):
    vs fantasy 68
    innate 54
    primal 54
    projective 91
    shared: *see* shared phantasy, concept of
        development of 57–58
    unconscious: *see* unconscious phantasy(ies)
Pickering, J. 6, 153
Pick, I. B. 162
Pincus, L. xxi, 1, 2, 3, 7, 8, 13, 57, 58, 59, 62, 65, 93, 95, 103
poetry 104
Poland, W. S. 153
post-depressive position 135
post-Kleinian theory(ies) xxi, 1, 24
preconscious identification 142
presenting problem, of couple 3, 17, 18, 24–27, 87, 160
primal phantasies 54
primal scene 54
primary object 60, 97, 127, 131
    relationship to 4, 130
primitive agglutinated nucleus 188
primitive anxieties 23, 188
    about survival of self 64
primitive defences 5, 98
primitive states of mind 98, 188
primitive symbiotic relationship 42, 188
projected parts of self, re-acquisition of 186–187
projection(s) (*passim*)
    intrusive 102, 104, 124, 182
    mutual, processing of 183
    withdrawal of 134, 183
projective gridlock 5, 23, 86, 88, 120–121, 124, 189
    concept of 103–104
    Stan and Frank (clinical example) 120
projective gridlock marriage 23
projective identification(s) (*passim*)
    acquisitive 91–93
    attributive 91–93
    and couple projective system 88–109
    in couple 95–96
    in couple relationship, Dilan and Radhika (clinical example) 105
    communication by 108

concept of 88–109
crossed 189
intrusive 99, 103, 105, 121
projective system with, Mario and Lula (clinical example) 94
as primitive mode of communication 89
as primitive phantasy of splitting 88
and projective system 7–8
projective phantasy(ies) 91
projective processes, defensive 102–103
projective system 2, 12, 38, 39, 61, 65, 76, 121, 124, 145, 152, 175, 177, 178, 187
couple 7, 8, 10, 25, 26, 59, 174, 189
developmental and defensive aspects of 97–98
and projective identification 88–109
creative functioning in 105
defensive 24, 95, 108
fixed 13, 26
flexibility of 3
functioning as container, Olivia and Jack (clinical example) 107
with intrusive projective identification, Mario and Lula (clinical example) 94
interpretation of, Harry and Bella, Kath and Christine (clinical examples) 165–166
interpreting 165–166
more creative functioning in, Rick and Sonia (clinical example) 106
powerful nature of 28
and projective identification 7–8
and shared phantasy 59–60
proleptic imagination 67, 77
pseudo-intimacy 104
psychiatric illness 30
psychic annihilation 115
psychic development 9, 25, 26, 57, 97, 98, 99, 185, 187
couple's 126–151
in becoming a couple 4
creative couple stage of 136–139
early stages of 134
from birth to being a couple 126–133
psychic equilibrium 74, 188
psychic leave of absence 116, 119
psychic pain 20, 105, 157
psychic reality 39, 115
inner 57
psychic retreat 189
psychic skin, undeveloped 188
psychic space (*passim*)
lack of 17, 159

sharing 6, 25
Antonio and Camila (clinical example) 116–119
couple's capacity for xix
developmental problems in 118–119
developmental problems in, Adam and Andrea (clinical example) 119
and narcissism 110–125
narcissistic adherence and narcissistic detachment 115–118
problems in 118–125
psychoanalytic couple assessment xix, 14
Psychoanalytic Couple Psychotherapy Group (PCPG) xvi
psychoanalytic psychotherapy, open-ended 27
psychoanalytic theories of development 127
psychoanalytic treatment, suitability for xxii, 27–28
psycho-biological system, mutual 58
psychodynamic sex therapy xviii
psychodynamic therapy 27
psychological state of marriage 6, 24, 97
psychosexual therapy 27
psychotic illness 30

questioning, and reflecting back 172–173

Racker, H. 163
randomised controlled trials (RCTs) x
rape 150
RCTs: *see* randomised controlled trials
reality testing 55, 167
reflecting back:
and analytic listening 172
and questioning 172–173
reflection process, and co-therapy relationship 48–50
regression, development, stages of 133–135
Reid, M. ix
reintrojection 94, 96, 108, 141, 186, 187
relating, complexity of 9
relationship(s):
couple:
nature of 24–27
as symbolic third 136
defensive 2
developmental 2
developmentally and dynamically in present 4–8
ending of, help with 181
nature of 1, 4, 24, 25, 98, 104

partners wanting to end 177–179
  as psychological container 3, 183
  repetition in 77–78
repetition compulsion 2, 73, 77, 78
Rey, J. H. 39
risk, technique in relation to 32
risk assessment xix, 19, 28–29
Riviere, J. 39
Rix, S. 139
romantic love 129
Rosenfeld, H. R. 96
Roth, P. 169
Rustin, M. 173
Ruszczynski, S. 3, 6, 52, 59, 61, 98, 110, 127, 133
  co-therapy xix, 42, 47–51, 76, 182
  countertransference, enactment of 77
  marital triangle 7
  shared defensive behaviour 60

sadism, shared fears of 146
sado-masochistic dynamics
  Johann and Anna (clinical example) 122
  in psychic space 121–125
sado-masochistic relationship 5, 23, 26, 38, 86, 92, 121, 123
same-sex/same-gender relationships 101, 147, 148
same-sex/same-gender couples 148
Sandler J. 74
Savege Scharff, J. ix, 7, 183
Scarf, M. 138
Schaefer, M. 67
Scharff, D. E. ix, 7, 100, 137, 138
Searles, H. 48
Segal, H. 111
Sehgal, A. 139
selected fact 22, 155
  conjoint 153
  emergence of 153
self-harm 31, 32
self-representing event 80, 170
separateness:
  vs. abandonment 60
  couple's unconscious struggle with 4
separating couples 85
separation, managing, Bill and Janet (clinical example) 179
separation-instigated violence 29
setting (*passim*):
  of assessment 15–16
  deep meaning of 186

management of, internal and external 40–42
symbiosis and 187–190
sex:
  and aggression 143
  aggression and transgression 142–145
  fear of 26, 170
  and gender and sexualities 126–151
  lack of 26, 147, 157
  outside marriage 139
  painful 145
  talking with couples about 146–147
sexual abuse 50, 146
  childhood 150
sexual behaviour, compulsive 146
sexual desire 26, 57, 142, 150
  loss of 126, 139, 140, 141, 145
sexual disorders 145
sexual dysfunctions 146
sexual identity and orientation 147
sexual indifference 143
sexualities:
  different 147–149
  and gender and sex 126–151
sexuality, enigmatic nature of 141–142
sexual pain 146
sexual play 150
sexual problem(s) 145–146, 150
sexual relationship xx, 25, 26, 36, 61, 83, 87, 120, 121, 150, 165, 170
  adult 128, 136
  couple's 126, 139, 145–147, 149
  meaning of 139–149
sexual trauma 150
shared unconscious phantasy, dreams as 170
shared defence 3, 54–72, 151
  and shared phantasy 60–61
shared defensive behaviour, Mr and Mrs Avon (clinical example) 60
shared phantasy 57–66, 152
  Mr and Mrs Frazer (clinical example) 63
  Mr and Mrs Smith (clinical example) 59
  and projective system 59–60
  and shared defence 60–61
  and unconscious choice and couple fit 61
  see also shared unconscious phantasy(ies)
shared problem, acknowledgement of 28
shared unconscious phantasy(ies) 3, 25, 54, 71, 72, 96, 170
  central, primitive and dominating 63–65
  and couple's ordinary unconscious relating 62–63

concept of 57–65
dominating 63–65
new 61–62
primitive and dominating 63–65
and reality 58–59
review of 59
specific, central, primitive and dominating 63–65
sharing, narcissistic relating, adherent and detached 6
Shmueli, A. 139
Sinclair, I. 23
situational couple violence 29
social dreaming 169
Spillius, E. B. 55, 91
split-off and projected parts of self, taking back 107
splitting 16, 23, 74, 88, 98, 116, 134
splitting behaviour, systems of 23
splitting mechanism, as defence 23
Steiner, J. 22, 24, 124, 153, 154, 174, 185, 186, 187, 189
Stein, R. 139, 141
Stockwell, M. 27
Stokoe, P. 38, 86, 114, 115
Stoller, R. J. 143
Strachey, J. 83
superego figure 163
critical, therapist as 83
symbiosis 41, 42, 120, 134
and setting 187–190
unconscious, with therapist 191
symbiotic part of self, working through of 188
symbiotic relating 189
symbol(s):
and dreams, interpretation of, Sadie and Paul (clinical example) 168–169
interpretation of 168–170
Charlie and Erica (clinical example) 169
symbol formation 104
symbolic act, deciding to go into couple therapy as 177
symbolic third 136
Symington, N. 57, 58, 61, 66

take sides, pressure to 85, 86
Target, M. 141
Tarsh, H. 64, 66
Tavistock Centre for Couple Relations xx
Tavistock Institute of Marital Studies xx
Tavistock Marital Studies Institute xx

Tavistock Relationships (TR) (*passim*)
Temperley, J. 13
Teruel, G. 13
theory, role of 22–24
therapeutic collusion 187
therapeutic couple countertransference xix
therapeutic couple transference xix
therapeutic transference relationship 75
therapist:
as critical superego figure 83
as idealised figure 177
initial contact with, responding to 17
as observer, Peggy and Jack (clinical example) 173
as parental figure 163
as particular kind of third 84
as superego figure 163
third position of xxii, 7, 22, 24, 41, 52, 72, 82, 83, 87, 131, 147, 156–163, 167, 171, 184, 185
unconscious symbiosis with 191
use of couple state of mind 39–40
therapy:
beginning of 39, 45–46, 53, 176
couple's decision to seek 34
ending of, planned 190
final phase of 190–191
final session 191–192
think, capacity to 52, 132, 157, 184, 186
third position:
observing partner in, Carly and James (clinical example) 159–160
therapist's xxii, 7, 22, 24, 41, 52, 72, 82, 83, 87, 131, 147, 156, 157, 159, 160, 162, 163, 167, 171, 184, 185
transference (*passim*):
and countertransference xix, 19, 26, 34, 73, 74, 75, 76, 78, 81, 84, 86, 87, 146, 149, 164
living inner world of couple 73–87
use of, Donna and Johnny (clinical example) 160
in couple relationship 25
Jimmy and Dale (clinical example) 164–165
in couple therapy 75–76
concept of 74–75
couple, therapeutic xix
early 35–37
erotic 82, 83, 87
gathering, Eva and John (clinical example) 79–81

idealising 84–85
interpreting, as vehicle of change 83–84
negative 36, 82
to partner 26
to therapist 35, 37, 79, 85, 87, 158, 163, 177
threatening 82–83
as total situation, including countertransference, dynamics and enactments 162
ubiquitous nature of 73
working creatively with 87
working with, in couple therapy 158–165
transference communication 178
transference dimension, of couple relationship 25
transference interpretations 158, 164, 169
transference object 73, 84
transference relationship, couple xix
translating, between couple 171–172
transsexual dynamics in couple, David and Cheryl (clinical example) 149
triangular configuration, in couple therapy 82, 132, 159
triangular setting, of couple therapy 159
triangular space xxi6, 52, 131, 136, 158
Turquet, P. 86

unconscious belief(s) vii, xix, xxi, 3, 5, 12, 76, 78, 102, 129, 145, 170, 172
concept of 65–68
and fantasy 54–72
interpretation of 167–168
rigid 25
unconscious blocks, internal working through of 183
unconscious choice 2, 7, 65, 73, 88, 96, 104
and shared phantasy and couple fit 61
unconscious communication 113
unconscious complementariness 97

unconscious partner choice, and couple fit 96–97
unconscious phantasy(ies) (*passim*):
concept of 54–72
Freud's 54
Klein's 55
and couple relationship, in present 4–8
group 87
interpretation of 167–168
and reality 55–57
shared *see* shared unconscious phantasy(ies)
unconscious symbiosis, with therapist 191
understanding, loss of 112

vaginismus 146
valencies 49
Vincent, C. 20, 48, 49, 64, 85, 120
violence:
coercive controlling 29, 30
couple, situational 29
partner, intimate 29
in relationship 29–32
separation-instigated 29
violent couples, psychoanalytic therapy with 29
violent resistance 29
Viorst, J. 138
Vorchheimer, M. 7, 112, 167, 172

Waddell, M. 133, 136
Wanless, J. 30
Willi, J. 97
Winnicott, D. W. 127, 129, 154
Woodhouse, D. 98
words, with symbolic references 172
working through, and repetition compulsion 77
Wrottesley, C. 132

Zinner, J. 102, 168

Printed in Great Britain
by Amazon